Two Worlds of Judaism

Two Worlds of Judaism

The Israeli and American Experiences

CHARLES S. LIEBMAN AND

STEVEN M. COHEN

Yale University Press *New Haven & London*

Designed by Richard Hendel.
Set in Simoncini Garamond type by
G & S Typesetters, Austin, Texas.
Printed in the United States of America.

Library of Congress Cataloging-in-Publication Data
Liebman, Charles S.
   Two worlds of Judaism : the Israeli and American experiences /
Charles S. Liebman and Steven M. Cohen.
      p.   cm.
   Includes bibliographical references.
   ISBN 0-300-04726-6 (alk. paper)
   1. Judaism—20th century.   2. Judaism—Israel.   3. Judaism—
United States.   I. Cohen, Steven Martin.   II. Title.
BM565.L54   1990
296'.095694'09045—dc20   89-28457
                              CIP

The paper in this book meets the guidelines of permanence and
durability of the Committee on Production Guidelines for Book
Longevity of the Council on Library Resources.

10 9 8 7 6 5 4 3 2 1

For Reut and Elad

and for

Edeet Dvora

Contents

Preface   ix

Chapter 1   Introduction   1

Chapter 2   Historical Familism:
             The Jewish Collective Consciousness   13

Chapter 3   Ethnocentrism and Anti-Semitism   35

Chapter 4   Land, State, and Diaspora   67

Chapter 5   Liberalism and Judaism   96

Chapter 6   Religious Life   123

Chapter 7   Are Two Judaisms Emerging?   157

             Notes   177

             References   185

             Index   195

Preface

This book is about the changing perceptions of American and Israeli Jews—their perceptions of Judaism and of what it means to be a Jew. We believe these changes represent important transformations of the Jewish tradition. But because the perceptions of American Jews are moving in one direction and those of Israeli Jews in another, the changes also raise important questions about the future unity of the Jewish people.

To interpret what Judaism means in the two societies is to address a very broad topic to which one book can in no way do justice. At the outset we therefore had to choose between two general foci in formulating our study. We could have looked at one aspect of Judaism—for example belief in the Messiah, or the meaning of Torah, or redemption, or the notion of the non-Jew—and asked how it had been transformed among Israeli and American Jews; even such a choice would have left room for a multivolume study. We could also have chosen to look at only one segment of each society or culture—for example intellectuals, or the press, or fiction, or school curricula. But we chose instead to explore many aspects of popular culture, and therefore have almost by definition cut a very wide swath. We have left room for countless further studies that we hope will pursue the direction we have taken, examine in much greater detail the topics on which we touch, add other topics we have omitted, and confirm or correct our very general observations and conclusions.

A word is in order about our methodology, the basis for our observations and conclusions about the nature of Judaism in Israeli and American society. We began with our own impressions as trained social scientists and active participants in American Jewish and Israeli society. We formed our impressions on our own and refined them in discussions with each other. It would be less than honest to pretend that we began our research for this book without a pretty good idea of what we would find; this is an important limitation. We believe that our impressions are correct because we have confidence in our own judgment and because our observations make theoretical sense. In other words, they fit into a larger framework that seems entirely credible, given what we know or believe we know about human behavior in developed societies in the twentieth century.

We tested these impressions against the results of survey research in the United States and Israel, mostly research that one or both of us directed. We were testing to see whether our impressions were confirmed by survey research data; we did not begin with survey research studies and ask what we could learn from them. Where one can assume considerable prior knowledge of a population, to rely exclusively on survey data is not a very effective way to study social attitudes; but of course our procedures subject us to the charge that we found what we were looking to find.

Finally, we relied on anecdotal evidence gathered from newspapers, magazines, pamphlets, speeches of public figures, and other sources of popular culture. We did not collect this material systematically or over an extended period, nor did we feel we had to: because we are dealing with popular tendencies in contemporary culture, if we are right about what we say then the evidence we are looking for should be all around us.

This is very much a joint study. One of us would draft a chapter, the other would revise it, and revisions would be continued into fourth and fifth drafts. But others must also receive credit for this enterprise. Most of our survey research data are based on studies undertaken on behalf of the American Jewish Committee and its Institute on American Jewish-Israel Relations, under the direction of Bert Gold and Selma Hirsch. In addition, the institute supported the study with a special grant that enabled us to employ the part-time services of a research assistant. This research was also supported by a grant from the City University of New York, PSC-CUNY Research Award Program.

Professor Richard Cohen of the Hebrew University read an early version of this manuscript and offered many valuable and insightful remarks. Professor David Segal of Ben-Gurion University gave valuable editorial advice on the early chapters. Ben Wizner of New Haven provided research assistance and capably incorporated many editorial comments into a single document on the word processor. We wish to thank Gladys Topkis and Fred Kameny of Yale University Press for their able editorial assistance.

There are also special debts that each of us incurred individually. Charles Liebman was assisted in this book as in everything else he has written by his wife, Carol. She read the manuscript, made cogent observations (albeit sometimes very critical ones), and did much to crystallize her husband's thinking. The manuscript was also read in part by the Liebmans' son, Aaron, who offered a number of important observations that found their way into the text. We are very grateful to them both.

Petach Tikvah and New Haven
February 1990
Shevat 5750

1 Introduction

The United Jewish Appeal proudly proclaims, "We Are One." In this pithy slogan, American Jewry's leading fund-raising organization expresses a powerful motif in Jewish organizational life, one widely shared among rank-and-file American Jews as well. On the most abstract level, "We Are One" asserts the worldwide unity of the Jewish people. Given the centrality of Israel to the UJA's campaign, the slogan "We Are One" makes another implicit claim—that Jews in the United States and Israel (and Jews elsewhere) are fundamentally alike, having the same history, the same destiny, and presumably the same basic understanding of what it means to be a Jew today. At least among American Jews, there is a widespread belief that the Judaism of Americans and that of Israelis are essentially the same: that notwithstanding the differences of interpretation between the modernist, secularist left and the traditionalist, religious right, the Jewish beliefs, practices, symbols, and myths of the American Jews and Israeli Jews are identical.

Recent events in Israel may erode this belief. The perception of religious coercion there and the Israeli reaction to the *intifada,* the Palestinian uprising that began in December 1987, may raise doubts among American Jews that Israelis share their beliefs and values. But most American Jews continue to subscribe to the slogan "We Are One" and take it for granted that being Jewish means the same thing to Israelis as it does to Americans. Israelis, on the other hand, believe that their own Jewish existence is fundamentally richer, fuller, more stable, and ultimately more significant than that of any diaspora community, including the one in the United States. But the primary distinction that Israelis draw between American and Israeli Judaism can be cast in quantitative terms: Israelis believe that the commitment of American Jews to Judaism is more fragile than their own and that most American Jews are likely to succumb to the allures of assimilation. In other words, Israelis believe that American Jews are the same kind of Jews they are, only less so—less firmly committed to Judaism and the Jewish people, less knowledgeable, and less proud, but not essentially different.

We believe that the differences between Israeli and American Jews are not simply quantitative. As we shall demonstrate, American Jews are not merely less (or more) Jewish than Israelis, but Jewish in a different way. Whether these differences are critical and whether they point to a divergence of the two communities are topics to which we shall return in the concluding chapter.

American and Israeli Jews not only give different answers to the same questions about the essence of Judaism but often ask different questions. In many cases what is an important aspect of Jewish identity to one community is Judaically irrelevant to the other. In addition, the Judaic vocabularies of the two communities overlap only partly. This does not simply reflect that one community speaks Hebrew and the other English; symbols, stories, concepts, and allusions that have meaning for one are often understood differently, if at all, by the other.

Even the same word can mean very different things in the two societies. The term *Zionism,* so crucial in the lexicon of modern Jewry, means one thing to American Jews and something else to Israelis. Most American Jews understand a Zionist to be one who believes that the state of Israel is central to Judaism and the Jewish people. To some Americans a Zionist is someone very committed to the Jewish state. To most Israelis, however, a Zionist is one who lives or aspires to live in the state of Israel, a view shared by only 4 percent of American Jews (Cohen 1987a, 102). In this case the disagreement between Israeli and American Jews does not necessarily create tension. On the contrary, it allows leaders in each society to call themselves Zionists and think that in doing so they have something in common with each other. And in one important respect they do: the nominal identification with a symbol, regardless of the differences in its referent, does provide a basis for unity and integration. But it can also have the opposite result.

The reasons for the differences between American and Israeli Jews lie in the social character of the two populations, as well as in the nature of the societies they inhabit. More specifically, part of the difference derives from the greater Westernization of American Jews and part from the very existence of the state and society of Israel. Thus the Israeli Jewish population contains far larger proportions of religious Jews, of those lacking a university education, and of Jews originating in

Islamic countries (Sephardim). Many of the Sephardim differ from Ashkenazi (European) Jews in never having felt the impact of Western modernization—the European Enlightenment, the emancipation by the Gentiles. Indeed, throughout this book we shall find that Israelis who are religiously observant, less well educated, and Sephardi more closely approximate the image of traditional Judaism than do the more secular, more educated Jews of Ashkenazi origin.

But the roots of the distinction between Israeli and American Jewry go beyond the social and demographic. Israeli Jews are a majority in the one Jewish state in the world; American Jews live as a minority in a modern, multiethnic, voluntarist society. Minority status, state sovereignty, and related environmental factors all operate above and beyond the differences in the character of the two populations to produce divergences in the nature of Israeli and American Judaism.

We do not wish to overstate our case. The Judaism of the two communities is tied to a common past; it has been influenced (albeit differently) by a shared recent history and by frequent interaction between American and Israeli Jews, both official and informal. Nevertheless, differences remain; the culture of American Judaism is in some cases sharply distinct from the culture of Israeli Judaism.

Judaism is a culture, certainly according to Clifford Geertz's definition of culture as a "historically transmitted pattern of meanings embodied in symbols, a system of inherited conceptions expressed in symbolic forms by means of which men communicate, perpetuate and develop their knowledge about and attitudes toward life" (Geertz 1973, 89). Judaism fits this definition whether one interprets its symbols as primarily religious, ethnic, or national (the interpretation depends to some extent on the perspective of the interpreter, as well as on how he or she defines religion, ethnos, or nation). What is especially attractive about Geertz's definition of culture is that it includes two dimensions: the dimension of tradition (culture is a system of inherited meanings) and the dimension of change, because at least by implication the symbols of the culture could not continue to serve the functions of communication, perpetuation, and development of knowledge unless they adapted to a changing environment.

Let us first consider the dimension of tradition. Like any other culture, Judaism has certain parameters. It is not whatever we say it is. It has symbols that are useful in communicating, perpetuating, and developing knowledge and attitudes toward life only if the members of the culture understand what the symbols signify and to what they refer. Holocaust, Israel, goy, Torah, along with Shabbat, seder, Hanukah, are all symbols of Jewish culture. They function in precisely the manner Geertz indicates because the terms carry roughly the same set of meanings for most Jews and evoke roughly the same set of responses from them. If they ceased to do so (as is true of the term *Zionist*), we should have to consider the possibility that there was more than one Judaism.

But the notion of change is also part of this conception of culture. Symbols are defined by the meanings people attribute to them. Because the ways people think and behave change, the meanings they attribute to cultural symbols also change. The survival of symbols is proof of their adaptability. Symbols of especially sacred character—which are most set apart from everyday life—may refer to orders of existence that are perceived as transcendent and eternal. But even these symbols require more concrete referents if they are to communicate, perpetuate, and develop knowledge and attitudes. And the more concrete the symbolic referent, the more rooted it is in time and space, the more it becomes subject to the vicissitudes of a changing environment.

God is the most dramatic example. The object of religious veneration by the masses of believers, the pillar of religious belief, is not the eternal, timeless God who has no form and cannot be imagined except by analogy. Instead every religious culture provides a conceptual if not a visual image of its god, including Islam, which ostensibly prohibits God from being represented. Not surprisingly, these images of God change from one generation to the next and from one society to another.[1] In Judaism God has been portrayed as the father, the master, the shepherd, the husband, the lover, the warrior, the judge, the betrayed, the avenger, the patriarch, and the scholar—portrayals that border on the forbidden and yet are unavoidable because human beings seek to attribute specific meaning to their symbols.

These myriad images obviously depend on the environment in which they are invoked. And if such is the case for God, what of all the other symbols that are less sanctified and by definition more susceptible to reinterpretation or transvaluation? The holiday of Shavuot (Pentecost) is another example. Projected in the Bible as a spring harvest festival, it becomes a celebration of the giving of the Torah at Mount Sinai in the rabbinic tradition, a holiday of produce in the revived Zionist tradition, and a holiday of Torah study in a renascent religious tradition. The dilemma is apparent. If the symbols are unchangeable, they cannot accommodate themselves to a changing environment. If the symbols are changeable, how can they form the basis of culture? How can they be inherited conceptions that function to perpetuate, communicate, and develop knowledge and attitudes toward life when their meaning in one generation differs from the one that prevailed in the generation from which they were inherited?

The answer is that symbols are to culture as a constitution is to a society. Both the symbols and the constitution may change; they may change so radically that they are eventually unrecognizable. But in general they change gradually and in accordance with norms peculiar to them. The changes themselves are often imperceptible. They may be unacknowledged, or seen as bringing about a more faithful understanding of the intent or spirit of those who devised the symbols or framed the constitution. Those prepared to acknowledge the appearance of change argue that the new symbols retain the essence or substance of the tradition even if they discard the dross. Thus even as symbols undergo change, they retain their image as unchanging and immutable. They support the myth of tradition. Tradition, after all, is not the past. The very term *tradition* is derived from a Latin root meaning to hand over, and the Hebrew term *masoret* connotes the same thing. The tradition is what the present generation perceives as the essential norms or values of the past. The power of the symbol resides in its capacity to evoke the sense that it is rooted in some ultimate reality, and that it provided the same meaning in the past as it provides today.

Judaism in Two Societies: The Divergent Impact of Modernity and Statehood

Our concern is with Judaism in Israel and the United States in our generation, and particularly with the changes taking place in Jewish culture—in the symbols and in the meanings that Jews impart to these symbols in both societies. Hence we are concerned with tradition and change.

Judaism is viewed as a religious culture by most Jews in the United

States and perhaps by most Jews in Israel. This means that a special sanctity attaches to the tradition. For those who conceive of Judaism in religious terms, its symbols derive directly or indirectly from God or from the interrelationship between God and the Jewish people. Even for those who view the Jewish culture from a secular perspective and interpret its symbols in ethnic or national terms, the tradition is a hoary one, sanctified at least by history and by the suffering of the Jews on behalf of the tradition (see chapter 2).

Under conditions of relative stability, the tradition is therefore not easily tampered with. It evokes powerful resonances among its adherents, counterreactions to any deliberate challenges. Accordingly the most successful changes take place unconsciously, through transvaluation of the symbols—that is, their reinterpretation or piecemeal transformation. The most effective changes generally take place through changes in relative emphasis: one symbol or the meaning attached to it gets more emphasis, another gets less. In periods of stress and crisis, under rapidly changing conditions or in a radically new environment, we should expect a quickening in the process of change. Radically new interpretations and meanings may be acknowledged consciously or unconsciously as necessary, and incorporated with a minimum of opposition.

This rapid change characterizes the last two hundred years of Jewish history. Western Jews in general and American Jews in particular live under conditions unique in Jewish history. American Jews not only suffer no disadvantages by virtue of being Jewish, but enjoy rather high status in some sectors of society. Further, the freedom and equality that American Jews enjoy are not the result of any special concessions, not a contradiction or reversal of tendencies within American culture: they are consistent with the basic values of the political system and with American traditions. If anything distinguishes American Jews today within the context of American society it is the special deference that society accords them. This does not mean that there is no anti-Semitism in the United States today or that a great deal more did not exist in the past (see chapter 3). But anti-Semitism was never endemic to American culture. At no point did Jews feel they were alien to the United States. On the contrary, they defended their rights in the name of American values, American principles, and American history.

Much that we shall report concerning American Jews is true of Western European Jews as well; we make no claim that the developments we note with regard to American Jewry are peculiar to them. But we suspect that the trends we observe generally are more pronounced in the United States: in part because the United States continues to be at the cutting edge of modern culture, but also because nowhere are Jews more integrated into society and quite so unselfconsciously Jewish. This means that Jews accept without question their status as Americans. It also means that to the extent that they choose to identify themselves as Jews, they display their Jewish commitments unashamedly.

All this is relative, of course; Jews still have qualms and fears. That Jews fear a resurgence of anti-Semitism and are not entirely secure even in the United States was evident when leaders of Jewish organizations discussed the possible anti-Semitic consequences in 1973 of the international oil crisis and the Yom Kippur war. And that some Jews still fear being charged with dual loyalty was clear from their reaction to the affair of Jonathan Pollard, an American Jew who worked in a sensitive job in the U.S. government and was convicted with his wife of spying on behalf of Israel. A full-page advertisement in the American Jewish magazine *Present Tense* cautioned Jews against helping to raise money for the Pollards, lest this "make it easy for others to raise the question of where American Jewish sentiments really lie." The uniqueness of the Israeli condition is no less obvious. The Jewish tradition, its major symbols, and the normative interpretation of these symbols all developed after the Jewish cultic center (the Temple) had been destroyed and the Jews had lost their political sovereignty and autonomy, been exiled from their homeland, and become a relatively powerless minority.[2] When Jews returned to the land of Israel in large numbers, achieved sovereignty, confronted problems of statehood, and exercised power over other minorities, they had to reformulate a tradition developed under dramatically different circumstances.

Both Israeli and American Jews have been undertaking radical reformulations of Judaism, although in many instances, especially among those more concerned with tradition, they have done so unselfconsciously. It is in this regard that we can speak of these communities as constructing or reconstructing Judaism.

A word of caution is in order. When we argue for different "constructions" of Judaism among Israeli and American Jews we do not pretend that either group or both groups have formulated a consistent

Jewish philosophy or program. It would be unreasonable to talk about two different Judaisms, not only because each group agrees with the other on many issues and has internal disagreements on some issues, but also because we do not foresee either group developing a total Judaic conception emerging exclusively from its particular condition. That is not how cultures develop, much less religious cultures. Rather, aspects of the tradition have undergone an interpretation or emphasis especially suited to the condition under which each group lives.

These differences should not be exaggerated. In many ways American Jews and Israelis are similar, which is somewhat surprising given their very different conditions. These similarities suggest that the tradition has a continuing power, and that not everything changes, certainly not rapidly, in response even to a very different environment. Other similarities suggest that whereas the tradition may change, it may change in the same direction in the two societies because certain aspects of the modern condition are common to Israeli and American Jews. We shall observe that neither Israeli Jewry nor American Jewry is homogeneous. Some of the differences between the two societies stem from the relative strength of one subgroup or another within each society. For example, that Orthodox Jews constitute about 10 percent of American Jewry and 20 percent of Israeli Jewry has implications for the construction of Judaism in each society. One question that arises is whether the differences between the societies are attributable to the relative weight of each group within them, or rather to overriding societal differences. In other words, do Orthodox Jews in the United States behave, feel, and think more like Orthodox Jews in Israel, or more like other American Jews? And what comparisons can we make between the less religiously observant or even secular Jews in one society and those in the other?

There is an additional problem of which we must be aware even if we cannot resolve it. Israeli and American Jews may have roughly the same Jewish symbols, but American Jews have some symbols that Israelis do not. The converse is less true: almost everything that Israelis do tends to be understood in both societies as having consequences for Judaism, and much of what they do and believe is seen both by themselves and by Jews in the diaspora as derived from an authentic Judaism, past and present.

Spiritual Israelis, Political Americans

Our focus is on symbols and on the meanings Israeli and American Jews attach to them. Perhaps by virtue of our training as social scientists, we focus on the cognitive meanings of these symbols. By rationalizing them, we necessarily diminish their meaning in some respect, denuding them of their emotional impact. But this may also lead us to overlook other aspects of culture, and the reader should be aware of this danger from the outset. We usually look at content, but differences in style are no less important. For example, the Israeli tendency, more pronounced among the religious but present even among the secular, is to spiritualize and mystify categories of thought; the American tendency is the opposite. As the late Uriel Tal observed, "We are presently facing the emergence of highly articulated and consciously conceptualized forms of consecration of the Land, the Nation, the State, the Wars—in fact of everything and everybody Jewish. A total and all-embracing sacredness of reality—a 'mystical realism'—has become a growing factor in Israeli life, education, and politics" (1986, 327). As Tal points out, Israelis do tend to view events in symbolic formulations and mythical paradigms. Things do not just happen: they are ordained by a transcendent power; they are a reliving of past events; or they are inexorable stages toward some predestined end. Events are not evaluated in their own terms, nor policies adopted for proximate ends. Israelis are more likely than American Jews to harbor the suspicion or even the conviction that their activity is of cosmological import. This is a perspective more commonly associated with the religious sector of the population (though not all the religious) but it is by no means limited to them. Its opposite is the American Jewish disposition, which is more pragmatic, less ideological, much less mystical, more likely to evaluate events without context, less conscious of such forces as history or destiny.

These differences have implications in turn for another aspect of the construction of Judaism: its politicization (see chapter 5). If there are tendencies in the Israeli construction of Judaism that mystify politics (to borrow Tal's formulation), then there are also tendencies among some American Jews to politicize Judaism, in particular among their organizational elite. Jewish symbols are reinterpreted in political terms, robbed of their essentially religious meaning, and turned outward to focus on ethnic interests (especially the defense of Israel's security and the plight of Soviet Jewry) and political considerations (especially the liberal political agenda of many American Jews).

Paradoxically, these two very different modes of conceiving Judaism have implications that emphasize points of continuity rather than distinction between the two communities. For they allow Israel itself to serve "as the principal symbol and prop of Jewish identity" for American Jews (Eisen 1986, 136). It is the very lack of interest of American Jews in legitimating their own reality in religious terms that enables them to incorporate support for Israel into their conception of essential Jewish obligations. If American Jews were indeed religiously oriented, if they insisted on interpreting their Jewishness in exclusively religious terms, it is unlikely that concern for the welfare of the state of Israel would play as critical a role in Jewish life as it now does. In fact such a scenario seems increasingly probable (see chapters 4 and 6). To the extent that American Jews insist on finding religious meaning in a Jewish tradition that speaks to their personal needs, Israel is likely to become of decreasing concern. Students of Jewish intermarriage already report that the partner who converts to Judaism is generally less interested in the ethnic and political aspects of the tradition (Cohen 1988a, 35–38). That partner may of course become socialized to the public aspect of Jewish life over time. But the opposite result is by no means precluded, and we suspect it is increasing in importance.

There are a number of ways we might have approached our topic. One would have been to compare influential thinkers in the two societies. This is the route Arnold Eisen follows in his book *Galut,* which is concerned with Israeli and American Jewish reflections on the topic of exile and homecoming. He observes moreover that the division between Israeli and American Judaism goes "far beyond the definition of exile and homecoming. It reaches to the very definition of Jewish commitment in our time" (1986, xviii).

A number of writers have remarked on features that distinguish Israeli scholars from non-Israeli scholars in their treatment of Jewish history. One American Jewish historian notes: "Israeli and diaspora historians hold fundamentally contradictory views of modern Jewish history . . . [and] call upon different memories. Their historians are writing, and I believe will continue to write, very different histories.

The unity and continuity of the Jewish past seems to me genuinely endangered by this division" (Meyer 1986, 16). Israeli scholars have made observations that are similar, although less sweeping. But they are also rather critical of the effort to "Zionise" Jewish history.[3]

There is certainly a need for a study comparing the conceptions of Judaism among leading Jewish thinkers in Israel and the United States, and for a comparison of Israeli and American Jewish historiography. But our method is different. We have looked at more popular conceptions of Judaism in Israel and the United States. Our primary data are derived from the press, from the literature of Jewish organizations, from our own impressions as participants in Jewish life and observers of it, from statements by people we consider representative, and from the social science literature. We have tested our observations against survey data gathered from nationwide samples of American and Israeli Jews.

The Sample Surveys

In 1986 we collaborated in designing parallel questionnaires on political and religious issues for surveys of the American and Israeli Jewish populations. The research, sponsored by the American Jewish Committee, resulted in two reports, one by Cohen on the American Jewish sample (1987a), the other by Mina Zemach on the Israelis (1987). The American sample consisted of 1,133 respondents and was derived from a self-administered mail survey of a Jewish subset taken from a large, nationwide "consumer mail panel" maintained by Market Facts, a survey research company. In its sociodemographic characteristics and measures of Jewish identity this sample is comparable to others selected by means of random-digit dialing, which is a more accurate and more expensive method.[4] Like most surveys of the Israeli Jewish population, the Israeli sample excluded Jews in the army or on kibbutzim, but in other respects was representative of the Israeli Jewish population.[5] This book reanalyzes the data collected for these two studies.

In addition to the studies conducted in 1986, we make frequent references to other national surveys of American Jews conducted by Cohen for the American Jewish Committee. Studies in 1983 and 1986 focused heavily on attitudes toward Israel and Israelis; studies in 1984,

1985, and 1988 concentrated on political and social attitudes. All contained much information on sociodemographic characteristics and measures of Jewish identity. The studies of 1983 and 1984 used Distinctive Jewish Name samples (Cohen 1983b, 1984), and the study of 1985 resurveyed the sample chosen in 1984. The study of 1988 used the consumer mail panel of Market Facts (Cohen 1989).

The use of surveys to refine and document our analysis of ubiquitous Judaic beliefs, attitudes, and behavior raises the question of what constitutes ubiquity. If 80 to 90 percent of American Jews attend a seder or light Hanukah candles (as they say they do), then we can call such acts normative for the vast majority of Jews, or say that there is an American Jewish consensus around attending a seder and lighting Hanukah candles. But what are we to make of the 60 percent who "see the Jewish people as an extension" of their family? What right do we have to use this as evidence that Jewish familism is a normative element in American Jewish consciousness?

We do so for two reasons. First, some American Jews and even Israeli Jews have virtually no Jewish commitments. Twelve percent of Israeli Jews and a slightly higher percentage of American Jews say that being Jewish is totally unimportant in their lives or almost totally unimportant (Cohen 1987a); more than a quarter of American Jews say that at least two of their three closest friends are non-Jews. If we are trying to understand the meaning of Judaism, then clearly we should focus on Jews to whom Judaism is of some import; and the 60 percent of all Jews who see the Jewish people as an extension of their family probably represent three-quarters of those to whom Judaism has meaning.

Second, we feel confident in drawing conclusions from our survey data when they are corroborated by our years of qualitative observation. The data refine our intimations, strengthen our confidence in our conclusions, and quantify trends and tendencies that otherwise lack precision and specificity. In no case do we rely on surveys for evidence that is not supported by qualitative observation, historical evidence, press reports, and the like.

2 Historical Familism

The Jewish Collective

Consciousness

By describing Judaism as a culture and Jews as the people who share it, we have attributed to Jews the characteristics of an ethnic community. Many Jews or even most may define their culture in religious terms, as Jews have done in the past, but they remain an ethnic community in the technical sense as long as that which binds them together is their culture. They are what Anthony Smith calls a "culture-based solidarity" (1983). According to Smith, such groups "betray a quasi-familial sentiment; even though the ethnic community subsumes many families and clans, it is, in the first place, an aggregate of such families and clans" (p. 156).

The myth of common ancestry implies both common biological traits and a common history (it matters not whether the myth is true, only that those who share the same culture believe it to be true). But a member of an ethnic group may also belong to other groups of common descent with whom he or she shares a sense of common history: hence American Jews may feel that the Revolutionary War or the Civil War is part of their historical heritage. As individuals they may also feel ties of kinship with non-Jews (through intermarriage). One measure of the strength of Jewish commitment is the extent to which ties to the Jewish past or perceptions of other Jews as part of one's extended family take precedence over other ties based in history or kinship or even exclude them.

That all those who are selfconsciously Jewish share some sense of history and family ties does not mean they all have the same sense of history or family ties. In this chapter we compare Israeli and American Jewish conceptions of history and family. We are interested not only in assessing whether these perceptions are stronger in one community than in the other, but also with charting the extent to which American and Israeli Jews have developed different ideas of what Jewish history is about and what it means to be part of the family of Jewish people.

A sense of shared history and a sense of kinship are not the only characteristics that define an ethnic group. Some ethnic groups attribute particular importance to such characteristics as language, territory, and religion. We discuss these attributes in the chapters that follow, but we begin with common ancestry and history because these are generally considered the central defining characteristics of an ethnic group, and because it seems to us that they are the fundamental attributes of Jewish identity in the contemporary world. At the very least, American and Israeli Jews share a sense of familism and of common history far more than they share language (if at all), religion (in terms of specific beliefs and rituals), or territory. Yet there are differences between Israeli and American Jews in their understanding of Jewish familism and Jewish historicity.

Jewish Historicity

When we say that Jews bring to their understanding of what it means to be Jewish strong historical elements, notions about their collective past and about its implications for the present, we do not mean that these notions are historically accurate. The critical dimension is not the history of the Jewish people per se but rather how contemporary Jews understand the history. As Yosef Yerushalmi argues in his book *Zakhor* (Hebrew for memory), a group's memory is only loosely connected with its history, and its history is itself a social artifact, the product of professional historians. Historical memory lends meaning, significance, and legitimacy to the lives that Jews lead in the present. Their understanding of the events that affected their real or putative ancestors helps shape their contemporary feelings toward one another, toward non-Jews, and toward the choices they face as political actors, as citizens of Israel, the United States, and other diaspora countries. In general, events of one, two, three, or even more generations ago (and, more precisely, Jews' understanding of these events) have very real consequences for Jewish public policy and Jewish attitudes toward public policy, in both Israel and the United States.

The "myths" that members of a group tell about themselves express the perception that the group has of its past, the way it remembers its past, and the significance it attributes to its past (which helps the group understand its present condition and decide what to do in its present condition). Myths are critical in helping the scholar decide what the group finds significant about itself. That is why we are eager to identify and compare the myths of American and Israeli Jews. Myths may be true in some objective sense, or they may be partly true; the social scientist who uses the term "myth" does not mean that what constitutes the myth is false. The stories of the Bible constitute central myths for the Jewish people, and the great sages of the Jewish past recognized this. They believed that everything written in the Bible was true. But they also realized that the Bible did not recount everything that had happened to the Jews. Indeed, the sages noted in the Talmud that "the deeds of the Fathers [the Biblical patriarchs] are signs to their children." In other words, the stories of the Bible are there so that we may learn lessons from them. This is precisely what we mean by "myth."

Myth refers to the structure and content of the story and also to the meaning it conveys. The story is fairly easy to ascertain; its meaning is far more difficult, conjectural, and sometimes impossible. Some myths are common to Israeli and American Jews. They contain the same basic ingredients, the same set of heroes and villains, the same basic events; but they do vary in nuance, so that when related to the environment and experience of one group or the other they carry different meanings. Other myths, both their story line and their moral, are obviously peculiar to one group or the other. Because they live under very different conditions, the two societies of Jews have each developed their own historical myths. Each has selected different aspects of Jewish history to elaborate, and at times each has lent its own understandings to the same events in their common past.

Hanukah is a good example of a common holiday that has different meanings in the two societies. American Jews relate the story of Hanukah as the account of a successful fight by courageous Jews against the forces of hellenization (assimilation). They celebrate the holiday as an alternative to Christmas. The lavish giving of gifts to children is intended to compensate for the absence of Christmas, and so represents a peculiarly contemporary battle against assimilation. To Israelis, on the other hand, Hanukah recalls a successful military struggle of national liberation. This version too is a drastic modification of the traditional Jewish conception, which emphasizes God's providence, and it is important to note that the nationalist transvaluation of the holiday has penetrated even into some religious and Zionist circles.[1]

Hanukah constitutes a shared myth, albeit one differently interpreted. Other myths and symbols are distinctive to Israeli or American Jews. One Israeli myth is that in the *yishuv* (the period before the state of Israel was established), Jewish settlements were established by night and in secret before the British authorities could prevent the construction of a wall and guard tower.[2] Once the wall and tower were erected, they provided quasi-legal status to the settlement, assured its existence, and strengthened the Jewish claim to sovereignty over the territory on expiration of the British mandate.

This myth embraces several aspects of Jewish settlement during the mandate. It has reinforced an important component in the contemporary Israeli system of beliefs: that it is essential to "create facts," and that once these facts have been created, once the Jews have demonstrated some physical claim, their claim is bound to be honored. This sort of mentality led to the settlement of the West Bank (Judea and Samaria) immediately after the Six Day War as well as to increased settlement in northern Sinai after the Camp David accords were signed. It was believed that such settlement would make impossible any Israeli surrender of territory. This belief nourishes in turn a larger conception of political life: in the words of Ben-Gurion, that it matters not what the Gentiles say, only what the Jews do.

Unique to American Jews is the major role they once played in the civil rights movement. The myth of this involvement enhances the self-image of the Jews as a caring, sensitive minority selflessly contributing to improve the lot of other minorities. Another myth peculiar to American Jews is what we call the myth of the Lower East Side, according to which Jews arrived in the United States as an impoverished group and by dint of hard work, sacrifice, and determination rose to prosperity. This myth also enhances the self-image of American Jews, credits the United States with being the land of opportunity (it allowed the Jews to use their talents), and at least indirectly casts aspersions on other minority groups, blacks in particular, that have not availed themselves of the opportunities the United States affords. It is not too far-fetched to suggest that this myth also alleviates the guilt that Jews may feel over their present prosperity and material comfort.

This sort of interpretation also suggests why many Sephardi Israelis reject the mythology of the settlement period. To them this celebration of the achievements during the *yishuv* of the Zionist settlers serves to justify the advantages enjoyed by the Ashkenazi children of the early settlers. But our major point is that both Israeli and American Jews derive much of their sense of Jewishness, and many principles of how to live their Jewish lives, by interacting with their ancient and recent history as they choose to understand it. The two communities have a shared heritage (though not an identical one), from which they draw a variety of contemporary lessons, some similar, some parallel, and some distinct.

Familism among American Jews

The second key element of the Jewish collective consciousness is familism, the tendency of Jews to see themselves as part of an extended family. Familism in turn has several elements, two of which merit our attention. The first is that of ascription: a family is a group into which a person is born and of which the person remains a part regardless of what he or she does. The second element is a sense of mutual responsibility: the members of a family care about each other. These feelings are suffused with a sense of compulsion, obligation, and permanence that characterizes the relationships of Jews.

There is nevertheless an element to the sense of Jewish belonging that is not familial. Although Jews see themselves as part of a larger family, they also see themselves as a people with a purpose. They have survived as Jews and feel they have a purpose beyond simply maintaining the group's boundaries. There is more to being Jewish than distinguishing between Jews and non-Jews. In this respect Jews are bound together not simply as members of a kinship group but as people who share a common and noble goal. In the language of the tradition, Jews have been singled out to serve as a kingdom of priests and holy people. Jews are bound by both kinship and consent (Elazar 1983). In many respects the notion of shared purpose or goal is the antithesis of the notion of common family, the members of which remain bound together regardless of what they do or feel or believe. But both dimensions of belonging to the group are present among Jews. The sense of common purpose or goal sometimes operates at cross-purposes with the sense of family, but sometimes it strengthens it.

The American Jews' conception of themselves as an extended family and the implications of this conception can be demonstrated in several ways. In our survey of American Jews, 60 percent agreed with the statement "I see the Jewish people as an extension of my family"; only 23 percent disagreed.[3] We wonder whether Italian-Americans, whose ancestors arrived in the United States at about the same time as the East European Jews, would refer to the "Italian-American people." And we doubt that as many Irish-Americans would say they regarded their community as an extension of their family.[4] Perhaps there are other American groups, new immigrant groups, nonwhite groups, or religious sects that display a strong sense of solidarity and of which large proportions see their group as an extended family. Jews are not entirely unique in this respect. But this sense of kinship is surely an important characteristic of Jews in the United States.

Familism is in some respects even stronger among Israeli Jews than among American Jews. But Israeli respondents in our survey were only slightly more likely than American Jews to report that they felt the Jewish people to be an extension of their family (64 percent rather than 60 percent).

That Jewish familism brings with it feelings of mutual obligation is exemplified by the wide support for this statement: "As a Jew I have a special responsibility to help other Jews." Among American Jews 74 percent agreed and only 14 percent disagreed. The obligation to help other Jews in need is a central motif in what Jonathan Woocher terms the "civil religion" of the American Jewish communal elite (1986). Woocher studied the attitudes and beliefs of the core group of American Jewish communal leaders, the heads of the central charitable and communal planning agencies found in virtually every sizable Jewish community in the United States:

> The rhetoric of the Jewish polity resounds with pleas for the Jews of America to attend to the physical and spiritual needs of all Jews, everywhere. "For us," asserts a UJA fundraising brochure, "there can be no rest . . . As Jews we recognize no boundaries on

the map of human need . . . we are responsible, one for another."
. . . The programs of [the philanthropic] agencies . . . are not
merely organizational endeavors, even "good works." They are
not the products of "a moment of compassion." They are expressions of the essential meaning of Jewishness. . . . The [American
Jewish] polity has come to accept responsibility for the spiritual,
as well as physical, well-being of Jews throughout the world. . . .
"Each person's destiny and fulfillment are tied to the well-being
of his community. He has basic obligations to the community."
(1986, 71–72)

The familistic sense of mutual obligation is an axiomatic principle of
public Jewish life. It has been a key ideological pillar of one of the most
elaborate infrastructures of voluntary social services in the United
States and is central to the campaign of the United Jewish Appeal,
which raises hundreds of millions of dollars annually for social services
in Israel, poorer diaspora countries, and the United States. The principle is also exemplified by the varied services established and supported under Jewish auspices. These include medical care (hospitals),
family counseling, vocational guidance, summer camps, schools, and
geriatric services.

In our survey 54 percent of American Jews agreed with this statement: "When I deal with a Jewish agency—like a synagogue or a federation agency—I expect to be treated in a more personal way than I
would by a non-sectarian agency." In other words, one crucial feature
of Jewish familism, the particularist relationship between individual
Jew and the Jewish community (or Jewish state), cuts two ways. On the
one hand, Jews attest to a special responsibility to other Jews. On the
other, they expect and demand special treatment from other Jews and
from organized Jewry. This relationship can indeed be likened to a family relationship, one that allows and even demands personalism and
mutual responsibility and obligations. Western society expects greater
distance and privacy; families expect greater engagement and intimacy.
The type of behavior appropriate in the family is often seen as rude,
intrusive, and overly personal in less intimate social contexts (such as
bureaucratic encounters); behavior that is polite in the wider society
would be seen as cold and impersonal in the family.

In their day-to-day functioning, the social agencies that embody

Jews' familistic obligations to one another are themselves subject to the norms of familism. Although Jewish social service organizations are bureaucratic, their clients, patients, members, and users relate to them as an extension of the Jewish family. This results in intriguing conflicts between them and the bureaucratic norms of professionals. Human service professionals—social workers, therapists, school principals—are trained to maintain some distance from those they serve, without reference to their personal relations with them; they are even urged to limit their friendships with those they serve. But those who avail themselves of Jewish communal services often expect a warmer, friendlier, and more individualized relationship with the agency professionals, precisely because the agencies are the very embodiment of Jewish familism.

That this familistic personalism can cause problems when it enters the quasi-bureaucratic domain is illustrated in the reports of Jewish day school principals. In a recent study these professionals complained of parents who were not merely demanding but quite intrusive, willing to overstep the boundaries that are supposed to protect the autonomy of professionals (Cohen and Wall 1987). The Jewish school principals were quite convinced that their students' parents behaved far more intrusively (or personalistically) than the parents of children in nonsectarian private schools. Parents call or visit principals to demand special attention of one sort or another. They urge that their youngsters be assigned certain teachers, that some teachers be fired, that others be hired. Many of them not only call principals at home but do so at inappropriate times.

This confusion of expectations in formal encounters, this normative dualism, has an instructive parallel in informal relations. In the social life of friends, neighbors, and acquaintances, Jews understand that mixed company (Jews and non-Jews) calls for greater formality and civility than company consisting of Jews alone. Jews view themselves as more gregarious and expressive than white American Gentiles; but more than that, one is simply more formal and civil in the company of those outside the family, in this case the Jewish extended family.

In *The Ordeal of Civility* (1974), John Murray Cuddihy writes of European Jewry's anxious transition into genteel society. He recounts a story told by Helene Deutsch, a pioneer in psychoanalysis, describing an incident from her childhood in Poland: "A Jewish wood dealer . . . barged into the upper-middle class Rosenbach apartment without knocking, with nobody home but little 'Hala' lying on the . . . couch reading, practically naked but for a light robe: 'I jumped up and demanded angrily, "Mr. Stein, couldn't you knock first?" The answer was: "Why? Isn't this a Jewish house?" All the Jewish tradespeople . . . had this same feeling of solidarity with us despite the fact that we were members of the "aristocracy"'" (p. 23). In other words, the rules of genteel civility are limited to Gentile society; the rules of personalistic familism apply to the extended Jewish family, to all members, rich or poor.

Jewish Familism among Israeli Jews

All of the foregoing is found in Israeli society as well, where familistic ideas underlie proposed policies for the state of Israel. And in their everyday lives Israeli Jews relate to one another and to the bureaucracy as to an extended family. Israelis have a reputation for bad manners; to the extent that this reputation is deserved it stems from the sense of familiarity that Israelis feel toward one another. Public expectations of the bureaucracy and bureaucratic responses to the public also reflect this sense of familism, such as in the frequent use of familial and personal connections to make the bureaucracy responsive, and in the familistic behavior of functionaries toward members of the public. As an American *oleh* (immigrant) to Israel remarked in 1981 to the anthropologist Kevin Avruch:

> In the U.S., when you go to a government office, the clerk is there to help you. He'll tell you the rules, and he'll help you follow the rules. Not here. The rules don't apply to everyone equally, so if the *pakid* [clerk, bureaucrat] doesn't know you, or God forbid doesn't like you, you're dead. This is really part of a whole Israeli complex. . . . The first thing you learn is to relate to the *pakid* differently. You don't relate to him as a clerk but as a whole person— "How's the family?" but also "Is your daughter Rivka married yet?" Now obviously you cannot know every clerk in the country. So let's say you have to go to the Ministry of Commerce and Industry on Tuesday. So you ask all your friends, acquaintances, and relatives if they know a *pakid* in that ministry . . . Some kids were playing ball and broke the windshield of my car. I couldn't get a

replacement in the country. So I go to *mekhes* [customs] to find out about importing one. But the guy I go to is the brother of a neighbor. I know, because I asked around of all my neighbors. So we talk, and talk, and then get to my problem—you can't rush, because, from *his* point of view, maybe you have a son who will marry Rivka. So we get to my problem. Now the import tax on a new windshield would have cost me around 1000IL—under one category, "glass," or something. So we talk some more. Then he tells me if I *let* him—get it?—let him import under *another* category—car parts—the tax would be about 600IL. So we talk. And I tell him how I'm going to *miluim* (military reserve duty) next month. Now we have a real *kesher* ("connection"), because every Israeli does that. So he says: "Look, your windshield is tinted glass, right?" I say, "Sure, but what's that got to do with it?" "Well," he says, "why don't we import it under *medical* glass? As medical equipment." Because then the tax is next to nothing. "Can you do that?" I ask. He says, "Sure, no problem." (Avruch 1981, 139–40)

Or elsewhere, in a discussion on obtaining a license: "I made the big mistake of trying to offer that *pakid* some money—to bribe him. Boy did I land on my ass. I thought he'd call the Marines in. In the States, a little cash to grease the wheels always worked, but I learned then and there you can't do that, by and large, in Israel. In fact, I think that because I tried to bribe him, the *pakid* really had it in for me. What did I learn? I learned *people* grease the wheels here, not just money" (pp. 147–48).

Avruch interprets this behavior as characteristic of a traditional society rather than a modern one. He argues that American Jews who successfully adjust to Israeli society are those who become traditionalized—who adapt themselves from a modern society to a traditional one. We have no objection to Avruch's basic thesis, to which we would add that in the extended family that is Israeli society, as in any family, not everyone will like everyone else. Family feuds can be more intense than other feuds, and family hatred can lead to the most violent behavior. But whatever the valence, familistic behavior means acting in a familiar manner, and familiar behavior means personalistic behavior, whether it is expressed as warmth, intrusiveness, rudeness, or even violence. To Israelis the officials of the state are in a sense their family members, and are related to accordingly.

Jewish familism has raised the emotional level of the question "Who is a Jew?" This question encompasses several others: Who is part of the Jewish family? With whom do Jews have a special relationship? *Halakha,* Jewish law, does not distinguish between those who are born Jewish and those who converted to Judaism; one is not even permitted to remind converts of their non-Jewish origins. Converts are assumed not only to be equal members of the Jewish people but to have acquired the genetic characteristics of the Jews by virtue of their conversion. According to the rabbis, the convert is literally reborn as a Jew in some mystical manner. Jewish law does not recognize the biological parents of converts as their real parents. If not for a special provision of rabbinical law, nothing in the law would prevent converts from marrying their biological parents.

Nevertheless, there is a distinction between what the law mandates and how people behave, not to mention how they feel. The strong familistic thrust among Jews has meant that converts have been treated with some degree of suspicion. At the very least, it has meant that Jews do not relate to converts in the same way they relate to those born Jewish. Among our American respondents 73 percent felt the same sense of identity with converts as with those born Jewish; among Israelis only 52 percent did. In other words, substantially more Israelis reported some reservations about converts.

There are two possible explanations for this, and both may be correct. When American Jews think of converts they are likely to think of people they know and with whom they share some degree of intimacy: friends, neighbors, the spouses of family members who converted to Judaism when they married. Israelis, on the other hand, are far less likely to be personally acquainted with a convert. We do not know what type of convert the Israelis had in mind when they responded to our question. They may have been thinking of an Arab who converted to marry a Jew, or of a European who converted for the same reason after meeting an Israeli on a kibbutz. In either case the convert would be remote and strange to the Israeli, and in the former case the question of conversion would have evoked the larger question of relations between Jews and Arabs, which is primarily national and ethnic rather than narrowly religious. Alternatively, our Israeli respondents may have been thinking of non-Jews in the abstract, with no particular referent; and non-Jews in the abstract are not highly regarded among Israelis.

This brings us to a second explanation of our findings, which is not at all inconsistent with the first. We believe that Israeli Jews have a stronger sense of familism than American Jews do. We have already noted that only slightly more of them view the Jewish people as an extension of their family. But this does not measure the intensity of their familistic feeling. Whereas Jewish familism is affirmed by a majority of Israeli Jews as well as by a majority of American Jews, we suspect that it means a great deal more to Israelis. Jewishness in Israel makes one part of the majority, part of the culture of the society; non-Jewishness makes one part of a minority that can never participate fully in a Jewish state, regardless of what civil rights may be accorded.

To cite the most trivial example, in the new year edition of *Ma'ariv*, one of Israel's two largest newspapers, the following headline was used for a story about a release from the Central Bureau of Statistics: "The Number of the State's Inhabitants is 4,375,000; 3,590,000 are Jews" (23 September 1987, p. 3). Public opinion surveys in Israel regularly exclude non-Jews, even though they make up roughly a sixth of the population. Joseph Burg, former minister of the interior, was asked by *Ma'ariv*, "What is an Israeli in your eyes?" He answered, "My wife and children, an Israeli is a Jew at home," completely ignoring his fellow citizens who are not Jewish (Weekend Supplement, 12 September 1986, p. 29). This sharp distinction in Israel between Jew and non-Jew would persist even if the Israeli non-Jew were not associated in the mind of Jews with an enemy who threatens the very existence of the Jewish people and its state. Until the recent increase in Arab-Jewish tensions arising out of the intifada and Israel's reaction to it, Israeli Arabs were in the eyes of Israeli Jews virtual nonpersons rather than enemies. (To be fair, a similar observation may be made about how some American Jews have felt toward blacks, who a generation ago were often referred to as "schvartzes" by immigrant Jews or their children.)

If the notion of family is taken seriously, it affirms a biological affinity. No amount of religious mystification can make biological Jews of converts, even those most scrupulous in observing the Jewish tradition. When Rav Amram Blau, leader of N'turei Karta (the most virulently anti-Zionist group of religious zealots in Jerusalem), sought to marry a convert there was widespread opposition within his own community of ultrapious Jews. No one questioned the Jewish credentials of his wife— she had already demonstrated her loyalty to ultrapietism by taking part in the kidnaping of a young boy, Yoselle Shuchmacher, from his parents, who sought to raise him in a nonreligious home against the wishes of his grandfather. Nevertheless, it was deemed inappropriate for a leader of Amram Blau's stature to marry a convert; and when he insisted on doing so he was exiled from Jerusalem to B'nei B'rak for a period. After he was permitted to return to Jerusalem he was prohibited from living in the heart of the *haredi* (pietistic) community for an additional time.

We might expect this wariness of the convert to be even stronger among those who conduct their lives in accordance with folk norms rather than the letter of Jewish law. In February 1989 the story was revealed of a Bedouin who was converted by Rabbi Ovadia Joseph, the preeminent religious authority of Sephardic Jews. The convert had served in the army, married a Jewish woman, and was accepted to membership in a moshav, a rural communal settlement. But when the members discovered he was a convert they insisted that he leave. The moshav was neither religious nor politically right-wing: in the elections of 1988, 83 percent of its residents voted for the Labour party or for groups to the left of Labour.

Among our respondents, the proportion who said they were somewhat alienated from converts was higher among Israeli Jews who defined themselves as just "traditional" (55 percent) than among those who defined themselves as religiously observant (46 percent). Those who defined themselves as nonreligious, whose level of observance was lowest, were the least likely to report alienation from converts (40 percent). This is not surprising, for this is the group that scored lowest on all our measures of Jewish familism. Rejection of the convert is therefore highest among those who are somewhat attached to Jewish tradition and Jewish familism but who do not feel constrained by their commitment to the requirements of Jewish law to welcome the convert.

The very importance of one's Jewishness in Israeli society makes Israelis wary of according the same sense of obligation and responsibility to the born non-Jew (converted or not) as to the Jew. We believe that this also helps account for some of the differences between Israeli and

American Jews over the question of accepting Reform or Conservative conversions.[5] Both samples were asked whether they agreed that "Israel should grant Conservative and Reform rabbis the same status as Orthodox rabbis." Although 79 percent of the Americans agreed with this statement, only 47 percent of the Israelis did. We suspect that the reason lies in the belief that conversion to Judaism ought not to be undertaken lightly. Being Jewish carries enormous consequences in Israeli society. It affects virtually everything people do and how they are perceived by others. Because conversion to Judaism is perceived, rightly or wrongly, as something that the non-Orthodox rabbis treat less seriously than the Orthodox do (the absence of traditional ritual among Reform conversions is taken as evidence of this), it is inappropriate in the eyes of many Israelis to regard the non-Orthodox convert as a real Jew. But as with the moshav, even Orthodox conversion will not make the convert a real Jew in the eyes of many who harbor intense familistic feelings about the Jewish people, especially if the convert is an Arab.

Restraints on American Jewish Familism

Unlike Israeli Jews, American Jews face pressures that militate against Jewish familistic feelings and behavior. American Jews need to square their Jewish familistic sentiments with American conceptions of equality and Western conceptions of liberalism and humanism. In these conceptions there is something archaic, unenlightened, and intolerant about asserting the primacy of one's kin or clan. In the liberal humanistic vision, the individual is the center of concern, not the family or the tribe or even the nation. And the primary attachments of people ought to be to their friends or coworkers or to those with whom they share acquired traits, not to those among whom they happen to have been born. Jews in the United States have to answer for the implicit particularism of the Jewish tradition, not to mention the notion of chosenness, which has implications of superiority.

A crucial aspect of Jewish familism—Jewish particularism, and especially the concept of a "chosen people"—has found its own resolution among American Jews. Arnold Eisen describes how American Jewish theologians have dealt with the problem (1983). Our concern is with how the problem has worked itself out in the popular mind.

Woocher notes that "the myth of chosenness" is a problem for Jewish denominational leaders but not for communal leaders (1986, 141).
He says that chosenness links the particular concerns of Jews with their
efforts to promote social justice and the welfare of all humanity. These
values are "on their face universal ethical norms, [but] civil Judaism
sees its ethos as the product and expression of Jewish distinctiveness"
(p. 142). Nevertheless Jewish elites, "like many modern Jews, often find
the traditional language of chosenness, and the implications of that language, discomforting" (p. 145).

Woocher's findings are reinforced by our survey of American Jews,
71 percent of whom agreed with this universalist statement: "As Jews,
we have special moral and ethical obligations." These obligations extend at least theoretically to non-Jews as well as to Jews: "As Jews we
should be concerned about all people, and not just Jews" (96 percent
agreed). And further: "I get just as upset by terrorist attacks upon non-
Jews as I do when terrorists attack Jews" (89 percent agreed). We find it
hard to believe that so many American Jews are as upset by terrorist
attacks on non-Jews as by attacks on Jews—such as those at Munich,
Entebbe, Ma'alot, and a Turkish synagogue. Perhaps the assertion that
they are as upset is testimony to the power of the rhetorical commitment to universalism: Jews are supposed to care or at least say they do
about all people (not just Jews), and especially about all victims. The
particularist struggle to defend Jews in a hostile world is universalized
to struggles against genocide, bigotry, and terrorism. The Jewish plea
for the support of righteous Gentiles is almost always phrased in universal moral terms. If Jews expect Gentiles to empathize with Jewish
victims of terrorism, Jews must at least say they empathize with Gentile
victims of terrorism.

The tension between the universal and the particular in Jewish life is
a favorite theme of Jewish commentators, both scholarly and popular.
Observers often note that on the one hand American Jews are renowned for their extraordinarily intense group life, communal solidarity, and sophisticated philanthropic structure aimed at caring for
the needy among them, while on the other hand they are known for
their involvement in universal causes (this is especially true of the
highly educated), such as civil rights, the antiwar movement, nuclear
disarmament, and feminism. In a peculiar way those who address Jew-

ish organizations will exploit for particularist ends this combination of universalist and particularist sentiments. They in effect lead their audiences in cheering the uniqueness of American Jewry, portraying it as the one American religious or ethnic group that combines a passionate concern for itself with an almost equally passionate concern for others. They adore invoking the epigram attributed to the Talmudic sage Hillel: "If I will not be for me, who will be for me? But if I am for myself alone, what am I?" Leonard Fein has echoed this theme: "We are the tribe that proclaimed the universality of God, but insisted on remaining a tribe. Others, not understanding why we have felt such urgency about remaining apart, have asked—and sometimes demanded—that we follow our universal insight to its logical conclusion and ourselves become universal. We have steadfastly refused" (1988, 168).

Accordingly, it is not at all contradictory that 61 percent of American Jews say, "In many ways Jews are different from non-Jews" and that 75 percent also say, "In most ways, Jews are no better than non-Jews." Most American Jews seem to be saying that they are a family, that they are obligated to each other as Jews, that they are special, and that they are different. But at the same time, they are saying that they are no better than non-Jews, and that they care about non-Jews as well. (The Orthodox and other traditionalists are of course more likely than other American Jews to conceive of chosenness in more traditional terms.) We understand these findings in terms of the idea introduced at the outset of our discussion of familism. In the qualified way in which American Jews reinterpret the traditional concept of chosenness, this ties into their conception of the Jewish people as having a set of common goals or purposes. Jews are not simply a family but a family with a purpose, and at least in the American Jewish version of Judaism this purpose has major universalist consequences. (We elaborate on these consequences in chapter 5, about Jewish liberalism.)

In contrast to Israeli rhetoric, American Jewish rhetoric emphasizes the purposeful or goal-oriented nature of Judaism at the expense of familism. American Jews are well prepared to ease the way of converts into the fold. Many accept as members of their synagogues even those who do not formally convert to Judaism, and accept their children as full-fledged Jews. They do so because their familism is less pronounced; one might say that they have ethicized the conception of family so that it now becomes a matter of ideological kinship rather than of biological kinship, even as the familistic conception remains central to their understanding of what it means to be a Jew.

As we might expect, the situation in Israel is not quite the same. There the public arena reinforces the uniqueness and even the feelings of superiority of Jews. These are preached in a selfconsciously ideological manner in certain sectors of society, the religious sector in particular. But even in the nonreligious sector, sensitive in the past few years to charges of racism, there is a tendency to emphasize Jewish uniqueness, with at least overtones of superiority. Thus, for example, Yitzhak Rabin, minister of defense and former prime minister, observed in a television interview that a bright future was in store for the Israeli economy as it developed technologically advanced industry built on "the Jewish brain" (*Erev Hadash,* 22 September 1987).

But the strength of familism in Israel also mirrors developments in the American Jewish community. Secular Zionism laid great emphasis on ideology. David Ben-Gurion, for example, constantly reiterated that a Jewish state was necessary not as an end in itself but rather to serve higher purposes. One purpose was particular to Jews: "ingathering of the exiles." Another was essentially universalistic: to serve as a "light unto the nations." The decline of secular Zionism as an ideology has left many Israelis without a common goal or purpose beyond survival. It is not surprising that under these circumstances a more familistic or narrowly biological definition of Judaism should assert itself.[6]

Assuming that American Jewish conceptions of Judaism are familist, although less so than those of the Israelis, we now want to introduce an important qualification. For American Jews the idea of Jewish peoplehood and of ties to an international Jewish people is more important than for the Israelis. Israeli Jewish familism is most vividly expressed in interactions with other Israeli Jews; the land, (Jewish) society, and the state of Israel are major components of the Israeli Jewish identity (see chapters 4 and 6). Relations with one's fellow Jewish Israelis undoubtedly crowd out and supersede ideological commitment to the Jewish people as an international entity. Israeli respondents were quite clear about this issue on our survey: 50 percent said that their "basic sense of identity and commitment is more [oriented] to Israel and Israelis than to Jews and Judaism"; only 31 percent disagreed.

As a minority seeking to justify to themselves and to their children their desire for continuity and survival, American Jews find it critical for their self-image to maintain the idea that they are different from non-Jews, although not better. It is more important for American Jews than for Israeli Jews to affirm differences between Jew and Gentile and to proclaim their mythical, ideological, and rhetorical links to other Jews throughout the world. The evidence from our surveys supports this assertion. Forty-seven percent of Israelis agreed that "in most ways, Jews are no better than non-Jews," compared with three-quarters of American Jews. Even secular Israelis assert more readily that Jews are superior to Gentiles, yet more American Jews than Israelis agree that "Jews are different from non-Jews" (61 percent to 47 percent). And given a list of reasons why being Jewish might be important to them; the statement "It provides me with a tie to other Jews" was chosen by more Americans (78 percent) than Israelis (64 percent). Jewish distinctiveness and Jewish connectedness are more apparent, accepted, significant, and genuine to Americans than to Israelis.

These differences are actually muted by the greater religiosity of Israelis and the greater secularism of American Jews. In both societies religiosity is linked closely to the assertion of differences between Jews and Gentiles, Jewish superiority, and a commitment to Jewish peoplehood. Holding religiosity constant reveals even more dramatic differences between American and Israeli Jewry in their commitment to Jewish peoplehood. Among American Jews the proportion deeply committed to Jewish peoplehood (as we defined the term) ranged from 34 percent among the nonobservant, to 60 percent among the moderately observant, to 71 percent among the non-Orthodox observant, to 90 percent among the Orthodox.[7] For Israelis the comparable percentages were 28, 40, 58, and 51. Thus at every level of observance the Americans scored higher than the Israelis.

The idea of Jewish peoplehood therefore looms larger in the American Jewish concept of familism, even as Jewish particularism (perhaps we can call it favoritism) is more unabashedly endorsed and practiced by Israelis. Rhetorically, Jews attribute to historic causes these concepts, as well as their putatively unique combination of particularism and universalism. As we have been suggesting, Jewish familism abides within a historic framework. It is a personalized, passionate commitment to a group conceived of as an extended family with a rich, articulated, and significant memory of its collective, tribal past. Hence the term *historic familism*.

Lessons of History: The Centrality of Victimization and Vulnerability

Many lessons are embedded in the Jewish historical consciousness, but one myth stands out as especially instructive: that Jews have been the victims of unrelenting persecution. The lesson begins with a central, formative event in Jewish history, the enslavement in Egypt, and continues until the Holocaust in Europe; in the interim it is punctuated with invasions, expulsions, and pogroms. "Jewish history is a series of holocausts, with only some improvement in technique," says the renowned Israeli author Aharon Appelfeld (1987, 4). This "lachrymose theory of Jewish history," to use a term coined by the Jewish historian Salo Baron, has implications for the present. It allows Jews to entertain images of their own nobility, one born of persecution, and it even allows them to make political and moral claims on the putative descendants of their ancestral oppressors.

Sociologists of knowledge have observed that society decides what constitutes knowledge and what kinds of knowledge are useful and valuable. It is in this sense that almost all American Jews (94 percent in the survey of 1984) can be said to "know" that "Jews have a uniquely long and tragic history of persecution." One critical element in this statement is the word *unique*. The image of Jewish victimization has its political and psychological uses, and as a result Jews often have a deep emotional investment in preserving their image as a uniquely long-suffering minority. Leading Jewish spokesmen have resisted efforts to deny Jews their history of extraordinary persecution and to diminish the singularity, the distinctiveness, of Jewish victimization. Nothing annoys Jews so much as to be told that other groups have also suffered. Not a few American Jewish spokesmen have bristled at the use of the words *Holocaust* or even *genocide* to describe tragedies that have befallen other minorities and nationalities in recent times, particularly when used to advance causes suspected of being anti-Zionist or anti-

Semitic. In Israel, to compare the tragedy of other peoples with Jewish tragedy is tantamount to anti-Semitism.

The story of Jewish persecution is a central element in the Jewish religious tradition, one that obviously influences American and Israeli Jews to varying degrees. The tale of Jewish slavery in Egypt is recounted at the Passover Seder, the most widely observed ritual practice in the Jewish calendar. One of the high points early in the Haggadah, the traditional Passover story, begins with these words: "We were slaves unto Pharaoh in Egypt." Not much later the Haggadah reads, "For more than once have they stood against us to destroy us." Who "they" are is not specified.

Still other religious holidays remind Jews of the dangers that Gentiles pose to their security. The story of Purim tells how the king's adviser, Haman, nearly succeeded in leading the masses throughout the Persian empire in a slaughter of Jews. Tisha b'Av commemorates the destruction of the first and second Temples, as well as other tragedies that presumably occurred on the anniversaries of their destruction (especially the expulsion of the Jews from Spain in 1492). The image of Israel, so central to the lives of American Jews, is projected as that of a country surrounded by enemies bent on its destruction. And the Holocaust itself, which along with Israel has assumed central symbolic importance in American Jewish life, reminds Jews above all of their precarious status among the hostile Gentiles.

These themes tend to be combined in appeals by Jewish organizations for funds. (We may assume that fund-raisers make it their business to know what arouses the emotions of potential contributors, and for this reason their fund-raising strategy is instructive.) In August and September 1987 a mass mailing appealing for funds was sent to American Jews by the Jewish National Fund, the special function of which is to plant trees in Israel. The letter reported that in July 1987 four fires had "ravage[d] 1,150 acres of forests" in Israel, that "arson is strongly suspected" (this was never confirmed, although nine months later some Arabs did set fire to Israeli forests), and that "Israel's enemies celebrate this conflagration." The Holocaust figured prominently in the letter: "Most heart-rending of all, 50 acres of the Children's Forest, in the B'nai B'rith Martyrs' Forest was utterly destroyed. It was planted by children in memory of the children who perished in the Holocaust."

Israel as an endangered entity is invoked in the last paragraph, before the reader is asked for funds: "Fourteen years ago, the Yom Kippur War broke out. We are reminded once again that Israel's battle for security is not over. Let's affirm that our transformation of the land can never be eradicated. It is a matter of national urgency." This paragraph is of special interest because it bears so little relevance to the planting of trees.

Since the trial of Adolf Eichmann (1960) and the Six Day War (1967), American Jews have made the Holocaust a central symbol. Scores of Jewish communities around the United States have erected Holocaust memorials, exhibits, and museums. Jewish fund-raisers regularly speak of the enormous responsibility that falls on the generation following the Holocaust to ensure the survival of endangered Jewry, whether in Israel, the Soviet Union, or elsewhere. University courses on the Holocaust are popular with students, and Jewish philanthropists are especially keen to endow professorial chairs for Holocaust studies. Eighty-six percent of the American Jews surveyed in 1985 agreed that "there's no doubt that the Holocaust has deeply affected the way I think and feel about being Jewish."

The Holocaust is no less significant to Israeli Jews. It has been referred to as the central myth of Israeli society (Liebman and Don-Yehiya 1983a), and we have demonstrated with survey data and by examining statements by the Israeli elite that the memory of the Holocaust pervades Israeli society and informs the policy decisions of its leaders. The myth of the Holocaust teaches that throughout their history of persecution the Jews have been blameless, their oppressors irrational. Pharaoh repeatedly "hardens his heart," even when confronted with plagues that make his refusal to let the Hebrews go costly and imprudent. The Crusaders take a detour from their route to the Holy Land to massacre Jews, and the Cossacks pillage Jewish villages even though it is the Polish noblemen who have been exploiting the Cossacks. The Nazis are driven by baseless hatred of the Jews to divert resources away from their war effort and toward their policy of genocide. Anti-Semitism is a mystifying disease—one with perhaps many permutations and with diverse origins, but at root one that is fundamentally irrational. This irrationalism only compounds the innocence of the Jewish victim.

It is not our intention to challenge the truth of these myths; we subscribe in good part to most of them. We wish only to point out that by recalling one's history in a particular manner, certain images of oneself and of others are conveyed. For the Jews these images have in turn become central cultural symbols, and they have affected the Jewish view of the non-Jew and of anti-Semitism.

3 Ethnocentrism

and

Anti-Semitism

In traditional times what it meant to be a Jew was intimately entangled with what the non-Jew meant to the Jews, and this remains true in modern times. Obviously the sense of distance from the Gentile, reinforced by a perception that the Gentile is antagonistic and inferior, has played an important role in shaping the nature and potency of Jewish solidarity and Jewish familism. Both Israeli and American Jews have inherited traditional images of the Gentile, but as they have done with other Judaic cultural elements, both communities have modified and recast what they have received from the past. In this context the concept of exile (*galut*) is important for understanding traditional Jewish attitudes toward non-Jews, or *goyim* (a term that in modern times carries pejorative overtones). From the mishnaic period in the second and third centuries of the common era until the last two centuries, the concept of "exile and redemption" more than any other provided the core integrating structure of belief for most Jews. Moreover, this theological construct subsumed an understanding of Gentiles and their character and what it meant for Jews to be living among them.

In traditional Jewish thought, galut is a metaphysical condition that evokes deeper levels of meaning than simply that of a people forcibly removed from their own land. Exile points to the sins of the Jews, the disordered nature of the cosmos, and the ultimate plan of God. Further, it points to the central role of the Jewish people in God's divine plan. The counterpart of exile is redemption, a time when Jews will return to their land, God will be reunited with His people, the Gentiles will acknowledge the greatness of God and His people, and the cosmos will be redeemed from its own disharmony. Secular Zionism ignored these deeper levels of meaning and defined exile in the purely political sense. But traditional conceptions pervaded Jewish thought at least until the modern period. Ben Halpern has observed that this religious mythos "gave the restrictions, subjugation and stigmas—the institutionalized anti-Semitism of [the Jews'] pre-modern status—a sublimated significance that made them inwardly innocuous if not benign, and not merely outwardly acceptable" (1987, 5). We would add that anti-Semites were not only "stock characters in the traditional drama of Exile and Redemption" (Halpern 1987, 7) but leading figures with necessary roles.

The Centrality of Anti-Semites in Traditional Jewish Consciousness

First, the suffering that non-Jews inflicted on Jews confirmed the reality of exile. Had Jews not suffered, the metaphysical meaning of exile would have been trivialized. After all, if cosmological disorder has no physical or material expression, it necessarily becomes a less serious matter. It stands to reason that the political fact of exile preceded the elaborate metaphysical conception of exile, although the concept is distinctly biblical in origin. The enormous importance that exile and redemption continued to exercise throughout the medieval period is probably related to the hostility that Jews endured in ancient times from the pagans and later from Christians and Moslems. This continued antagonism (which Jews called anti-Semitism) confirmed the validity of the Jewish myth of exile and redemption. Jews developed this myth to account for their miserable material conditions, to console themselves, and to provide them with a program for enduring their persecution and poverty. The perpetuation of these conditions confirmed in turn the Judaic conceptions of the reality of exile and redemption.

Second, although anti-Semitism was a tragic fact in the lives of the Jews, it also reinforced their ethnocentric self-image as a "chosen" people. The special animus of non-Jews toward Jews demonstrated the truth of the Jewish claim that they were different, privy to a special status in divine creation—in short, superior to the Gentiles.

Jane Gerber has noted that Jewish chroniclers depicted Jewish tribulations in a way that left the reader "with an impression that Jewish life in the Diaspora [was] uniformly and eternally plagued by the irrational, unpredictable, and all-encompassing evil of anti-Semitism" (1986, 74). The image of insecurity, of the permanent threat of anti-Semitic eruption, of the hostile Gentile, was so deeply embedded in Jewish thought by the late medieval period that we find it even in periods of relative security, tranquility, and prosperity. Recent writers, for example, have challenged the assumption of earlier Jewish historians that the condition of Polish Jewry from the sixteenth century to the eighteenth was one of continued oppression, poverty, and humiliation, and have demonstrated that in fact Polish Jews enjoyed relative security and prosperity. M. J. Rosman accepts this assessment, but he shows that Jewish leaders of the period nevertheless did not view their condition as secure (Rosman 1986). Although Rosman does not say so, we suggest that for them to have believed otherwise would have revolutionized Jewish theology.

A theological revolution did take place in the nineteenth century, when Rabbi Zvi Hirsch Kalischer (1795–1874), harbinger of the Zionist idea, accepted the reality of the emancipation (J. Katz 1979). He believed that Gentiles really were offering Jews civil liberties; it was no illusion or trick. Because in Kalischer's mind the political emancipation of the Jews could have proceeded only from a divine plan, the emancipation itself signaled a new stage in Jewish history, indeed in world history. It was the beginning of the redemption and therefore it justified and even necessitated such activity on the part of the Jews as resettling the land of Israel and restoring sacrifices that they were heretofore constrained from undertaking.

The fear of Gentile hostility was of course only part of the manner in which Jews before the emancipation understood non-Jews. In addition, Jews harbored many unflattering images both of Gentile individuals and of Gentile culture. These negative images were constituent elements in traditional Jewish identity, reinforcing Jewish notions of their own individual and collective superiority, and contributing to the sense of Jewish familism (the belief that Jews were all part of one extended family) and Jewish chosenness.

Most Jews regarded themselves as spiritually superior to non-Jews. As Jews they enjoyed a special relationship with God, combining special obligations with special privileges. Rabbinic attitudes toward Christianity were not monolithic. They varied from one rabbi to another, from one period to another, and from one location to another. Some viewed Christianity with contempt, seeing it as no better than idolatry. Others saw it as a valid monotheistic religion containing values compatible with Judaism, albeit inferior to it. But there was never any doubt that Christianity was the backward religion, that Judaism enjoyed the approbation of God, and that among all God's creatures Jews had a special relationship with the Maker. The contempt of traditional Jews for Christianity was paralleled by a disdain for Christians as individuals. Jacob Katz notes that rabbinic attitudes toward Christian individuals changed in the modern period (1961, 165). He cites the work of Moses Rivkes, a seventeenth-century Lithuanian authority who "drew the conclusion that, regarding the obligation to save life, no discrimination should be made between Jew and Christian; the same degree of merit was attached to saving either." The conclusion only demonstrates the depth of historic Jewish hostility toward the non-Jew and the legitimation that this hostility received within the religious tradition. Rabbi Rivkes's positive evaluation of Gentile lives (one that not all Orthodox rabbis today share with equal conviction) is itself testimony to the popularity of the antithetical view among his rabbinic contemporaries and predecessors.

Zborowski and Herzog (1952) provide additional evidence that Jew and Gentile have continued even into the modern period to see each other as completely different. Their study is based on the memories of former residents of *shtetlach* in Poland, and although these memories may not be completely accurate (a point that critics of the study have made), the study is useful in describing how East European immigrants to the United States a generation ago recalled the nature of relations between Jews and Gentiles. "Reciprocal attitudes are reflected in linguistic usage. Each group will use animal terms in speaking of the other, implying it is subhuman. If a Jew dies a [Gentile] peasant will use the word for animal death in reporting the event, and a Jew will do the same for a peasant. . . . The peasant will say, 'That's not a man, it's a Jew.' And the Jew will say, 'That's not a man, it's a goy.' To each group the other represents the unbeliever. 'A Jew and a dog have the same creed,' say the Ukrainians. And the Jews say [direct quote from informant]: 'The peasants don't have a God, they just have a board they call an icon and they pray to that'" (p. 157).

The images of Gentiles that these immigrants from Eastern Europe recalled were constructed so as to enhance a self-image of Jewish superiority and convey communal norms. "The children are constantly reminded that a 'real' Jew is moderate, restrained and intellectual," Zborowski and Herzog write. "The chief reason for prohibitions is 'because it is un-Jewish' or, as the shtetl puts it—goyish." The Gentile is the mirror image of the Jew: "A series of contrasts is set up in the mind of the shtetl child who grows up to regard certain behavior as characteristic of Jews, and its opposite as characteristic of Gentiles. Among Jews he expects to find emphasis on intellect, a sense of moderation, cherishing of spiritual values, cultivation of rational, goal-directed activities, a 'beautiful' family life. Among Gentiles he looks for the opposite of each item: emphasis on the body, excess, blind instinct, sexual license, and ruthless force. The first is ticketed in his mind as Jewish, the second as goyish" (1952, 152).

The traditional Jewish understanding of the Gentile world combined several elements that were mutually reinforcing: (1) life among the Gentiles is galut—a state of physical and spiritual exile for the Jew, a state of homelessness among foreigners; (2) Gentiles hate Jews, and anti-Semitism constitutes an ever-present and serious threat to Jewish security; (3) Christianity, or more broadly Christian culture and civilization, is spiritually inferior to Judaism and unattractive compared with Jewish culture and civilization; (4) individual Gentiles have several negative traits, and Jews have many admirable ones. Clearly, contemporary Jews in both Israel and the United States have modified these conceptions of anti-Semitism and the non-Jew. Ben Halpern notes in his essay cited above how the modification of traditional Jewish belief necessitated new responses to anti-Semitism. He argues that Jews of the modern period, lacking the mythos of divinely ordained exile and redemption to account for anti-Semitism, could not respond with detachment and passivity to the shame and degradation that anti-Semitism now imposed on them as a result of their modern consciousness.

Zionism was one outcome. But Zionism implied pessimism about Jewish security in the diaspora. It retained an image of continuing threats to Jewish survival as long as Jews had no country of their own. What about those Jews committed to living in the West (and thus in the diaspora)? Almost by definition, they must believe that Jewish disabilities can be overcome. We would expect them to become convinced that Jews and Gentiles are basically similar and can live in harmony. And we would expect their understanding of the Gentile world to embrace the following principles: (1) America (or England, or France, or Germany) is home for the Jews—Jews are no longer alien to the larger society, and Gentiles are no longer alien to the Jews; (2) most Gentiles (especially the better educated and more modern) harbor no particular animus toward Jews, and anti-Semitism is not the threat it once was; (3) Western culture is very attractive and in some ways more sophisticated and appealing than Jewish culture; (4) Jews are neither better nor worse than Gentiles.

Despite movement toward these four principles, traditional views of the Gentile and the fear of anti-Semitism persist, even among Jews who accept the reality of emancipation. Indeed such notions have been strengthened in our generation, particularly as a result of the Holocaust and of Arab hostility to Israel (Liebman 1983). This sense of estrangement from the non-Jew and fear of the non-Jew remain not only for Israelis and not only for those most deeply committed to the Jewish tradition. Our first task is to explore notions among American Jews of the Gentile, of anti-Semitism, and of ethnocentrism and ask whether anything about them distinguishes American Jews from Israeli Jews.

Mostly at Home in America: The Denial of Exile

The clue to the emergence of new American Jewish conceptions lies in the unwillingness of many American Jews to come to terms with their own acceptance in American society. (As Abba Eban has remarked, Jews are notable for their inability to take yes for an answer.) Jewish ethnocentrism has declined, but American Jews continue to believe or at least to say they believe that anti-Semitism in the United States remains widespread. Without denying that there is some anti-Semitism, we nevertheless find it striking that Jewish concern over anti-Semitism is as great as it is. After all, there is persuasive evidence that Gentiles accept American Jews and hold them in high esteem, the record of Jewish achievement in the United States is extraordinary, the anti-Semitism that does exist is primarily social rather than economic, and physical abuse of Jews is rare. Further, surveys repeatedly show a continued decline in hostility toward Jews on the part of Gentiles.[1]

Jewish acceptance into the mainstream of American life today seems beyond dispute.[2] Several studies indicate that Jews may be the most affluent and best educated group in America. Charles Silberman reports that about a quarter of the "Forbes 400" (the wealthiest Americans) are Jewish, as are about a third of those with self-made fortunes rather than inherited wealth (1985, 143–44). Although they constitute less than 3 percent of the American population, Jews account for at least a quarter of the most influential journalists in the United States (Alba and Moore 1982). Another study suggests that they make up half of the most influential intellectuals (Kadushin 1974), and scattered anecdotal evidence suggests that in the last two decades little has changed in this respect. The pro-Israel lobby in Washington, led by the American-Israel Public Affairs Committee, is often thought of as the most influential lobby of its kind (Tivnan 1987).

In many ways the sense of American Jews that they are truly at home in America is stronger and more pervasive today than ever before. Not only are younger Jews today relatively well-off, but many of their parents were, and inherited privilege bestows a greater sense of security than privilege only recently achieved. The 1970s and 1980s saw the maturation of large numbers of Jews whose parents and even grandparents were born in America. The stigma of foreignness experienced by the immigrants and their children no longer applies to most of American Jewry.[3]

The growing sense of ease in the United States felt by Jews is reflected in the changing tenor of Jewish political activity. Until 1967 the style of those who represented Jewish political interests in the United States bore many similarities to that of Jews in modernizing Europe or premodern societies. In the first two-thirds of the twentieth century, the agents of American Jewish influence relied heavily on coalition building, high-level intercession, and supplication. Jewish politicians rarely stood for election outside densely populated Jewish areas. Some communal leaders and intellectuals, sensitive about appearing collectively to be at odds with the larger society, bristled at any suggestion of a "Jewish vote" or at the idea that Jews might be overly clannish or excessively loyal to Israel.

Since the late 1960s Jews have been elected in increasing numbers to public office in areas with relatively few Jewish voters. Jewish activists have been more assertive in demanding that elected officials support Israel and the rights of Soviet Jewry. Politicians have complained about unabashed pressure tactics that threaten critics of Israel with political defeat. There is some evidence that Jewish political action committees were able to make good on their threats; the defeat of Sen. Charles Percy of Illinois in 1984 is probably the best example of how Jews used their political muscle. American Jews succeeded in placing the issue of Soviet Jewry on the agenda of Soviet-American relations and contributing to the movement that resulted in the emigration of 300,000 Soviet Jews since 1968.[4] Jewish pressure certainly helps account for the government's support of Israel. All this stands in marked contrast with the inability of Jewish leaders in the 1940s to get American leaders to save European Jewry from slaughter by the Nazis.

Despite all this, fears of anti-Semitism persist. Notwithstanding their faith in America and their appreciation of it, and their extraordinary social, economic, and political achievements, American Jews remain anxious about anti-Semitism and threats to their security. In 1984, 92 percent of American Jews agreed that American Jews must be vigilant in combating any signs of anti-Semitism; in 1983, 1984, and 1986 from two-thirds to more than three-quarters agreed that anti-Semitism in America might become a serious problem in the future; and in 1988, 65 percent rejected the proposition that virtually all positions of influence are open to Jews, and 76 percent rejected the proposition that anti-Semitism is not a serious problem for American Jews today. In 1985 as many as 37 percent of the Jewish respondents characterized American Christians as generally anti-Semitic. On a related issue, in 1988 57 percent agreed that "when it comes to the crunch, few non-Jews will come to Israel's side in its struggle to survive." One is forced to conclude that at least half of all American Jews harbor anxieties about the amity of their Christian neighbors; among those who identify more strongly as Jews the proportion is even higher. One reason for the broad perception of anti-Semitism is that in the American Jewish mind, anti-Semitism connotes many forms of conflict or of antagonism to Jews, severe or inconsequential, real or imagined.

The claim made by Jewish organizations that they are successfully combating anti-Semitism or opposition to Israel (which American Jews often define as anti-Semitism) is one of the most effective instruments for mobilizing Jewish financial and political support. The American

Jewish Congress, the most politically liberal of the major Jewish "defense" organizations, experienced its most successful direct mail fundraising campaign in 1984, when its letters highlighted the ostensible threats to Jewish security posed by the rise to prominence of the Moral Majority, a Christian fundamentalist organization led by the Rev. Jerry Falwell. Four years later the congress apparently thought the same sort of appeal would still be effective. In May 1988 it mailed an appeal for funds in an envelope bearing the legend "If the Christian Right wins, you haven't got a prayer." The letter reads, "There exists in this country today a powerful political religious movement that is fundamentally hostile to the basic principle of religious freedom."

In the 1960s the Anti-Defamation League and the American Jewish Committee had comparable budgets and staffs. In the last two decades the ADL has grown substantially, and it is now considerably larger than the AJC in budget and staff, and arguably in influence. Observers credit the expansion of the ADL to its emphasis on exposing and combating anti-Semitism, a function that the AJC regards with some disdain as pandering to the fears of the Jewish masses.

The memory of persecution in general and of the Holocaust in particular is deeply embedded in Jewish consciousness (see chapter 2). This accounts at least in part for persistent anxieties about anti-Semitism. But collective memories are inadequate to explain contemporary levels of concern about the antagonism of Gentiles. Modern Jews selectively retain or abandon elements of the traditional Jewish past in accord with their contemporary needs. That perceptions of an unfriendly world persist among at least half of all American Jews suggests that the fear of anti-Semitism not only derives from powerful collective memories but plays a vital role in the Jewish identity of contemporary American Jews. In sociological parlance, it has certain "functions" for American Jews that bear further examination.

The view of the non-Jew as essentially hostile serves the financial and political interests of several communal institutions, particularly the Jewish "defense" agencies. There is no question that the agencies are sincere when they warn of threats to the security of American Jews. But neither is there any question that the perception of hostility on the part of non-Jews strengthens the agencies themselves, and makes it difficult for them realistically to assess positive developments in the social climate.

In the world of public discourse, the assertion that anti-Semitism is historic and persisting serves other functions, one of which is to provide a basis for Jewish claims to moral privilege. Jews would say (and do) that their persecution has given them special moral insights. To take one telling example, 80 percent of Jewish respondents in 1984 agreed that "the Jewish history of persecution has made Jews especially sensitive to the needs of minority groups." American Jews frequently claim that blacks fail to appreciate the extent to which Jews have helped the civil rights movement and are committed to eradicating prejudice in all its forms.

In fact, two popular Jewish writers and lecturers say that anti-Semitism itself is a function of the higher moral standards and behavior of Jews. According to Prager and Telushkin (1983), one reason the Jews have been persecuted is that they sought to change the world for the better and thereby made moral demands on others. These demands contributed in turn to tension with the Gentiles. In addition, "as a result of the Jews' commitment to Judaism, they have led higher quality lives than their non-Jewish neighbors in almost every society in which they have lived. . . . To cite but a few examples: Jews have nearly always been better educated; Jewish family life has usually been far more stable; . . . and Jews have been far less likely to become drunk, beat their wives, abandon their children, and the like. . . . This higher quality of life among Jews, which . . . results from Judaism has challenged non-Jews and provoked profound envy and hostility" (1983, 23). The contention that there is a link between anti-Semitism and superior Jewish morality is not at all novel. But American Jews have usually asserted that persecution has made them sensitive to the needs of others and to the importance of moral behavior. We find surprising by American standards the suggestion that the reverse is true: that persecution is the result of a higher Jewish morality. But this position too has powerful roots within the older rabbinic tradition.

Beyond moral privilege, the Jews feel that their suffering entitles them to special consideration from the non-Jewish world. Groups (and individuals) often make much of their history of suffering as a way of strengthening their claims to certain rewards. Like family members in a therapy session, members of conflicting groups feel an urgent need to explain to outsiders how they have suffered at the hands of other groups; they compete to demonstrate how each has suffered more than his or her opponent. In 1986, 46 percent of American Jews agreed that "the Jewish history of persecution is one important reason why non-Jews are obligated to support the security of Israel."

The rhetoric of American Jewish leaders may be seen as both a response to these sentiments and a reinforcement of them. This is most evident in the weight that American Jews in general and their leaders in particular attach to the memory of the Holocaust. This preeminent Jewish symbol for contemporary American Jews serves many functions, but above all it reminds Jews of the potential of anti-Semitism, the ultimate horror of anti-Semitism, and the necessity to remain vigilant against its recurrence. According to Jon Woocher, "When leaders of the Jewish polity speak of survival they mean, first and foremost, the physcial survival of Jews and the Jewish people. Since the Holocaust, no leader . . . is prepared to take even this level of concern for granted. . . . Wherever Jews are perceived to be in danger—and especially in Israel, which is seen as an embattled nation surrounded by implacable enemies—the American Jewish polity feels a responsibility to offer its support. A constant vigilance is maintained against manifestations of anti-Semitism, heightened by the conviction that the anti-Semite's ultimate aim is Jewish extinction. Such is the lesson of Jewish history, ancient and contemporary" (1986, 73).

Woocher demonstrates throughout his work how the theme of recurring anti-Semitism promotes feelings of Jewish solidarity, tangibly expressed in charitable donations to the United Jewish Appeal and local federations of Jewish philanthropy. This inference is confirmed by in-depth interviews with Jewish donors, who say that perceived anti-Semitism is one of their two most important reasons for giving to local Jewish federations (Dashefsky 1989).

Fear of Anti-Semitism:
The Private Dimension

The fear of anti-Semitism functions in the private sphere to buttress Jewish identity and enhance feelings of Jewish familism. For example, parents opposed to the marriage of their child to a Gentile point to the latent anti-Semitism that they assume resides in every non-Jew, even the non-Jew who wishes to marry a Jew. For many Jews even today, marrying a Gentile, to say nothing of converting to

Christianity, connotes "joining the enemy," and the Gentile remains an enemy despite his or her willingness to intermarry. (Rising intermarriage may in time weaken this traditional view.) The Gentile world is to be feared and rejected, because for so long the Gentiles have feared and rejected Jews: "In addition to whatever other objections they may harbor, Jews reject Christianity at the emotional and affective levels. Jewish socialization transmits a sense of membership in a distinct ethnic group. In the western world, a significant defining characteristic of being Jewish is *not* being Christian. This awareness is continually reinforced by the lessons of a long history of Christian anti-Semitism and persecution, supported by Christian theology, which believed that Jews suffered divine rejection for their obstinate refusal to accept Christianity" (Medding 1987, 28).

Fear of anti-Semitism is commoner among the more traditional, but it is not confined to them. Among Jews who lead less intensively Jewish lives (in terms of ritual, friends, communal affiliations, and so forth), images of antagonistic Gentiles are certainly present. Even marginal Jews may use anti-Semitism to motivate their own identification as Jews and to help to explain to themselves what it means to be Jewish. Ellen Willis, a columnist for the *Village Voice,* has described this tendency as follows: "Being Jewish was not problematic for me in the way I think it always was for my brother who grew up being subjected to anti-Semitism from an early age. . . . My parents were not religious. We were not even particularly culturally Jewish in any kind of concrete way. . . . When I first started getting really self-conscious about Jewishness, Jewish identity and anti-Semitism was in the late sixties when I came up against anti-Zionism on the Left. . . . Another thing that also upset me very much . . . was that there was a lot of very overt anti-Semitism among black nationalists and nobody on the black or white Left seemed to be ready to criticize it" ("Pride, Prejudice, and Politics," 6–7). Willis then explains that she remains a secular Jew, but one conscious of her attachment to "a persecuted minority that's subject to this complicated form of oppression." In her view, Jewishness consists of belonging to "a big extended family." She denies that being Jewish connotes a set of divinely ordained obligations: "To me the status of Jews as outsiders and as persecuted outsiders is at the core of what Judaism and Jewishness is all about. It's what all Jews—religious and secular, Zionist and non-Zionist, conservative and radical—have in common" (p. 17).

The autobiographies of Jews who were once only minimally involved in Jewish life testify to the critical role that anti-Semitic encounters, the Holocaust, centuries of persecution, and contemporary anti-Semitism played in increasing their interest in things Jewish. In 1978 the novelist Anne Roiphe published an article in the *New York Times Magazine* entitled "Christmas Comes to a Jewish Home." The piece provoked an outpouring of angry letters from Jewish readers upset by Roiphe's embrace of a Christian holiday. Stung by the reaction, Roiphe undertook to learn more about Judaism and began to take part in conventional Jewish life. She published her reflections on her journey to an intense Jewish identity in *Generation without Memory* (1981). Significantly, Roiphe attributes enormous importance to the suffering and persecution that Jews experienced at the hands of non-Jews, and her feeling of responsibility to perpetuate the faith that her persecuted ancestors retained through centuries of hardship.

Similar stories can be told about thousands of Jews in the United States and other diaspora countries. Although only marginally involved in conventional Jewish life, many Jews report that anti-Semitic experiences or anxieties have led them to a strong sense of attachment to Jews and Jewishness. And the content of their Judaism, their sense of what a Jew ought to feel, believe, and do, derives heavily from the view of Jews as victims, as a persecuted minority, and as potentially threatened even in contemporary America. At the same time, such feelings obviously seem compatible with the relatively high rates of intermarriage among the more marginally Jewish. Jews in mixed marriages are less likely to hold traditional attitudes toward Gentiles, but it is fair to say that for many of them their sense of Jewish identity still embraces feelings of otherness, marginality, and victimization, all of which are fed by perceptions of widespread anti-Semitism.

Despite their material success in America and the evidence that America has been quite good to them, Jews retain feelings of insecurity and vulnerability. The best explanation we can offer for this feeling is that it derives from a "collective memory," a family history that American Jews continue to nourish (see chapter 2). It is a history of Jews being weak and vulnerable while their Christian neighbors are strong and secure. The residue of this traditional image is clearly visible in the way Jews characterize themselves and others. In the survey of 1985, American Christians were seen as "generally powerful" by 89 percent of Jewish respondents; American Jews were seen as powerful by 55 percent. American Christians were also seen as more secure (87 percent to 35 percent) and as less "vulnerable" (13 percent to 73 percent). These perceptions of Christian power and security feed perceptions of Jewish weakness and vulnerability, or are perhaps fed by them: those who see Christians as powerful, secure, and invulnerable tend to see them as anti-Semitic; and those who see American Jews as vulnerable or lacking in power also tend to see American Christians as anti-Semitic.

Historical images of the goyim and of their relationship to Jews also nourish American Jewish notions of who is likely to be anti-Semitic. During the nineteenth century, when European Jews were struggling for political and social rights, the political left tended to support their effort, whereas the political right, the Church, and conservative nationalists resisted lifting legal and social barriers to full Jewish participation in the economy and polity. Although this is not necessarily the American experience, American Jews remain far more suspicious of groups on the political right than of those on the left. For example, 20 percent of all respondents in 1988 felt that many or most Republicans were anti-Semitic; only 7 percent felt the same about Democrats. And 22 percent said many or most conservatives were anti-Semitic; only 9 percent said this about liberals.

The collective Jewish memory points to another source of anti-Semitism. In the same survey, respondents were asked whether most members of various ethnic and religious groups were anti-Semitic. The affirmative responses were remarkably high: for Hispanics, 30 percent; for Catholics, 38 percent; for mainstream Protestants, 34 percent; for fundamentalist Protestants, 50 percent; and for blacks, 36 percent. Here we have a curious contradiction, for many Catholics and almost all blacks are liberal Democrats, especially on economic issues. More than a third of the Jewish sample apparently regarded the religious and racial identities of these groups as grounds for suspicion, even though they perceived their typical political label (vague as it might be) as a sign of friendliness to Jews and Jewish interests. The answer to this paradox may lie in the lesson Jews have learned from their mythic past.

Strong nationalist, ethnic, or religious loyalties of Gentiles increase the likelihood of their being anti-Semitic. The safest goy is one devoid of strong group commitments.

In addition to instructing Jews about the persistence of anti-Semitism and the likely identity of their adversaries, their collective memory also tells them what circumstances are likely to engender anti-Semitic outbreaks. According to the conventional understanding of the European past, Jews have a stake in an orderly society. The peasants, whose virulent anti-Semitism could bring about pogroms, constituted a grave threat to Jewish security. When the authorities lost control of the masses of downtrodden peasants or needed to distract them, the masses would act out their hatred for the Jews in pogroms and violence. Whether accurate or not, this memory of the past has very real implications for the present. In 1985, 86 percent of American Jews agreed that bad economic times and major social unrest in the United States could easily lead to increased anti-Semitism, and 55 percent agreed that one good reason for Jews to support government spending on social welfare programs was that in the long run they helped deter social unrest and upheaval.

The collective memory of persecution is alive among American Jews. Most see anti-Semites around them, and they find them where their traditional consciousness tells them to look: in the camp of the religious and politically conservative, and among Gentiles who are strongly identified with their own religious, ethnic, or racial groups. Although this consciousness influences contemporary Jewish understandings of Gentile anti-Semitism, it must compete with rival ones. About half of American Jews express anxieties about anti-Semitism, but it is just as significant that about half do not. In addition, many Jews who do believe that Gentiles are anti-Semites also believe that the form of anti-Semitism prevailing in modern America is less virulent than that which prevailed in other places or at earlier times.

A nationwide survey of more than three hundred Jewish respondents conducted in 1987 by the social psychologist Simon Herman focused on opinions of anti-Semitism. Where his questions replicated those in our earlier surveys, his responses were nearly identical to ours. About half his respondents said that anti-Semitism in America was a serious problem for American Jews, or disagreed that virtually all positions of influence in America were open to Jews. About half said they had personally encountered anti-Semitism. More than a quarter said that many Americans were anti-Semites, and an additional 50 percent said that at least some of them were. A third said that anti-Semitism was increasing in the United States, and only 13 percent said it was decreasing. Nevertheless, most of those concerned about anti-Semitism in the United States do not fear for the physical security of American Jews. Only 17 percent in Herman's survey said there was a real possibility of a holocaust in the United States, whereas more than half said there was such a possibility in Argentina, Poland, the Soviet Union, Syria, and Iran.

Images of the violent Gentile persist among only a minority of Jews. As many as 61 percent of our respondents in 1985 characterized American Christians as "peace-loving," and only 12 percent characterized them as "violent"; 62 percent said Christians were generally honest, and only 11 percent said they were not. In addition, the Jewish ethnocentrism expressed as Jewish superiority and Gentile inferiority was not in evidence: although three-fifths of American Jews in 1986 agreed that Jews were different from non-Jews in many ways (see chapter 2), 75 percent agreed that in most ways Jews were no better than non-Jews.

We cannot be sure whether such benign notions of today's Gentile represent mere rhetoric or genuine sentiment. Perhaps in the inner recesses of their consciousness Jews still retain an exalted image of their own intellectuality and morality while outwardly professing the socially approved notion that Jews are no better than non-Jews. But even as rhetoric, the data suggest a shift away from the traditional idea of Jewish superiority and Gentile otherness.

Receding Notions of Gentile Inferiority and Hostility

The image of Gentiles has improved over the last three decades. The way Jews of the 1950s spoke of Gentiles seems antiquated today, and the way Jews describe non-Jews today would have seemed to their predecessors of thirty or forty years ago artificially universalist or excessively naive. Wayne Clark, a young, non-Jewish writer, distilled the essence of numerous anti-Gentile remarks she and her Gentile friends heard, and constructed a composite "Portrait of the Mythical Gentile":

The nucleus of the stereotype *goy* is, of course, his omnipresent anti-Semitism. It is rooted so deeply in him that he is almost without responsibility for it. Like his libido, it acts in every situation. . . . *The Gentile Intellect* is a rough-hewn, primitive mechanism with no more than a gloss of civilization that inevitably dulls in crises. It has few resources, the slenderest mnemonic endowment, and a debilitating torpor; it reaches elevated points only by a kind of brute patience. . . . The Gentile suspects conceptual thinking because he has no capacity for it; . . . Even the educated Gentile seems somehow to evade the consequences of intellectuality . . . *The Gentile Family* is a strained, loveless complex without devotion and therefore without friction. The children leave it without pangs, never return, do not believe in establishing stable families themselves. . . . *The Gentile in Business* is unscrupulous in dealing with Jews, but with his own "sort" he is usually honorable and trustworthy. He is also slow-witted, conservative, and unimaginative. . . . All Gentiles are drunkards. . . . The Gentile drinks enormously, but without savor, being insensitive to vintage and admixture. He sets a sparse, inept table based on a compulsive repetition of plain meats, vegetables, and scarcely sweetened fruit pies. . . . The *goy* has mastered little of the technique of voluptuousness. He cannot relax or spin out a pleasure. . . . This is the face of the Myth-Gentile. I know few Jews who believe he exists as a whole, but there seem to be few, also, who do not believe some of these traits are typical. (1949, 547–48)

We agree with Clark's final observations. Her description of American Jewish images of the Gentile in 1949 is all the more significant because she moved in intellectual circles (she was a writer and editor) and was therefore associated with the most acculturated Jews. There is the ring of truth in the images in Clark's article, only a few of which are presented here. They are directly derived from those cited earlier by Zborowski's and Herzog's respondents. And like those reported by the former residents of the shtetl, they are the reverse of Jewish self-images. Each negative stereotype of the Gentile above is counterbalanced by a positive stereotype of the Jew.

In interviews conducted in 1957 in a fashionable suburb of Chicago populated predominantly by Reform Jews, Sklare and Greenblum found additional evidence of Jewish estrangement from Gentiles. These findings are especially striking because the population was far less involved in conventional Jewish life than the less wealthy, less native, and heavily urbanized Jews who made up the bulk of American Jewry at the time. A few remarks are illustrative: "We have Gentile friends, but we'd never think of mixing with them. It wouldn't work. We're very small drinkers. We like to have a nice dinner and play cards. We'd feel self-conscious, especially if they lose" (Sklare and Greenblum 1979, 282). To translate: Jews and Gentiles are different, so different we can't really be close friends. They drink to excess; we don't. We're refined and intellectual; they're crude. What's more, we're smarter—at least in cards, if not in other ways too.

Sklare and Greenblum cited the example of "an active alumna of a leading Eastern women's college, who is also involved in several Jewish and non-sectarian groups." She reported "intellectually stimulating" friendships with both her closest Jewish friend and her closest Gentile friend, but she remarked about the former relationship: "It's like being [in] a family without the tension" (1979, 283). Note again the emergence of the family as a metaphor for relations among Jews, and the sense of unbridgeable alienation from the Gentile. For this person, Jewish familism and Gentile otherness were intimately related, as they are for Jews generally three decades later.

Using the data from 1986, we cross-tabulated a measure of perceived anti-Semitism with an index of commitment to Jewish familism.[5] Of those scoring low on Jewish familism (about a quarter of the sample), only 23 percent scored high on perceptions of anti-Semitism; of those scoring high on Jewish familism (also about a quarter of the sample), nearly twice as many scored high on perceptions of anti-Semitism (43 percent). As might be expected, Jewish familism and Jewish ethnocentrism also are strongly related. Among those scoring low on Jewish familism, only 15 percent doubted that Jews were no better than others; of those scoring high on familism, 35 percent did so. Identifying with the Jewish family often means accepting the group's historically based fears of Gentiles and feelings of Jewish superiority; and we strongly suspect that this generalization was as true in the 1950s as it is in the 1980s, even if the average levels of familism and the fear of anti-Semitism have declined.

But around the middle of the twentieth century (the period covered by the surveys), Jews became increasingly uneasy about expressing the negative images of the Gentile that so many of them shared. In a study by Charles Snyder, Jewish respondents were asked in the early 1950s about differences in the drinking habits of Jews and Christians. They offered these mixed responses:

Definitely [Jews drink less], but I can't think in those [ethnic, group-oriented] terms.

That's something I wouldn't say, I couldn't say, but I think they do [drink] less. There are very few drunkards among the Jewish race.

I don't think it has anything to do with nationality. I don't want to bring it in. If Christians were raised in a non-drinking environment they wouldn't either.

There's an old saying among Jews of my class—my father has an old theory that Jews drink less than Christians. It's hard to say. It might be so. I don't mean this with a racial bias, it just might be that Jews drink less. (1958, 575)

Negative images of the Gentile persist, but they are less widespread than they were three or four decades ago. Survey data reveal less uneasiness about intimacy between Jews and Gentiles and less of a sense that the two groups are fundamentally different. In 1986 only 24 percent of respondents in their twenties scored high on our index of perceived anti-Semitism; the figure was 31 percent for those in their thirties, 37 percent for those in their forties, and roughly 40 percent for those over fifty. Another measure of these changes is the weakening opposition to intermarriage. Until the 1960s most American Jews would have been extremely upset at the prospect of a close family member marrying out of the faith (Axelrod, Fowler, and Gurin 1967). Since then opposition to intermarriage has plummeted: in 1965, 70 percent of respondents in the Boston area said they would "strongly oppose" or "discourage" their child's intermarriage; the figure fell to 34 percent by 1975 and to 31 percent by 1985 (Israel 1987, 60).[6]

Closer relations with Gentiles are enjoyed not only by Jews who marry outside the faith (who make up about a third of recently marrying Jews). In 1984 about 40 percent of all respondents said they had a very close Gentile friend, around 60 percent said they had a close Gentile neighbor, and more than 80 percent of those employed said they had a close association with a Gentile at work. These relationships are testimony to the mutual acceptance of Jew and Gentile, and also play an important role in softening and modifying the traditional views held by Jews that Gentiles are hostile and inferior.

American Jewish Attitudes: Complex Patterns, Partial Answers

How are we to interpret our findings about American Jewish attitudes toward non-Jews and anti-Semitism? On the one hand, images of the non-Jew among about half our respondents demonstrate strong continuities in traditional Jewish images. At the very least there remain echoes of fear and insecurity, and of a belief that Jews are hated, that there is a potential for violence, and that Jews have a special status. This is of some significance, because it contrasts so sharply with our optimistic assessment of the condition of Jews in the United States and our observations about the dramatic improvement in their social standing in the last several decades. Further, persistent Jewish suspicion of the Gentile stands in contrast to other things: the assessments that Jews make of their status, their sense of prosperity, their assertive behavior (which reflects confidence in their political equality), and not least their declining opposition to intermarriage and growing social ease with non-Jews. Putting matters baldly, if things are so good and Jews know that they are so good, why are Jews still so afraid?

There are a few possible answers to this paradox, more than one of which may be true. One possibility is that negative images of the Gentile and fears of anti-Semitism are associated with only one group of American Jews. Our data are consistent with this explanation, for they show that roughly half of all American Jews have abandoned traditional Jewish conceptions of anti-Semitism and ethnocentrism, so central to traditional Jewish notions of exile and redemption and to what were once core conceptions of Judaism and Jewish identity. Some of those who have abandoned these traditional conceptions may also be seen as having assimilated—as lacking any significant involvement with other Jews and any commitment to Judaism or Jewishness, however broadly defined. There is no point in asking what images of the Jew and non-Jew have replaced the traditional ones. Assimilated Jews have no new or reconstructed conception of Judaism. They do not seek to substitute new meanings of Jewish existence. Their Jewish affiliation is accepted as a fact, but it remains largely devoid of meaning and of little consequence to their lives.

On the other hand, as many as half of all American Jews continue to adhere to traditional Jewish images of the non-Jew. The images have to some extent been moderated, but it is remarkable how traditional images are sustained despite their tenuous relation to the objective conditions and experiences of American Jews. We suspect that these images have retained their resonance because they remain central to conceptions of Judaism and to what it means to be a Jew. One cannot choose to remain Jewish, least of all in a society that offers the option of not remaining Jewish, unless one has a positive conception of Jewish self as opposed to Gentile other. One way to sustain such a conception is by maintaining the image of the anti-Semitic Gentile, or at least the potentially anti-Semitic Gentile.

This explanation finds support in the distinctions between the types of Jews who believe in Gentile anti-Semitism. Those who are more Jewishly involved (in terms of ritual observance or associating primarily with other Jews) are more likely to fear anti-Semitism. Fears of anti-Semitism and more intense Jewish commitments reinforce each other. In 1984 those reporting a greater number of close Jewish friends and neighbors more often expressed fears of anti-Semitism; and those with a greater number of Gentile friends and neighbors reported fewer fears of anti-Semitism. The perception that Gentiles are hostile may lead Jews to avoid non-Jewish social intimacies and neighborhoods; the absence of such friendly contact may well sustain a historically imprinted fear of Gentiles. Both processes are probably at work.

Jews with more familistic attitudes, those who feel part of an extended family and who feel close and especially obligated to other Jews, are also more fearful of Gentile antagonism and more likely to see American Christians as anti-Semitic. This perception of anti-Semitism legitimates the ethnically segregated life of many American Jews.

Throughout the surveys the Orthodox in particular, who are most closely associated with traditional Judaism, frequently express concerns about the antagonism of non-Jews.

A second explanation for the paradox is that this is a peculiar time to describe American Jews, for a transition is being made from a more traditional form of Judaism to a more modern, American one. The image of anti-Semitism that we found among so many American Jews may simply be a vestige of an older mode of thought. The studies we have cited of Jews in the 1950s document the presence of greater discomfort, alienation, and insecurity about socializing with Gentiles than we suspect we would find today (unfortunately, there are no strictly comparable data). The absence during the last few decades of widespread anti-Semitism of any kind in the United States and the integration of Jews into the larger society through intermarriage and close friendships have spurred many Jews to abandon their fears of anti-Semitism. The residue that remains may result from a kind of cultural lag and will disappear in time as long as anti-Semitism remains submerged.

A third explanation for the apparent paradox is that it reflects the emergence of a new American Judaism, one oriented on the one hand toward tradition and on the other toward American society. Some Jews are more committed to Judaism and others less, some are on the verge of assimilation and others rooted in the tradition or in a reconstruction of the tradition, and some are distant from the tradition but still situated in communities of fellow Jews. This entire book assumes that like any living religion Judaism is always in transition and being transformed and reformulated, by turns slower and faster, unintentionally and consciously.

Hence although the first two explanations are correct, they are only partly so. According to this third explanation, one can also speak of a Judaism unique to America and in which all American Jews partake. Not all of them partake of it in the same way, nor is this American Judaism a coherent religion that is ideologically and ritually distinct from the Judaism of the past or of other societies, Israel in particular (see chapter 1). It is instead composed of bits and pieces of the past transformed to varying degrees by the American experience, and bits of Americana transformed to varying degrees by the Jewish experience. And nowhere is this more evident than in American Jewish attitudes toward the Gentile, toward differences between Jew and Gentile, and toward the threat of anti-Semitism. The American Jew professes to feel at home in the United States but is not certain that this will always be so, numbers Gentiles among his or her best friends but does not believe that all or even most Gentiles like Jews, and feels a kinship with liberals but feels that anti-Semitism taints every Gentile with strong particularist commitments—to race, to ethnicity, or of course to religion.

There is no question that much of the traditional Jewish past has been abandoned in this new imagery. The conceptions of the Jew as distinct from the non-Jew and of the reality of anti-Semitism have been eroded, at least among major segments of American Jews. The erosion is least noticeable among the most committed sector—for example the Orthodox, or the ethnically embedded Jews with close friends who are exclusively Jewish. Their images may therefore still support in attenuated form the traditional mythos of exile and redemption, of superior Jew and hostile Gentile. Among the least committed and the least involved the erosion may be complete, and no substitute is necessary. But among the middle group of American Jews, we suspect that the negative image of the Gentile and the reality of anti-Semitism no longer support deeper conceptions of Jews as a special people. Thus these Jews have no peculiarly Jewish notion of redemption or of a better world, because Jews today do not require relief from persecution and misery. The traditional images of Jews and Gentiles are not as powerful as they once were, nor are they compatible with America's integrationist and pluralist ethos.

In this case American Jews must construct a new meaning of Judaism, according to which such concepts as exile and redemption are at best irrelevant and at worst counterproductive. The Jewishly identified but Judaically nontraditional Jew has had to develop a new mythos, one that is consistent with the benign condition of American Jews but that will legitimate Jewish distinctiveness. The problem is to provide content to a belief that Jews are different but not necessarily better. (Recall that 61 percent of our respondents in 1986 said that in many ways Jews were different from non-Jews, and that 75 percent said Jews in most ways were no better than non-Jews.) For many of these Jews the solution to the problem lies in liberalism (see chapter 5). And as one would expect, there are similarities as well as differences between the way American Jews adapt traditional images of Gentile antagonism and inferiority and the way their Israeli counterparts do.

Israeli Attitudes: Blame the Goyim or Blame the Jews?

Anti-Semitism and conceptions of the hostile goy were building blocks in the central Jewish myth of exile and redemption. Even after Zionism transformed the myth, anti-Semitism continued to play a crucial role. Anti-Semitism was in fact more central in Zionist ideology than in traditional Judaism's conception of reality.[7] As Eliezer Don-Yehiya points out in a forthcoming book, Zionism transformed the conception of exile from an existential condition to a material one defined by the continued threat this condition posed to the security and status of the Jews.[8] Yet in classical Zionist thinking the non-Jews are not really to be blamed for their hostility to the Jews. The fault lies in the unnatural condition of Jews living as strangers in a host society that understandably harbors suspicions of them and their intentions. The Zionist answer, the creation of an independent and autonomous Jewish society, is the only solution to the problem of anti-Semitism.

Thus even though anti-Semitism was central to the purpose and meaning of Zionism as formulated by several thinkers in the late nineteenth century and the early twentieth, Zionism was neither ethnocentric nor necessarily hostile to the non-Jew; it claimed to understand the non-Jew. In its conviction that an independent Jewish state was the solution to anti-Semitism, Zionism ascribed rather benign motives to the non-Jew, who simply could not accept and incorporate the diaspora Jew into the emerging nation-states of Europe. So powerful was the force of this ideological formulation that David Ben-Gurion continued to adhere to it even as the last of the European Jewish communities was being transported to the death camps: "The cause of our troubles and the anti-Semitism of which we complain result from our peculiar status that does not accord with the established framework of the nations of the world. It is not the result of the wickedness or folly of the Gentiles which we call anti-Semitism" (cited in Liebman and Don-Yehiya 1983a, 104).

However naive and unrealistic it appears in retrospect, Ben-Gurion's statement is a faithful reflection of classical Zionist ideology. Nevertheless, not all Zionists or even all Zionist ideologues were quite as universalistic as this ideology suggests. Berl Katznelson, the preeminent ideologue of the Labour Zionist movement until his death in 1944, barely reflected in his private life the resonant universalism that characterized

Zionist ideology. But perhaps this is also because he maintained ties and associations to the tradition that were stronger than those of many Zionist leaders. According to his biographer he harbored "instinctive hostility towards the stranger, the Gentile, the ruler—whether Russian, English or Arab. These emotions were as much second nature to Berl and his friends as their Yiddish speech, as the pages of the Talmud they had learned by heart in childhood" (Shapiro 1984, 99–100). In a letter to a friend abroad he wrote: "One should not, in my opinion eat with Gentiles. And, generally speaking it is best to stay as far away from them as possible" (1984, 68). Alongside the official Zionist ideology, which understood, predicted, and even excused Gentile hostility, some Zionists retained traditional, more particularistic, and ethnocentric images of the Gentile.

The role of anti-Semitism in formulations of Zionism and (since 1948) in the importance attributed to the existence of the Jewish state has not diminished. What has changed is the benign image held by Israeli leaders of the Gentile. It is no longer the Jew who is indirectly to blame for being hated. Anti-Semitism is no longer the expected hostility of the hosts toward their uninvited guests.[9] As in the traditional Jewish past, anti-Semitism is now attributed instead to the Gentile's irrational hatred of the Jew. The state of Israel is no longer projected as the solution to anti-Semitism so much as the haven for the oppressed Jew. The origins of anti-Semitism are no longer explained in terms of Jewish estrangement from their host societies, but as endemic to the non-Jew.

Two Types of Gentiles: Those Who Only Hate Us, and Those Who Try to Destroy Us

Rabbi Moshe Zvi Neriyah, the head of the network of religious Zionist yeshiva high schools in Israel and a former member of the Knesset, cites with obvious approval the statement of a sixteenth-century Jewish leader, the Maharal of Prague (Rabbi Judah Loew Ben Bezalel, 1525–1609). Neriyah noted that there are two types of non-Jews, "those that simply hate us and those who attempt with all their power to destroy us" (*HaZofeh,* 14 September 1981, p. 2). In a weekly bulletin published in cooperation with the National Religious party and distributed in Israeli synagogues each Sabbath, the editor cites, also with obvious approval, a homily on the biblical phrase "Let all the nations praise the Lord, for his mercy has overcome us." The phrase is interpreted to mean that the nations (goyim) praise the Lord because they are aware of miracles of which the Jews are unaware. The Gentiles know how often they have sought to harm the Jews and how "God has saved [them] from [the Jews'] hands" (*Shabbat B'Shabbato,* 18 March 1988).

Some religious Zionist formulations portray Gentiles as demons; these formulations reconceptualize the notion of exile so that its greatest harm is that it obliges Jews to live near Gentiles, unable to significantly dissociate themselves from them (Don-Yehiya, forthcoming). Ancient and medieval Jewish conceptions that attribute inferior biological characteristics to the Gentile have been revived in religious Zionist schools. Thus students in some of these schools learn that the first two patriarchs, Abraham and Isaac, each had two sons so that the Jewish son might inherit pure genes whereas the corrupt, inpure genes that Abraham inherited from his idolatrous ancestors could be passed on to the non-Jewish son. Only Jacob's sons—those of the third generation—inherited pure genes and were worthy of being Jewish. Such racist views were held by only a minority of rabbis even in the middle ages; that there is no outcry against their being part of the religious Zionist high school curriculum suggests the level that Jewish ethnocentrism has reached in some quarters.

It is interesting to observe the differences between prominent Israeli and American religious scholars in this regard. In a lecture before advanced Talmudic students at Yeshiva University in the late 1960s, Israel's chief rabbi spoke on the question of whether a Jew was permitted to violate the Sabbath to save the life of a Gentile. He concluded that this was permitted "for the sake of peace," in other words because not doing so might lead to interreligious friction and the persecution of Jews. At the conclusion of the lecture an eminent Talmudic authority from Yeshiva University ordered his students to return to class. He then informed them that the chief rabbi of Israel had erred. He said that the principle that the Sabbath could be violated to save the life of any person, Jew or Gentile, was integral to Jewish law and was not merely an expedient intended to prevent harm to the Jews (see Liebman 1983b).

Although the most extreme expressions of racism and ethnocentrism are generally confined to religious Zionist spokesmen in Israel, non-religious leaders indulge in them as well. These milder forms often surface during commemorations of the Holocaust or with reference to Arabs specifically rather than Gentiles generally. For example, according to the former minister of education: "The Holocaust is not a national insanity that happened once and passed, but an ideology that has not passed from the world and even today the world may condone crimes against us" (cited in Liebman and Don-Yehiya 1983a, 184). In 1988 the Israeli press reported that Minister of Justice Abraham Sharir told an audience of American Jews that all Arabs were liars. When the former Israeli chief of staff referred to Arabs as "drugged cockroaches" and a member of the Knesset spoke about "tearing out their eyes," this did occasion some comment but no widespread condemnation outside the political left.[10]

A personal experience in this regard is instructive. An article in one of Israel's largest circulating daily newspapers condemned the sale of land by Jews to Arabs, arguing that because Israel was a Jewish state it was improper to sell land to non-Jews (Strassman 1985, 10). One of us wrote a letter to the editor accusing the writer of racism. In a personal reply the editor explained that he refused to publish the letter because the term *racism* ought not to be used so freely. In his own reply the author of the article likened his position to that of Americans who refused to sell land to Indians, and called it a perfectly natural assertion of national interest.

By and large, however, one hears not expressions of enthnocentrism but rather pronouncements that the Gentile still hates the Jew. Menachem Begin was famous for such utterances, which are very often associated with the idea that Jews who live in the diaspora are continually subject to threats and lack the power or right to defend themselves (see chapter 4).

This rhetoric is reflected only partly in the attitudes of most Israelis, which in some ways correspond to earlier Zionist formulations and in others represent the assertion of a special role for the state of Israel, one quite different from that envisioned by early Zionist leaders. Most Israelis affirm the classical Zionist linking of anti-Semitism to the condition of galut. In a recent survey conducted by Simon Herman, anti-Semitism was attributed by 41 percent of Israelis to the condition of the

Jews as a minority, by 36 percent to characteristics of Jews, and by only 22 percent to characteristics of non-Jews. In response to another question, 64 percent of the respondents said that the Jews' condition as a minority accounted at least to "a great extent" for anti-Semitism (Herman 1988). The association of anti-Semitism and life in the diaspora is interesting, because it reinforces our own impression that when Israelis think about anti-Semitism they do not automatically think of the Arabs. Israelis certainly believe that Arabs are anti-Semitic, and according to Herman's study they believe that anti-Semitism accounts in good part for the Arabs' hostility to them. But Israelis also bear a distinct image of the generalized anti-Semite who is not an Arab.

Blaming Jews or the Jewish condition rather than Gentiles for anti-Semitism points to classical Zionist ideology. But contrary to the universalism implicit in Zionist ideology, a universalism that denies that there is any special animus toward Jews on the part of Gentiles, today's Israelis are suspicious of Gentiles and their motivations. According to Herman's survey a third of Israelis said that all or most non-Jews were anti-Semitic, and another 41 percent said that many of them were; only a quarter of the sample said that but a few non-Jews were anti-Semitic. Herman also asked his respondents to assess the chances of preventing anti-Semitism. Fewer than a third thought the chances were good; the rest thought there was little or no chance of preventing anti-Semitism. Like classical Zionist ideologues, most Israelis blame anti-Semitism on Jewish life in galut. Unlike the classical Zionists but in keeping with traditional Judaism, most Israelis have no hope for its resolution. Anti-Semitism is apparently perceived as inherent in the nature of the Gentile. Israel is not the solution, and in addition it is itself the focus of anti-Semitism. According to an unpublished survey conducted in 1986 by the political scientist Asher Arian, 58 percent of all Israeli Jews believe that the criticism of Israel heard in the world today stems from anti-Semitism (a view often shared by pro-Israel American Jews as well). This belief is especially prevalent among the more religious Israelis, Sephardim, and the less educated.

Israel the Redeemer

Even Israelis who do not believe that most Gentiles are hostile to Jews acknowledge the existence of anti-Semitism. Anyone

socialized within Israeli culture and subject to the continuing remind-
ers of the Holocaust must be sensitive to anti-Semitism. In addition, the
Israeli press always reports with special interest any stories of anti-
Semitism in the diaspora. But surprisingly, the generalized anti-Semitism
that Israelis perceive is less threatening than the anti-Semitism that
American Jews perceive. Indeed, Israelis generally express greater feelings of security about the threat of anti-Semitism in the United States
than American Jews do. In our survey of 1986, only 24 percent of Israelis expressed concern that the United States would stop being a firm
ally of Israel (as opposed to 40 percent of American Jews); 50 percent
of Israelis and 67 percent of American Jews said that anti-Semitism in
America might become a serious problem for American Jews in the future; 51 percent of Israelis and 37 percent of American Jews said that
virtually all positions of influence in America were open to Jews. The
same proportion of Israeli and American Jews (46 percent) said that in
a struggle for Israel's survival only a few non-Jews would come to
Israel's help. In other words, on every question but one pertaining to
Gentile hostility, Israelis saw non-Jews as less anti-Semitic than American Jews did.

What is especially important for our purposes is the manner in
which statehood has become intertwined in the Israeli mind with anti-
Semitism. We recall the traditional concept of exile and redemption:
exile is a cosmological as well as a human condition, and redemption is
the act of God that would restore the cosmos to its rightful order and
the Jews to their proper status. It is not too far-fetched to argue that
this concept has been transformed, with exile now interpreted as the
condition of Jews who live outside the borders of the state of Israel and
redemption as their return to their land, or at least their protection by
the state. God the redeemer has become Israel the redeemer. In this
paradigm redemption is directed in different ways at different sorts of
Jews. For Jews who are persecuted Israel serves as a refuge. In recent
years the arrival of Soviet and Ethiopian Jews in Israel was a source of
genuine enthusiasm among Israelis. As the press reported at the time,
not least of the reasons was that their arrival confirmed Israel's redemptive role.

Israelis are however aware that many Jews live free from persecution,
especially in the United States. That Israelis are less likely than American Jews to perceive anti-Semitism as a threat to American Jews may be

because they interpret anti-Semitism to mean physical violence, but it may also be because anti-Semitism in any particular area, even the United States, is less crucial to their conception of Judaism than it is to the conception of American Jews, who are oriented almost exclusively toward the United States and Israel. But in the minds of Israeli Jews the state of Israel has a redemptive role to play among Jews of the free world as well. It provides a stimulus to Jewish identity and a source of pride for these Jews. In a survey of the Israeli public taken in 1983, roughly two-thirds of the sample agreed that "support for Israel" was the focus that united American Jewry, that American Jews would always support Israel, and that when Israel's name was smeared American Jews were also hurt (H. Smith 1983). Both objectively and subjectively the fate of American Jewry depends on the fate of Israel, and the strength of American Jewry depends on the strength of its commitment to Israel. It is consistent with this image of Israel the Redeemer that most Israelis believe Israel's existence has diminished anti-Semitism (51 percent), and that most believe Israel strengthens the stance of Jews to "a great degree" (61 percent—of the remainder most believe that Israel strengthens Jews to at least a small degree; see Herman 1988).

Israelis agree that there is a great deal of anti-Semitism in the world. They differ over its origins and its virulence, but they tend to see the state of Israel as playing a central role in the story of anti-Semitism. A majority espouse a view consistent with classical Zionist ideology: that Israel's existence diminishes anti-Semitism. But in contrast to the expectations of classical Zionism, a majority also believe that the state of Israel is a focus of anti-Semitism and suffers from a hostility that stems from anti-Semitism.

These two points of view are not inherently contradictory. But they are rooted in two larger ideologies that are contradictory, the ideology of classical Zionism and that of the traditional Jewish world view. The former sees anti-Semitism as the consequence of Jews' living outside the land of Israel; the latter ascribes it to the nature of the Gentile or the destiny of the Jew. According to classical Zionism the establishment of a Jewish state will remove the cause of anti-Semitism, not transform the state into its target; in the traditional Jewish world view the establishment of a Jewish state would be irrelevant to the existence of anti-

Semitism but would presumably provide a convenient target for it. Most Israelis seem to have adopted elements from each of these world views. Our question is whether there is some new, unifying image or conception of Judaism that rests behind these attitudes and serves to integrate them.

Our data suggest that there is an answer: the centrality of the state of Israel. To Israeli Jews the state of Israel is central in whatever happens to all Jews, for better or worse. It is critical in combating anti-Semitism and is also the target of anti-Semitism. In the minds of most Israelis, neither classical Zionist universalism nor the traditional myth of exile and redemption explains the origins of anti-Semitism or offers solutions to it. The problem and the solution rest instead in the state of Israel itself, which is becoming the central focus of Israeli images of Judaism (see chapter 4).

This is neither a coherent nor a logically satisfactory solution to the question of what anti-Semitism is and what causes it, but this is less problematic than one might expect. First, the question of anti-Semitism is not critical or even troubling for Israelis. Now that they enjoy state power, Israelis do not suffer from anti-Semitism as individuals; they suffer from the hostility of their Arab neighbors, which threatens their existence, and from the perceived hostility of the world, which is a source of discomfort, economic hardship, and potential danger. Anti-Semitism is perceived not as the immediate cause of these problems but as the explanation for them.

The usefulness of portraying Israel's adversaries as anti-Semites is obvious. It delegitimates the grievances of the Arabs and the criticism of outsiders. It provides a rationale for the Israelis' refusal to compromise with Palestinians and their demand, in the words of a member of the Knesset, that "all the free world . . . show its repentance . . . by providing diplomatic-defensive-economic aid to Israel" (cited in Liebman and Don-Yehiya 1983a, 184). Anti-Semitism is not seen as a major problem requiring resolution but as a factor that contributes to the hostility of the Arabs and to international support for the Arabs, both of which pose a more real and consequential threat to Israeli security.

Second, the attitudes we have reported are those of the general population. The elite have clearer views of the nature of anti-Semitism, which stem from either a traditional Jewish position or a classical

Zionist position. Among the Israeli masses a coherent, logically consistent ideology is not needed to explain reality or guide behavior. All that is needed is some generalized conception that provides meaning and legitimacy to one's pattern of life. To the extent that Israeli Jews look to Judaism to provide such a conception they increasingly associate this with the state of Israel itself. It is to this conception that we now turn.

4

Land, State,

and Diaspora

"The ethnic homeland is far more than territory. As evidenced by the near universal use of such emotionally charged terms as the motherland, the fatherland, the native land, the ancestral land, the land where my fathers died and, not least, the homeland, the territory so identified becomes imbued with an emotional, almost reverential dimension" (Conner 1986, 16). Israeli Jews use all these terms to refer to Israel (for example *moledet,* native land). The word *aretz,* literally "land," is a synonym for Israel. The phrase *chutz la'aretz,* literally "outside the land," means "abroad." (Israeli soldiers stationed in Lebanon joked that they were serving in chutz la'aretz.) Only a small minority of the most dedicated American Jewish Zionists refer to Israel in these terms (and it does not seem to us that most American Jews readily use such language to refer to the United States). The absence of linguistic parallels reflects a deeper conceptual gap between the two Jewish communities with respect to investment in the land of Israel and attachment to it.

The territory of Israel is of major importance to Israeli Jews, but decidedly peripheral to American Jews. Sixty-five percent of our Israeli respondents agreed with this statement: "It is impossible for me to think of what it means to be a Jew without thinking of *Eretz Yisrael*"; only 26 percent disagreed. We have no comparable survey data on American Jews, but we know that Eretz Yisrael plays a minimal role in the rhetoric of American Jewish leaders (Woocher 1986) and in the writing of leading American Jewish thinkers: "The Land's existence is accorded significance, . . . but not its historical or physical reality" (Eisen 1986, 149).

Eretz Yisrael:
From Traditional Jewish Conceptions
to Modern Israeli Conceptions

To some it may seem peculiar to refer to territory or to Eretz Yisrael, the land of the Jewish people, as a conception. It may be argued that this is surely a physical reality, not a concept. But this is not quite true. As Hans Kohn has indicated in his study of nationalism, territory as a focus for national sentiment is an artifical construct (1944). One can love an immediate village or neighborhood, but a larger region one cannot know intimately (although one may pretend to). In a statement that bears a striking resemblance to contemporary Jewish religious formulations about Eretz Yisrael, a Cherokee Indian spokesman is quoted as having said: "In the language of my people there is a word for land: Eloheh. This same word also means history, culture, and religion. We cannot separate our place on earth from our lives on the earth nor from our vision nor our meaning as a people" (cited in Matthiessen 1984, 119).

Although Eretz Yisrael was a central component of Jewish culture throughout Jewish history, its meaning underwent enormous change after the second Temple was destroyed in 70 C.E. and the Bar Kokhba revolt failed sixty years later. Eliezer Schweid notes that because most Jews no longer lived in the land of Israel, the sages found it necessary to retain ties to the land without questioning the legitimacy of Jewish life outside it: "Thus ritual patterns were created that perpetuated the memory of the land of Israel and endowed it with supreme *symbolic* significance . . . The idealization of the land culminated in its absolute spiritualization . . . For most of the people, the land of Israel became an imagined place that was the focus of emotion, speculation, and ritual. Even the memories of the land from the time the nation dwelt there underwent mythologization and became displaced by messianic and apocalyptic hopes and dreams" (1987, 538; italics added). Eretz Yisrael became so spiritualized that it ceased in the minds of many Jews to represent an earthly reality. Ehud Luz cites the accounts of eighteenth-century settlers, who before they came "could not imagine that Eretz Yisrael actually existed in this world. On the basis of everything written in the books about its holiness, they had imagined that the land 'was in an entirely different world'" (Luz 1987, 373–74).

Some of the Haskala (Jewish Enlightenment) writers of the nineteenth century sought to revive both the Hebrew language and the love of Eretz Yisrael. Their work began the process of demythologizing the land, even as they placed renewed emphasis on its importance. The early Zionist settlers welcomed the encounter with the land, but the importance they too attributed to it suggests that it meant more to them than territory, particularly since it was a land that was barren and that they acknowledged as strange and in some ways alien. Even so, "Going back to the land of Israel was a return to the people's point of origin, its place of birth. The people's way of life would be reconstituted right from the beginning, and this time it would grow in the natural way" (Schweid 1985, 150). Young artists wrote of the land, put its scenery into verse, sang of it, and "danced their efforts to strike roots in the soil" (1985, 151). In the culture they created, land was the content and determined its style.

Schweid and others have commented on the quasi-religious character that land assumed to the early settlers; it has even been suggested that land provided an alternative expression of Judaism for the settlers, who were primarily secular. According to Shaul Katz, the Zionist movement "transformed the religious, non-territorial basis for Jewish identity to a Jewish-Israeli ethnic-territorial one" (1985, 67). Katz also suggests that Israeli Jews have accorded a central position in their culture to three land-related elements. The first is ancient Jewish history, "most of which is identified with Israeli territory." This element is expressed in the enormous interest in archaeological research in Israel (most Israeli newspapers have a special correspondent for archaeology). The second is the geographical history of the land, demonstrated in the growing popularity of "Eretz Yisrael studies" in Israeli universities. The third element is regional natural history, especially that related to realistic interpretation of Jewish holy scriptures. Katz points out that "the various consecutive editions of the *Analytical Flora of Palestine* have been on the list of best sellers for the last fifty years or so" (1985, 67).

Further support for the centrality of territory in contemporary Israeli culture is the publication of a remarkable series of volumes beginning in 1982. Many of Israel's outstanding historians worked on the ten-volume series, entitled *The History of Eretz Yisrael.* This is not a history of the Jewish people in the land of Israel but rather a history of the events that took place in Eretz Yisrael regardless of who lived there.

The book was written at a popular level and is obviously intended for a mass audience. The enterprise is remarkable, because as far as we know there has been no such effort in any other society: it is difficult to conceive of a history of the North American continent written not for the scholar but for the popular reader, and that focuses not on one ethnic or national group but rather on what has happened in North America during the course of human history. The study of Eretz Yisrael is also a central part of the elementary school curriculum, and it is supplemented during the school year by frequent trips and hikes. These culminate in an annual trip (the *tiyul shnati*), which for many is the major social event of the school year. As the student progresses from class to class the tiyul shnati grows in duration and rigor until the junior year of high school, when students spend several days and nights in what is for them a remote part of Israel.

All this fascination with the land evokes images of the Canaanite movement, a group formed in the early 1940s. In their zeal for a new Hebrew culture, its adherents expressed hostility toward the Jewish religion and traditional Jewish culture.[1] They evoked the myths of the Canaanite tribes, who lived in the land in the prebiblical and biblical periods. The religion of these tribes was centered on nature, more attached to the land itself than the religion of the Israelites. The Canaanite movement was never large, but because its adherents and fellow travelers included an important group of artists and writers it did leave an impact on Hebrew literature. The Canaanites were ultranationalist in their insistence on self-rule for the nation and on preserving the territorial integrity of the entire land of Israel. Yet they claimed allegiance not to the Jewish people but to the Hebrew nation; this was a fiction, though one no greater than those entertained by some other modern nations in their embryonic stages.

Canaanite sentiments can be perceived in the statement attributed to Moshe Dayan, who is said to have contrasted his own basic loyalties with those of Golda Meir: "She loves *Am Israel* [the Jewish people] and I love *Eretz Yisrael* and therefore I feel closer to a Palestinian *fellah* than to a Jewish tailor from Brooklyn" (Milson 1986, 17). These sentiments also find echoes on the Israeli political right, which objects to any territorial compromise with the Arabs. In the elections of 1984 the Likud as well as the more extreme Tehiya used such slogans as "the faithful of Eretz Yisrael," implying that their opponents on the left were not loyal to the land. The vision of the political right is that the land of Israel is exclusively for the people of Israel, the Jews.

Despite the fears voiced by Zionist thinkers in an earlier period, land or territory has not come to compete with Judaism or the Jewish people as a focus of loyalty. Certainly the political right expresses keen attachment to both the land and the Jewish people, but the left believes with some justification that attachment to the land of Israel contributes to a reluctance to withdraw from territory acquired in the Six Day War. Within the Labour movement, support for establishing settlements on the West Bank (and even for annexing the disputed territory) has been especially rife among those associated with efforts to increase public knowledge of the land and attachment to it, with those who write the best-known guide books and run schools for Israeli guides; it has also been associated with the rural rather than the urban party centers, and with some legendary leaders of the kibbutz movements in particular.

At least since 1967 sentimental attachment to the land has therefore been correlated with a sense of attachment to the Jewish people. This applies not only to the political elites but also to the population at large. In our survey of Israelis we examined the pattern of answers to the statement "It is almost impossible for me to think of what it means to be a Jew without thinking about Eretz Yisrael." We measured attachment to the Jewish people according to answers to questions about seeing the Jewish people as an extension of one's family and about Judaism being important because it provides a tie to other Jews. Among the least attached to the Jewish people only 53 percent saw Eretz Yisrael as indispensable to their Jewish identity, among those more attached 61 percent did, and among the most attached 70 percent did. Commitment to the land of Israel had an even more striking correlation with religiosity: of the least observant 49 percent said they were committed to the land of Israel, among the moderately observant 66 percent did, and among the most observant 78 percent did. Not only is attachment to the land correlated with attachment to the Jewish people and to religiosity, but attachment to the people and religiosity are themselves correlated. Israelis with more than an average commitment to the Jewish people accounted for only 28 percent of the nonobservant, for 40 percent of the moderately observant, and for about 53 percent of the most observant.

Whereas territory assumed a quasi-religious status among the early

Zionists and was an alternative to more traditionally central components of the Jewish religion, the traditional religious elite protested its transformation by the Zionists into a sanctified object independent of God, the sanctifier (though the elite never denied the centrality of Eretz Yisrael to the Jewish tradition).[2] Nevertheless, because so many commandments can be fulfilled only in the land of Israel, the land could never lose its significance for those faithful to the halakhic tradition. In recent years the holiness of the land has transcended its original halakhic meaning, and religious Zionists are the foremost interpreters of its new meaning: "According to the original meaning . . . the Land is holy because only there is it possible to fulfill the *mitzvot hateluyot ba'aretz* [commandments dependent on the land], i.e. to observe the religious and ritual laws concerning agriculture, socio-economic customs and ways of life related to rural economy. Now, however, following ancient or medieval folklore and folkways, the Land itself becomes holy rather than merely pointing to a metaspace; the space has actually become the incarnation of metahistorical holiness" (Tal 1986, 321).

At least as much as secular Zionists, religious Zionists have transformed Eretz Yisrael into a pillar of Judaism. The central spiritual figure for religious Zionists is Rabbi Abraham Isaac HaCohen Kook (1865–1935), a multifaceted personality whose writings are largely unpublished. What has been published, for the most part posthumously, was edited by his son and his son's followers, making it impossible to know the extent to which the nuances, subtlety, and complexity of Rav Kook's thought were distorted. Our interest is not in Rav Kook himself but in how he is perceived by religious Zionists. Among the qualities attributed to Rav Kook are love of all Jews and love of the land of Israel. For Rav Kook the land of Israel had a sanctity, a holiness, that imparted magical qualities to it:

> It is the air of the land of Israel that makes one wise, that illuminates the soul to enlighten that element which is derived from the world of unity. In the land of Israel, one draws upon the light of Jewish wisdom, upon that quality of spiritual life which is unique to the people of Israel, upon the Jewish world-view and way of life . . .

> In the impure lands of the gentiles, the world view of unity is imperceptible, and the divided world rules with force . . . The

impure soil that is everywhere outside the land of Israel is thus suffused with the stench of idolatry, and the Jews there are worshipers of idols in purity. The only way in which we may escape the disgrace of idolatry is for the Jewish people to gather in the land of Israel, as it is written, "to give you the land of Canaan, to be your God." (Lev. 25:38).

The lands of darkness may be capable of sustaining the trivial discussions brought up by the world's divisiveness but enlightened wisdom is to be found only in the land of light; there is no Torah like that of the Land of Israel. (quoted in Schweid 1985, 171–72)

This vocabulary and the conceptions that it expresses are quite foreign to American Jews, even the Orthodox. Schweid observes that for Rav Kook the image of the land of Israel as a loving mother was no mere metaphor: "The face of the land, its physical image, is that of a mother. A sympathetic heart beats within her. A Jew returning to the land feels, by his physical contact with it, her loving embrace. In the flavor of its crops and its water he senses her consolations, which are directed exclusively toward him. This sense that in the physical contact between man and the land their inner souls are responding to one another—this only the land of Israel can give to the Jews, and this sense alone is a sufficient foundation for the true revival, both physical and spiritual, of the people's national life" (1985, 184–85). This belief was shared by Kook's son, Rav Zvi Yehudah Kook (1891–1982), spiritual leader of Gush Emunim and the religious ultranationalists: "This is a land 'whose fruit is holy' and the working of the land is equivalent to the command of putting on phylacteries . . . This is how matters have been determined: this is a holy land and this is a holy people" (Kook 1978, 144)

The spirit of Rav Kook clearly lies behind the determination of the religious settlers in the West Bank (Judea and Samaria) and in particular of the leaders of Gush Emunim to resist any territorial concession, even in exchange for peace. In the words of the present leader of Gush Emunim, "The wholeness of the Jewish people cannot be obtained without the wholeness of the land."[3] Or, as another leader observed in a newspaper interview, "The central point is the understanding that the object of our generation is to settle the Land of Israel not as a refuge for a people who only seeks a place to live but as the redemption of the chosen people."

According to one settler (who we believe overstated the matter), the aim of those who have settled the West Bank is to turn "the Land of Israel into the sole content of Judaism and Judaism into the sole content of the Land of Israel."

The centrality among religious Zionists of Eretz Yisrael is not confined to the ultranationalists but has become almost universal, as is clear from two recent examples from the popular weekly pamphlet *Shabbat b'Shabbato.* (This four-page pamphlet, distributed free of charge in hundreds of synagogues throughout Israel, is published by a cultural organization associated with the National Religious party and deals primarily with the weekly reading from Bible and random news of a religious and cultural nature likely to interest a lay person.) The issue of 8 January 1988 mentions a new book that focuses on the "central idea of the Torah"—that is, "the place of *Eretz Yisrael* in the covenant that God made with His people." The following week *Shabbat b'Shabbato* described another book, *Sarvaney Geulah* (Dissenters from redemption). The reference is to those "who don't want to see the land of Zion and Jerusalem where the divine people walk in the vision of the prophets that will exist for all eternity."

The centrality of Eretz Yisrael may have been seen by early secular Zionists as an alternative to Jewish peoplehood and the Jewish tradition, but this is no longer the case; ties to land, people, and religion among Israeli Jews are all correlated. In sharp contrast, the vast majority of American Jews have little appreciation for the centrality of the land of Israel in Jewish tradition, nor do they appreciate the extent to which Israelis, even secular Israelis, have invested land with a sacredness all its own. It is fair to say that to most American Jews, even those with strong interests in Jewish life and Israeli matters, land constitutes an instrument of Israeli security; to the Israeli, it is often an end in itself.

"State" and "Community" among Israelis

In contrast to the powerful images in Israeli conceptions of Judaism of Am Yisrael (the people of Israel, the Jews) and Eretz Yisrael (the land of Israel), there is some evidence that Israelis have a very weak image of their state. Baruch Kimmerling has observed that in 1977 Israeli leaders began to use the concept of Eretz Yisrael rather than that of the state of Israel to define, however unconsciously, the collectivity's identity as rooted in a moral community based on primordial symbols and ties rather than in a civil community based on impersonal and universalist standards of conduct and governance (Kimmerling 1985; the orientation to which Kimmerling refers in fact began before 1977). One might infer from this attachment to land rather than state that Israelis attribute rather less importance to the state as an institution. But our argument is instead that many Israelis do not share the Western image of the state: they view their state in "communitarian" terms, or as an extended family.

Political scientists make frequent use of the term *state*. There is little agreement on its definition, but the term does evoke what one political scientist describes as "the sense of an organization of coercive power operating beyond our immediate control and intruding into all aspects of our lives" (Skowronek 1982, 3). The sense of state includes impersonal law and physical sanctions (Lewellen 1983, 35), but it is primarily the sense of an entity detached from the citizens. The modern state "is a remote public set of institutions, often appearing cold and impersonal to individual citizens. Its bureaucratic rationale and *modus operandi* hardly inspires sentiments of affection or solidarity" (A. Smith 1983, 156). Citizens of typically modern states therefore assume generally that the state has interests of its own that are independent of the interests of its citizens and that it may legitimately pursue.

The term *community* also refers to an abstraction: a group of people who believe that they share a set of characteristics, values, or needs that define the nature of their relationship. The basis of community is interrelationship, and that which supports and strengthens the members' interrelations is most highly valued. Unlike the state, the community has no interest independent of its members. Jewish Israelis have a rather weak sense of state in the Western sense and a rather strong sense of community. Whether they refer to the state of Israel or to Eretz Yisrael, they are imagining a community and not a state.

This phenomenon has been observed in differing forms by many others, although the terminology has varied. It lies at the heart of Ehud Shprinzak's analysis of Israel's culture of illegalism (1986). Shprinzak observes that the concept of rule of law is relatively weak in Israeli society: not only do many Israelis violate the law, but they feel that it is legitimate to do so, particularly if it serves the interests of their group or community. He traces this aspect of Israeli political culture to a variety of factors, including the Jewish tradition itself, the experiences of the vast majority of Israelis who originate from Eastern Europe or Arab countries, the socialist traditions of Israel's founders, and the legitimation of extralegal procedures during the British mandate.[4] In our terminology, Shprinzak demonstrates the weak value that Israelis attribute to state and the strong value they attribute to community.

The significance of community in contrast to state comes through very clearly in a column by Yonatan Gefen in the weekend supplement to Ma'ariv, one of Israel's two mass circulation newspapers (3 October 1986, pp. 10–11). Gefen writes that he and his friends dislike the country's leaders and government and are loyal to the hevreh (a slang term for one's circle of friends). A homeland "is primarily the love of the people who live there. . . . I don't know the meaning of state. It's too big for me. But a platoon I understand, it's easy for me to love. . . . Yes, we are a state [composed] of hevreh . . . I am here because of my hevreh . . . And there is nothing to do about it. This is the only state in which there is a hevreh and hence it is your fate to continue to hate it but to remain here forever."

In keeping with the precedence that it gives to community over state, Israeli society places a low premium on efficiency, a value overshadowed by that of caring for the welfare of individuals. Examples abound. In 1985 the Israeli cabinet ordered all government ministers to reduce the number of their employees. When the Ministry of Education planned to dismiss 270, Minister Yitzhak Navon was criticized; it was charged that many on his department's list of dismissals were "hardship" cases. In a radio interview on 28 July 1985 Navon denied this. He said that he had ordered his department heads to retain all employees who were ill or handicapped, who were the heads of families that had lost members in a war, or who were the sole sources of their families' support. Navon said that efficiency was not to be a criterion for dismissal: "We will make the inefficient more efficient."

Such instances are not unique to Israel. The expectation that government will employ those who are otherwise unemployable is well-known in Western society. But for a high government official to make preeminent the welfare of individuals rather than the pursuit of efficiency expresses starkly that the interests of state are virtually unknown in the lexicon of Israelis. This can have important consequences for policy. A dramatic example came in summer 1985, when after lengthy negotiations Israel agreed to exchange 1,150 imprisoned terrorists for three Israeli soldiers captured during the war in Lebanon of 1982. The soldiers were being held by a terrorist organization identified with an extreme faction of the Palestine Liberation Organization; the released prisoners were chosen by the terrorist organization and included some serving life sentences for the murder of Israelis.

Virtually all Israelis and their leaders now recognize that the exchange was a grave mistake. It undercut Israel's claim that governments should not make deals with terrorist organizations. It freed more than a thousand hardened, trained terrorists, with no guarantee that they would not conduct terrorist activity in the future. It provided the terrorist leaders with enormous prestige. It strengthened the morale and resolve of terrorists by sending the message that no matter how heinous their crime, if captured by Israel there was a good possibility of their being released. It discouraged captured terrorists from cooperating with Israeli authorities. It demonstrated how high a price Israel was willing to pay for the release of its own prisoners, thereby setting a standard for future exchanges that Israel would find hard to meet.

The exchange was approved without objection by the national unity government in 1985. Only one minister, Yitzhak Navon, abstained. In a private communication, the pollster Mina Zemach told us that her survey of public opinion taken the day after the exchange was announced revealed that a great majority of Israelis approved of the exchange. But the exchange did come under public attack from the news media as soon as it was announced. It is interesting to examine the defense of the exchange offered by public officials. Enormous importance was attributed to the pressure that the parents of the imprisoned soldiers exerted on the minister of defense. One spokesman for the army asked, "How could he look these parents in the eyes?" Others said that public criticism of those responsible for the exchange was illegitimate, and asked how the critics would feel if their sons were held prisoner. What came through dramatically in the defense of the exchange was the idea that no sacrifice was too great in the interest of the Israeli prisoners. Calculations of prestige, of future cost, of responsibility were all secondary to the communal, quasi-familial sentiment that one does whatever is possible for one's child. The exchange of prisoners was precisely what one expects of a family, not what one expects from a state.

There are other examples of the relative devaluation of the state. Government buildings in Israel have none of the grandeur or awesomeness of government buildings elsewhere. Only the contributions of the Rothschild Foundation brought about the construction of one of Israel's most imposing edifices, the Knesset building, and enabled a new Supreme Court building to be in the final stages of planning forty years after Israel became independent. Perhaps the ascetic, socialist ethos of Israel's early political elite may be partly responsible for the modesty in government buildings, but so is a modest regard for the state.

The lack of respect for the state and its institutions is dramatically expressed in the crude manner of address used by members of the Israeli government and legislature. This behavior may be accounted for by the political culture, which personalizes relationships and harbors very weak images of a remote state somewhat alien to the members of the society. The ritual forms of speech and stylized behavior that characterize governments of the Western world are foreign to the Israeli mentality. After all, they are not characteristic of how a quasi-familial community projects itself.

Of all the instrumentalities of the state, the one most remote and alien from the general public would seem to be the courts. At best they may be trusted to dispense justice and treat all equally; but they are not institutions with which the public feels intimate. Their procedures are the most stylized of all government institutions. They would appear to personify statist rather than communitarian values, and it is among the statists in particular that Israeli courts are most popular. Yet note how the attorney for an arrested Jewish terrorist addressed the court in appealing for leniency in the sentencing of his client: "Your honor; you are a Jewish judge in the district court of Jerusalem. You are not the judge in the International Court in The Hague" (*Ma'ariv*, 15 June 1984, p. 4). The very impersonality of the Western state suggests the applicability of universal law. Its independence from its citizens implies their equality in the eyes of the state: all are equally distant. Community, on the other hand, is personal. It is built on status, on past performance and future expectations, on degrees of kinship ties, and on loyalty and commitment, which suggests that not all are equal. And because membership in the community of Israelis is defined by Jewish identity, those who belong to the non-Jewish minority become almost by definition second-class citizens.

The belief that the rights and opportunities of non-Jewish citizens of Israel ought to be limited does not derive from the idea that Jews have a superior right to the land (although Israeli Jews do believe that their rights to the land of Israel supersede those of the Arabs). Nor is it the Jewish experience of persecution that justifies the suspicions of the Israelis about the Arabs' intentions toward them, although perhaps most Jews are convinced that the Arabs seek to destroy them. But there is a feeling that the state of Israel is the state of the Jewish people; it is a nation-state in the narrowest meaning of the term, of which non-Jews are not really a part. They may benefit from the civil rights that Jews grant them for reasons of humaneness, pragmatism, or ideology, but Israeli non-Jews are not Israelis by natural right: they are something else, a something generally left unspecified and unclear.

To associate one's ethnicity or religion with one's state is common throughout the Middle East and most parts of Asia. But this non-Western notion is difficult to understand for those brought up in Western societies, especially Jews. After all, the political emancipation of the Jews was based on the modern, liberal ideal that ethnicity and religion are irrelevant to membership in the polity, to citizenship in the Western sense.

The conceptions of Israeli Jews about the subordinate place of the Arab find expression in survey evidence, both our own and that of other researchers. Sammy Smooha, a sociologist at Haifa University, writes of a survey conducted in 1980: "At first glance, Jews appear receptive to Arab minority rights. A majority of 55% of the Jewish public . . . grant the Arab minority the right to live in Israel with full civil rights. . . . Upon closer examination, however, Jews are actually less accepting of Arabs. Many Jews who agree to allow the Arab minority full civil rights have in mind a status quo in which Arabs are formally afforded such rights but denied them in practice. . . . This interpretation is borne out by the fact that an overwhelming majority of Jews favor preferential, rather than equal, treatment of Jews by the state" (1989, 57). Smooha cites findings from another survey conducted in 1980, according to which at least two-thirds of Israeli Jews rejected equal treatment of

Arabs in several specific areas, including university admissions, employment, social security payments, and provision of agricultural loans (1989, 140).

In our survey roughly half of all Israeli Jews rejected the proposition that full citizenship should be enjoyed by Israeli Arabs (those who live within the boundaries that defined Israel before 1967, who enjoy full civil rights under Israeli law). As many as 38 percent agreed that "since Israel is a Jewish state, its Arab citizens are not entitled to the same rights and opportunities that Jewish citizens receive"; 14 percent were unsure. In contrast, only 6 percent of American Jews agreed with a similarly worded statement, and 10 percent were unsure. Further, the wording of this statement in Hebrew virtually precludes the possibility that some liberal Israelis were merely assenting to a statement of fact (Arabs do not have the same rights) as opposed to a statement of norms (Arabs should not have the same rights). Responses to another question on the same survey fortify our conclusion that nearly half of Israel's Jews oppose granting to Arabs the same rights as Jews have in Israel. Only 60 percent of the sample agreed (and 25 percent disagreed) with the following statement, which embodies a principle of Western democracy worthy of a civics textbook: "The State—its laws and officials—should treat all citizens equally, irrespective of their background, and without differentiating between Jews, Arabs, and Christians."

The social characteristics of the 25 percent who rejected this universalist statement are by now predictable. Unequal treatment of non-Jews was endorsed by more *dati'im* (those who identify themselves as "religious," which in the Israeli lexicon means Orthodox) than nonobservant Jews (37 percent to 19 percent; among the somewhat observant the figure was 25 percent), by more people without a high school diploma than with some university training (31 percent to 16 percent), by more Sephardim than Ashkenazim (of those born outside Israel, 33 percent to 20 percent; of those born in Israel, 28 percent to 17 percent).

Israeli Jews wish to curtail the rights and status of Israeli Arabs principally because they fear for their own security and feel threatened by neighboring Arab countries. But the reluctance of so many Israelis to view the Arabs as equal members of their society stems also from the political culture, which encourages conceptions of community at the expense of conceptions of state and sees the Israeli state as an expression of historic Jewish familism, and entertains the possibility of denying equal rights to Israeli Arabs (although the threats to Israel's survival may themselves feed communitarian conceptions of the society).

The phenomenon of Jewish statehood is at variance with two thousand years of Jewish tradition, which emphasize loyalty to one's community of fellow Jews rather than to an impersonal entity to which one is subject. Ben-Gurion recognized and feared the consequences of his compatriots' relatively limited loyalty to the state. He sought to counter the parochialism of community, although his concern was chiefly to undermine the subcommunities formed around political party and country of origin rather than to counter the Jewish particularism of the state. Ben-Gurion was the father of what has been called *mamlakhtuit* ("statism"), a term that he himself frequently invoked.[5] We are not concerned with tracing Ben-Gurion's specific conception of statism. He was not always faithful to the blueprint of a statist society in some of his actions, especially not in his insistence on imposing military rule in areas where most Israeli Arabs lived, his compromises with the demands of religious parties for a virtually independent school system, and his tolerance of some corruption in his party. But at least in broad outline, the concept of a strong state in the Western sense is not totally foreign to Israeli political history.

How influential are statist orientations in Israeli political culture today? The question is difficult to answer, and much of what we say here is speculative. It seems that statism in the Western sense is important only to a minority of the Israeli population. Statism is an important value primarily to those who are secular rather than religious, Ashkenazi rather than Sephardi, of high educational status, and in the legal and military professions (the foreign service in particular). Most other Israelis have a communitarian image of the state of Israel. This image is not necessarily a weak one, but according to it the state is an extension of the community; it is not some abstract or alien entity with interests of its own, independent of its citizens.

This image is very noticeable in attitudes toward the Israel Defense Force (IDF). The Israeli army commands respect on the one hand, but elicits a mixture of familiarity and contempt on the other. There is an element of fear in the relationship between the average Israeli and the army, but the army is also something of a home. It is not alien. The IDF is the army of the people, the power of the community. Hence the well-known Israeli resistance to the rituals and mannerisms of traditional armies, the insistence on informality, and the involvement of families in army ceremonies—as an audience if not as participants.[6]

In this conception the state of Israel represents the authority of the Jewish community and exercises power on its behalf. To those who hold this conception of state, the state of Israel plays a very important role in the meaning they attribute to Judaism. As one historian points out, "Israel's leaders might have interpreted Jewish statehood as the expression of a national liberation movement, something every former colonial people would have understood. The term was scarcely mentioned, however, in the addresses and writing of Ben-Gurion, Sharett, or Eban. Rather, the Israeli statesmen chose to discern a profounder explanation for the 'miracle' of rebirth in the historical and theological roots of the Jewish people" (Sachar 1976, 471).

The state of Israel plays an important role for the communitarians in their conception of Judaism, but like the ultranationalist, religious Zionists they may be disappointed that Israel does not behave in accordance with their image of a Jewish state. Rav Zvi Yehudah Kook, spiritual leader of the religious right, attributed sanctity to the state of Israel as well as to the land of Israel; he even argued that this sanctity extended to all the instrumentalities of the state, including the army (Kook 1978). But these ideas were predicated on the state of Israel being endowed with a purpose: according to the resolution adopted by the Council of Jewish Settlements in Judea, Samaria, and Gaza, should Israel surrender sovereignty over Judea or Samaria this would "represent a prima facie annulment of the State of Israel as a Zionist Jewish state whose purpose is to bring Jews to the sovereign Land of Israel, and not, perish the thought, to remove them from the Land of Israel and replace them with a foreign sovereignty."[7]

This is not the statement of a group to whom the state of Israel is unimportant but of a group with a particular image of what the state of Israel represents. Among religious Zionists the state assumes particular significance. Some, like the ultranationalists, have a vivid image of its role and therefore may argue that the present leadership or government is subverting its purpose. Like those arrested for committing terrorist acts against the Arab population, they will insist that they are serving the true interests of the state. More moderate elements in the religious Zionist camp are far more accommodating to the state as it exists. One spokesman argues in a leading religious Zionist journal: "Education for military service, study of science, and respect for the rule of law must serve, in a principled manner, as the basis for all religious values. . . . That is the purpose of religious Zionism which finds its expression in expanding the concept of religion until it includes service to the needs of the national state" (Nehorai 1987, 6).

Seventy-two percent of our Israeli Jewish respondents agreed with the statement "It is almost impossible for me to think of what it means to be a Jew without thinking about *Medinat Yisrael* [the state of Israel]." The attachment of Jewish importance to the state of Israel is clearly a matter of near consensus, even more so than the consensus about the land of Israel. Those who dissent from this view share the characteristics that have been so predictive in other contexts: those who disagreed with the statement cited above or were undecided about it tended to be the nonobservant rather than the most observant (41 percent to 18 percent), to have a university education rather than a high school degree alone (32 percent to 21 percent), and to be Ashkenazim rather than Sephardim (35 percent to 27 percent among those born in Israel; 35 percent to 17 percent among those born outside it).

The state of Israel is indeed a major component in the meaning that Judaism has for Israeli Jews. But at least to most Israelis the state of Israel does not mean a state in the Western sense of the term but rather the power and authority of the Jewish community. It is worth asking to what extent American Jews share this view of the state of Israel, and how this view has been incorporated into their conceptions of Judaism.

"Israel" among American Jews

For Israelis who live in the land of Israel and are subject to the authority of the state of Israel, the distinctions among people, land, and state are clear. For American Jews, living six thousand miles away or more, the distinctions are less clear. "Israel" is a symbol with a functional significance to American Jews that may well make it unnecessary to distinguish people, land, and state. In addition, most American Jews are ignorant of even the most rudimentary features of Israeli life. For example, fewer than a third of our sample of American Jews in 1986 knew (or guessed) that Menachem Begin (a former prime minister and the veteran leader of the right-wing Likud bloc) and Shimon Peres (then prime minister and head of the Labour alignment) were members of different parties. This ignorance does not mean that most American Jews are indifferent to Israel. Quite the contrary: Israel has been a major source of ethnic pride for American Jews, roughly two-thirds of whom say they care deeply about Israel and regard it as a very important part of being Jewish. Although quite a few maintain articulated and distinctive relationships with different aspects of Israel, there is in broad terms an American Jewish conception of Israel and of its meaning for Jewish identity.

Any assessment of American Jews' relationship with Israel and of how Israel is understood in Judaic terms needs to recognize the presence of two contrasting themes. On the one hand, particularly since 1967, organized American Jewry has made Israel the centerpiece of Jewish public life. News about Israel certainly occupies most of the space that Anglo-Jewish newspapers devote to news of the Jewish world. Many organized Jewish political groups in America—lobbyists, campaign contributors, and activists—decide which candidates to support, and to what degree, largely on the basis of the candidates' attitudes toward Israel. Israel is the mainstay of every community's annual fundraising campaign for Jewish philanthropy, and roughly half the money raised is allocated to causes related to Israel. The concern for Israel has been so pervasive and passionate that it has led many to observe that Israel is the core of the religion of American Jews.[8]

But the pro-Israelism of American Jews is limited in a number of ways that observers of American Jewish life often overlook. In quantitative terms the commitment to Israel varies considerably. On the basis of several surveys, we feel comfortable dividing American Jews into three broad categories: about one-third are relatively indifferent to Israel, another third are moderately pro-Israel, and a third are passionately pro-Israel. In the first group are those who say in their responses to our questionnaire that they do not "often talk about Israel with friends and relatives," or have no intentions of ever visiting Israel, or are not interested in having their children visit Israel, or reject the view that "caring about Israel is a very important part of my being a Jew," or see themselves as "not very close" to Israel, or do not agree with the statement "If Israel were destroyed, I would feel as if I had suffered one of the greatest tragedies in my life." About two-thirds of American Jews answer such questions in a way that shows support for Israel; about one-third do not.

Among the two-thirds of American Jews who are pro-Israel, almost half respond affirmatively to a more stringent set of questions. They have visited Israel, they claim to have had personal contact with an Israeli during the preceding twelve months, they want their children to spend a year in Israel, they plan to visit Israel in the next three years, and they call themselves Zionists. To be sure, even among this more passionately involved segment of the population only a fraction would qualify as Zionists by the typical Israeli's criterion, which emphasizes commitment to *aliyah,* resettlement. Only 15 percent of American Jews say they have given some thought to settling in Israel, and an even smaller number say they could "live a fuller Jewish life in Israel than the United States."

Support for Israel dominates public life, is part and parcel of the American Jewish consensus on what it means to be a Jew, and is voiced by a large majority of American Jews. But only about a third of all American Jews express what we would call a very passionate involvement with Israel, and only about a sixth express what might be called a truly Zionist commitment. The limited commitment to Israel is reflected in the recently published credo of the Conservative movement, entitled *Emet V'Emunah: Statement of Principles of Conservative Judaism* (New York: Jewish Theological Seminary, 1988). According to this document, a good Conservative Jew supports Israel but sees no compelling reason to live there and denies that the primacy of Israel is important for Jewish life (what the primacy of Israel does mean is not specified): "This zealous attachment to *Eretz Yisrael* has persisted throughout our long history as a trans-national people in which we transcended borders and lived in virtually every land. Wherever we were permitted, we viewed ourselves as natives or citizens of the country of our residence and were loyal to our host nation. Our religion has been land-centered but never land-bound; it has been a portable religion so that despite our long exile (*Galut*) from our spiritual homeland, we have been able to survive creatively and spiritually in the *tefutzot* (Diaspora)" (p. 38). Significantly, American-born Conservative rabbis who have settled in Israel have found their movement's statement far too noncommittal on the centrality of Israel and on the imperative to settle there. At the same time, many of their American colleagues thought the statement had gone about as far as they would have liked in elevating the ideological position of Israel and by inference denigrating the role of diaspora Jewry.

Our argument about the dual nature of Jewish involvement with Israel goes beyond these quantitative considerations. We believe that American Jewish involvement with Israel has for the most part relatively few consequences for the construction of Jewish identity in the private sphere. This statement presupposes a distinction between public and private Judaism, each with its own orientation toward Judaism. Private Judaism assumes a "cultural-religious-spiritual model which takes the individual as its starting point," an individual for whom "Judaism is a meaning system [providing] the adherent with an orientation to . . . questions of ultimate concern"; public Judaism assumes a "political-secular model [which] takes the Jewish people as its starting-point and concerns itself with its collective existence" (Liebman 1981). Public Judaism is what is conducted by communal organizations, primarily in the philanthropic and political spheres. Here political and financial support for Israel is the dominant feature, the one constant and commanding cause of public American Judaism.

But the massive philanthropic and political lobbying apparatus has had relatively little impact on the private Jewish lives of most American Jews, even the two-thirds who say that Israel's destruction would be one of their "greatest personal tragedies." As a society, culture, state, language, or sacred concept, Israel has little meaning for American Jews at the times in their private lives when they feel most keenly Jewish: at important events in their lives (marriage, divorce, birth, mourning) and family celebrations (the Passover Seder, the lighting of Hanukah candles, the High Holidays). Paradoxically, this observation remains true even though echoes of Israel from the Jewish past and future are incorporated into traditional Jewish ritual. Whatever anthropological explanations may be offered for the breaking of a glass by a Jewish groom under the wedding canopy, the Jewish tradition ascribes the custom to the need to remember even on the happiest occasions the destruction of the Temple. Few worshipers pay serious attention to passages in the liturgy that express the yearning of Jews for their physical ingathering in the Holy Land; and few Passover celebrants regard as a literal obligation the concluding chant of the seder, "next year in Jerusalem." (In fact several thousand Israelis annually set out to spend next year—and more—in New York and at other American destinations.)

Because few American Jews have a real familiarity with the currents of Israeli cultural and political life, these currents are not integrated into their own cultural life, even in an English-language version. (Very few American Jews are fluent in Hebrew.) An informal scan of the adult education programs sponsored by synagogues and Jewish community centers reveals few lectures and classes devoted to Israel, and most of these focus on the external threat to Israel rather than on the internal features of Israeli society. As a rallying point or as a locus for travel and study, Israel is at best an instrument to further Jewish identification. Yet little of the substance of Israeli life enters into the thinking and activities of most American Jews, even among the one-third who have been to Israel.

Others have expressed similar ideas. A Conservative American Jewish educator now living and working in Israel observes in the *Jerusalem Post:* "Today, while support for Israel is conceived of as an integral part of being Jewish, it stands somewhat apart from American Judaism. It is as if the influences of American life have exorcised the spiritual meaning of Zion from the political reality of Jerusalem. What remains is an urgent sense of obligation to support Israel, with only faint echoes from the tradition as to the reasons why. Israel in American Jewish education has become an entity to be learned about, to be supportive of and devoted to, and to identify with. But it is not a reality with implications for Jewish self-understanding" (Breakstone 1988, 11).

There is yet another way to view the limited extent to which Israel is integrated into conceptions of American Judaism. Phillip E. Hammond advances the idea that personal identity generally and religious identity specifically operate on two levels: one more intimate, essential, and constant, the other more peripheral, voluntary, and changeable:

We use the concept of identity in two quite different ways in the social sciences. The first way of looking at identity suggests the immutable, or at least the slowly changing core of personality that shows up in all of a person's encounters, irrespective of differing role-partners. The second way suggests the transient and changeable self as persons move from one social encounter to another, offering a somewhat different identity, as it were in each place. The first notion of identity suggests that it is involuntarily held; the second, that it can be put on and off. The first is nourished in primary groups, probably early in life; the second exists precisely because much of life is lived outside of primary groups. (1988, 2)

This division of identity into two spheres raises the question of whether the identification of American Jews with Israel is in fact part of the core Jewish identity of most American Jews. Alternatively, it may be fair to say that pro-Israelism is primarily situational, likely to ebb and flow principally in response to threats to Israel's security and Jewish efforts to strengthen it with philanthropy, political activity, and public relations. Undoubtedly the answer varies from one individual or community to the next, though unfortunately we lack hard evidence that it does. Nevertheless, we are willing to speculate that for the most part identification with Israel remains in the situational compartment of the identity of most Jews.

Diaspora or Galut in Traditional and Israeli Terms

The conceptions of exile and redemption were linked, and at least until the modern period they afforded Jews an explanation for their persecuted condition and hope for its radical transformation: "The religious mythos of Exile and Redemption in its Jewish version gave the restrictions, subjugation and stigmas—the institutionalized antisemitism of [the Jews'] pre-modern status—a sublimated significance that made them inwardly innocuous if not benign, and not merely outwardly acceptable" (Halpern 1987, 5). Further, "If exile had been ordained by God Himself as the lot of His chosen people, there was honor and purpose in apparent disgrace. If exile would end only with the coming of God's Messiah to all the world, the millennia of waiting could be endured and lent significance" (Eisen 1986, xi). But Halpern notes that "the stock characters in the traditional drama of Exile and Redemption" lost much of their meaning in the modern period. Other than the Zionists, those Jewish thinkers who dealt with the meaning of exile deprived it of its ties to the land. In this respect they developed a line of thought that can be found in the traditional rabbinic literature, but one that modern thinkers transformed into a major theme. After all, for the sages exile connoted the alienation of man from God, and this was a condition that prevailed in the land of Israel as well. But as Arnold Eisen observes, in the modern period homelessness was stripped of layers of imagery, just as the land of Israel was:

> The meaning of exile and return was universalized. Jerusalem came to connote the state of perfection centered there in the imagination of the prophets; it could rise "in England's green and pleasant land" or anywhere else. Exile indicated the human condition short of that perfection, and so, in the minds of many Jewish thinkers in the West, bore no relation to the real land of Israel, where Jews no longer lived. Dispersion was in fact a blessing and not a curse: the ground on which God's work would be planted and come to fruition . . . Exile signified a lack of rights or equality to be remedied in the countries where Jews were at present aliens, but in the future would be citizens. Redemption would come with emancipation rather than ingathering. (1986, 23)

Exile is therefore a basic Jewish concept that has undergone transformation among both Israeli and American Jews.

Galut is a term of opprobrium in the Israeli lexicon. To live in galut means to be adversely influenced by the surrounding environment, which diminishes and distorts not only one's Jewishness but one's humanity. To most Israelis, Jewish life in galut (outside Israel) is not only distorted but tenuous, subject to the ravages of assimilation and anti-Semitism. There are many expressions of such views. After the massacre of Jews in a synagogue in Istanbul by a group of Palestinian terrorists in 1986, Shmuel Shnitzer, a former editor of *Ma'ariv* and an important figure in popular circles in Israel, wrote a column entitled "The Meaning of *Galut*." (It is important that the title was not something like "Jewish Life in an Authoritarian Society" or "Jewish Life outside the West.") The column was devoted to what it means to live as a Jew outside the state of Israel: "The destiny and life of the Jew is in the hands of the rulers, who, under the best of circumstances are not overly concerned to save a Jew from death. The Jew cannot do a thing to save his own life and that which is sacred to him. That would be against the law. Nor is [the Jew] permitted to rely on [the state of Israel]. That would raise doubts about his loyalty to the host society. He is permitted to be fearful, but only in the recess of his heart because even fear smacks of the absence of loyalty" (*Ma'ariv*, 12 September 1986, p. 25).

When applied to Jews in the democratic West, the statement is absurd. But such hyperbole is not unusual and is not seen as hyperbole. Israelis who make similar statements say they are based on personal experiences, and they may indeed be a faithful record of perceived experiences. This only reminds us again of how myths and images shape perceptions of reality. For example, Uri Ben-Ari, a retired Israeli general who had served as an Israeli consul in New York, was quoted as follows in a long article in *Ma'ariv:* "I am a Jew. Not religious, not traditional. A Jew. But a different kind of Jew than one who lives in Boston or Chicago. I'm not an exilic Jew [*yehudi galuti*]. I won't swallow insults. I have many friends in the diaspora [*golah*]. When they are called 'fucking Jew' [the words are transliterated in the Hebrew text]— they swallow it" (*Ma'ariv*, Weekend Supplement, 18 March 1988, p. 14).

Religious Zionists to whom the state of Israel is at least the beginning of the "flowering of redemption" are particularly apt to vilify the galut by attributing exclusively negative characteristics to Jewish life there.[9] But secularists do so as well, employing the term *galut* to condemn the behavior of other Israelis. The nonreligious leader of an ultranationalist group refers to Israeli doves as embodying "neo-*galut* reactions" (*Ma'ariv*, Weekend Supplement, 28 November 1986, p. 13). And the prominent secularist author Amos Oz observes that "the combination of whining and self-righteousness . . . in Israel of late is the identifying mark of *galut*," because "the exilic Jew could not look a Gentile in the eye, but either squinted from below in self-abasement or looked down from above in superiority" (cited in Eisen 1986, 134).

Most remarkable, however, and a tribute to the ubiquity of the negative connotations of galut in Israeli society, is to find it used as a term of opprobrium by the *haredim,* the religious non-Zionists. In a debate that need not concern us, one religious Zionist leader critical of a religious Zionist school principal said about him, "There are people who have left the *galut* but whom the *galut* has not left." The non-Zionist religious weekly *Erev Shabbat* came to the defense of the principal. Its haredi writer charged that the person who made the statement was guilty of galuti (exilic) behavior because he complained to the minister of education about the conduct of the school principal. (Complaining to an outsider exemplifies galuti behavior, whether the outsider is a goy in galut or a secularist in Israel; see *Erev Shabbat,* 28 August 1987, p. 15.)

In the use of the term *galut* in the examples we have offered, the context of galut is somewhat vague. First, no distinction is drawn between periods of time—medieval or modern, before statehood or after statehood—or between different diaspora societies. Galut is a powerful symbol, because it serves to distinguish between appropriate behavior (the way a modern Israeli ought to behave) and inappropriate behavior (that of a Jew before statehood or a non-Israeli Jew). In this sense the use of the term strengthens the notion that Israeli Jews live in the best of all possible places in the best of all possible times. Of course only a little reflection will suggest that behavior defined as galuti is not necessarily characteristic of non-Israeli Jews today or of Jews in the past. And because it is not really grounded in reality, *galut* has become a general term of contempt bearing no relation to where one lives.

Second, modern Israelis' use of the term *galut* contrasts with traditional usage in two very important respects. No longer is galut a metaphysical or spiritual status shared by all Jews; it is rather a physical status referring to Jews who do not live in a particular place—the land of Israel. In addition, galut does not mean life outside Eretz Yisrael but life outside the state of Israel. The attributes of statehood—power and pride in one's Jewishness in particular—characterize Jews who live in modern Israel rather than in galut.

Finally, the term does not distinguish between those who live in galut by choice and those who live there for lack of an alternative. In the case of the United States, the disparagement of galut by Israelis is a disparagement of American Jews as well, for it encompasses the notion that even if American Jews are not faced with immediate threats to their physical safety, they are destined to assimilate. Among our Israeli respondents, the majority agreed that "assimilation poses serious dangers to American Jewish survival" (58 percent); that "American Jews can lead a fuller Jewish life in Israel than in the United States" (54 percent);

that they were "troubled that American Jews do not make *aliyah*" (52 percent); and that "when an Israeli meets an American Jew, he should urge him to make *aliyah*" (60 percent). (In all four instances roughly a quarter to a third disagreed, and the rest were undecided.) Granted that each of these questions measures a different dimension, and that none of them expresses the kind of intensely negative feelings toward galut that were characteristic of the early Zionist settlers. But all point to the centrality of life in the state or land of Israel and to the negative quality of life for Jews elsewhere.

American Jews may be surprised or disappointed to learn that most Israelis feel this way. But in the light of statements by Israel's cultural and political elite, the surprise is that so many Israelis dissent from this conventional Zionist rhetoric. Who are the dissenters? First and not surprisingly, they are those distinguished by their personal attitude toward *yeridah*. Israelis who have seriously considered leaving Israel are those who feel most positive about the diaspora and who are least likely to feel that Israelis should encourage American Jews to emigrate to Israel. Nineteen percent of our survey sample said they had given some thought to leaving Israel and settling abroad. (The rate was 27 percent among the nonobservant, 18 percent among the moderately observant, and 7 percent among the dati'im.) By combining answers to the questions about encouraging aliyah we devised a scale of commitment to aliyah. Of those who had thought of emigrating only 28 percent scored high on this scale, compared with 55 percent among those who had not thought of emigrating.

The dissenters from the rhetoric of Israel's leaders are also distinguished by religiosity, education, and ethnicity. Thirty percent of our entire Israeli sample scored in the lowest category on the scale of commitment to aliyah. Low scores were achieved by more nonobservant Jews than dati'im (44 percent to 18 percent), by more respondents with some university training than respondents with no high school degree (39 percent to 21 percent), and by more Ashkenazim than Sephardim (among the Israeli-born, 40 percent to 28 percent). Religious observance is central to variations by education and ethnicity: Sephardim are more strongly oriented toward aliyah than Ashkenazim, and the less well educated are more strongly oriented toward it than the university-educated, in large measure because Sephardim and those with less education are more religious.

The Meaning of the Term *Exile* to American Jews

The term *galut* has virtually no meaning for American Jews: "The Jewish homeland was meant only for Jews who unlike Americans, had no other home. By attempting to secure such a home for his persecuted brethren overseas, the American Zionist became a 'better man and a better American'" (Eisen 1986, 157; the quotation is from Louis Brandeis). To the extent that the term *exile* plays any role at all in contemporary Jewish thought (and Eisen demonstrates that even among Jewish theologians its role is negligible), it is encapsulated in the statement that "all of us are in *galut*" and that "those are most in *galut* who think they are already at home" (Eisen 1986, 160). The quotation above summarizes the sentiments of most of the American Jewish thinkers who took part in a symposium on the meaning of galut sponsored by *Midstream,* which published the proceedings in March 1963.[10] Eisen observes that even among American thinkers whose ideological position recalls that of Israeli intellectuals, the topic of exile is devoid of angst:

> Israel's religious significance is not a principal theme. When the subject does arise—most often, in the past decades, in the aftermath of the crises of 1967 and 1973—it is Israel's *existence* which matters decisively, providing rescue from the despair of the holocaust and indispensable reassurance for the worth of Jewish life and faith. But this inspiration conveys no imperative to live in the Land rather than gaze reverently from afar; more important, it does not take in the actuality of the Land or the state. The revolutionary character of modern Zionism is in effect denied. In short: Israel is a homecoming, but not a home. America may be somewhat less a home than Israel, but it is far from exile. Israel does not challenge American Jewish life but rather undergirds it. (1986, 164)

Most American Jews reject the Israeli notions of exile. Accordingly, they reject the Israeli image of Jewish life outside Israel (in the diaspora) as precarious, distorted, and incomplete, and the Israeli claim that Israel offers a genuine home to the Jew, who can lead a full Jewish life there without fear of alienation from the larger society. The differences between Americans and Israelis over these issues are highlighted by their different responses to a statement we posed to samples of both populations: "American Jews can lead a fuller Jewish life in Israel." Fifty-four percent of our Israeli respondents and about 15 percent of our American respondents endorsed this statement. American Jews find foreign the classical Zionist understanding of the diaspora in general and America specifically as galut, just as they find foreign the notion that Israel is truly their home, the one place where they can be full Jews.

At first glance, we are struck with the gross disparities between Israeli and American Jewish understandings of some very basic concepts in Judaism and Jewishness. Israelis distinguish the separate dimensions of "Israel": people, land, state. Despite their passion on the subject of Israel, American Jews make no such distinctions. Israelis both secular and religious, from the political left as well as the right, feel a special tie to the land of Israel, with implications for their core identities as people, as Jews, and as Israelis. Hardly any American Jews even realize that the land of Israel played an important role in traditional Judaism, in part because many lack a strong interest in the fine points of Jewish tradition. And few American Jews appreciate the land's special meaning for Israelis beyond its instrumental functions. Israelis maintain a concept of the state of Israel according to which Israel is subsidiary to their notion of Jewish familism. For American Jews, the only alternative to the Western liberal conception of the state is an antidemocratic, racist, or authoritarian one. For Israelis galut is still a powerful term, one appropriated from the tradition and constructed so as to lend legitimacy and meaning to their national purpose. For American Jews America is home, the notion of exile meaningless.

Similar observations can be made regarding universalism and political liberalism, but in reverse (see chapter 5). These two concepts are central to American Jewish formulations and essentially meaningless to the Israeli. The differences between Israeli and American Jews are therefore not over what is Judaically right or Judaically wrong; they are differences in emphasis. Each group has in effect chosen to attribute Judaic value to its own environment. For Israelis this means Jewish people, land, and state; for American Jews it perforce includes not just Jews but the larger society of non-Jews as well. At the risk of oversimplifying and overstating our conclusions, in the next chapter we suggest that at the heart of American Jewish liberalism lies the belief that life among Gentiles serves some essential Jewish purpose, and that the kind of relationships Jews establish with Gentiles are based not only on strategies of survival but on principles of Judaism. This belief is also embedded in the Jewish tradition, although one almost never hears it expressed in Israeli society. Neither is it the way most American Jews would formulate their liberalism or their Judaism, but we believe it is inherent in much of what they say they believe and in what they do.

5   Liberalism and
Judaism

There are many important differences between Israeli and American Jews in their understanding of Judaism. Israelis are more familistic in their orientation to their fellow Jews (see chapter 2). The concept of exile has lost its meaning for American Jews, and although they still regard non-Jews as anti-Semitic, Jews are not as ethnocentric as their traditional forebears were. The symbol of exile continues to have meaning for Israelis, though it has undergone a conceptual transformation. Israelis see the diaspora as an exile threatened by assimilation and anti-Semitism, in which Israel plays a central, redemptive role (chapter 3). The state and land of Israel occupy a far more central position in the Jewishness of Israelis than of Americans (chapter 4). Not surprisingly, sharp differences extend to the realm of political behavior and attitudes as well. In adopting contrasting political orientations, Israelis and American Jews use different political values that reflect very different ideas of what it means to be a Jew in the modern world.

American Jews are overwhelmingly liberal, and their liberalism is central to their conception of Judaism. In many important respects most Israeli Jews are not liberal. More significantly, the core elements of liberalism are rather marginal to their conception of Judaism. These propositions are more easily advanced than demonstrated, for there are methodological problems in comparing the political orientations of American and Israeli Jews. The issues and contexts are so different that identically worded survey questions can have different meanings to the English-speaking American and the Hebrew-speaking Israeli. Nevertheless, we believe a convincing argument can be made that American Jews are liberal and Israelis are not—or, more accurately, are less liberal (although they may have been more liberal in the past).

The contemporary difference in political orientation is the result of different perceptions with regard to several questions: What constitutes genuine Jewish group interests? What lessons are to be learned from Jewish history, in particular the history of political interaction with non-Jews? Which Jewish political values are authentic and compelling? And how should those values be applied?

American Jews, the non-Orthodox in particular, perceive political liberalism as a constituent element in their understanding of what it means to be a good and caring Jew. In their survey of Jews in a suburb of Chicago in the late 1950s, Sklare and Greenblum asked what it meant to be a "good Jew" (1979, 322). Two-thirds of their respondents said it was essential to "support all humanitarian causes" and "promote civic betterment and improvement in the community," and almost a third said this was desirable. Helping "the underprivileged improve their lot" was rated almost as highly. Almost two-thirds said it was at least desirable to be "a liberal on political and economic issues" in order to be "a good Jew." The authors conclude: "At first glance the ideal of Jewishness predominating in Lakeville seems to be that of the practice of good citizenship and an upright life. To be a good Jew means to be an ethical individual; it also means to be kind, helpful, and interested in the welfare of neighbors, fellow Americans, and of humanity-at-large" (p. 324).

More than thirty years later, a nationwide survey of American Jews by the *Los Angeles Times* confirmed that liberalism or a variant of it was integral to how American Jews understood their Judaism. Respondents were asked: "As a Jew, which of the following qualities do you consider most important to your Jewish identity: a commitment to social equality, or religious observance, or support for Israel, or what?" Fifty percent chose "equality"; the rest were equally divided among religious observance, support for Israel, and miscellaneous other responses. As one might expect, denominational traditionalism was inversely related to the liberal response: equality was seen as most important by 18 percent of the Orthodox, 44 percent of the Conservative, 65 percent of the Reform, and 63 percent of the nondenominational. At least for the non-Orthodox American Jews, liberalism is not merely a characteristic but clearly a major component of their understanding of what it means to be a Jew.

Both Jewish liberal ideologues and their conservative critics acknowledge this. But many Israeli liberals as well as their political opponents believe that Judaism and liberalism are in tension, or even incompatible. To many Americans a good liberal is a good Jew; to many Israelis the liberal Jew is less Jewish—because he or she is less nationalistic, less particularistic, and less religious—or perhaps a weaker Jew. For the more religious and politically right-wing, the liberal Jew is often seen as a "self-hating" Jew.

Both Israeli and American Jews have reconstructed or reformulated traditional Judaism. But insofar as one can measure such things, American Judaism departs more dramatically from the traditional past than Israeli Judaism does. As the tree of modern Judaism has grown, the Israeli branch has remained closer to its traditional Jewish roots.

There is one important exception. Before the emancipation Jewish relations with the Gentile authorities were the responsibility of Jewish elites—community leaders, generally wealthy, and rabbis. The masses of Jews were hardly ever interested in the major political questions facing the societies in which they dwelled, much less mobilized to respond to them. Political emancipation in the modern era meant the participation of the Jewish masses in the politics of their societies: "Politics has been an avocation of the Jews for a mere two hundred years. . . . Modern Jewish politics was forged in the crucible of 19th-century Europe, in the striving for liberty and political equality that swept the European continent from West to East" (Dawidowicz 1985, 25). As they became integrated into society Jews realized that they had a stake in the outcome of the political debates swirling around them. Not only would the resolution of the debates affect Jews indirectly by shaping the societies in which they lived, but the large political conflicts impinged directly on the Jews' struggle to secure the promises of the Enlightenment and the emancipation—namely, equal rights in the economic, social, religious, and political realms. Different groups of Jews chose different political options: conservative and liberal, socialist and nationalist, Zionist and cultural autonomist.

The liberal political orientation of the Jews of Western Europe and the United States is pronounced. Since the late 1960s some Jewish intellectuals and communal leaders in the United States have questioned the wisdom of this orientation. On the other hand, liberals maintain that Jewish history, values, and interests all mandate continued Jewish participation in the liberal camp in American politics. They in effect argue that American Judaism and liberal politics reinforce each other. But some go further and argue that they cannot conceive of themselves as American Jews without simultaneously identifying as liberals.

Conservatives are aware of the historic association between Judaism and liberalism. They criticize what they perceive to be the failure of Jewish liberals to reassess the demands of Jewish interests in light of recent political developments in the United States:

> It is instructive to note the kind of explanation that has been offered to account for the continuing identification of many Jews with liberalism. One prominent historian has suggested that this closeness derives from the residual, latent strength of the Jewish religious heritage, including utopian moral philosophy. Another . . . has argued that the Jewish community . . . is in quest of a new, messianic secular faith. A third explanation is that the Jews [are motivated] . . . to transcend ethnicity . . . [to overcome] the commandments for group solidarity . . . of the ghetto [with] . . . the seemingly universalist moral imperatives of liberalism. . . . *Each of the three suggests that an affinity for liberalism by Jews is part of their personal self-identification,* and therefore cannot be abandoned when confronted by new events and circumstances. (David Sidorsky, *Commentary* 1980, 71; italics added)

For Sidorsky, the observation that Jews' liberalism runs deep is a point of polemic. His charge is that most American Jews are constitutionally incapable of abandoning their liberalism even though they ought to. Liberal polemicists attribute the strong allegiance to liberalism of American Jews as a reflection of the Jewish authenticity of liberalism, not of the political obtuseness of American Jews. Both sides agree that liberalism is a key to the group identity of American Jews. But are American Jews really liberal?

The Breadth and Persistence of American Jewish Liberalism

No one doubts that American Jews were liberal before the early 1970s, by any reasonable definition of the term. What is a matter of some dispute is whether American Jewish liberalism endured into the 1980s. The impression that Jews have abandoned their historic commitment to political liberalism has been strengthened by the emergence of a good number of prominent Jewish conservatives (perhaps best represented in the pages of *Commentary*), the anxiety felt by Jews about affirmative action, their passion for strong American military and diplomatic support of Israel, their concern over the Soviet Union's treatment of Jews, and their affluence.

But the evidence is that American Jewish liberalism persists. The Jewish political center remains to the left of the ever-shifting American center. The American political road may have veered rightward in the last two decades, but Jews are still disproportionately in the left lane: "Studies of Jewish attitudes and political behavior continue to find that Jews remain the most liberal white ethnic or religious group in the nation" (Seymour Martin Lipset, *Commentary* 1980, 54). The political inclinations of American Jews are even more surprising when we consider that income differences have emerged as a very powerful axis of political differentiation, with the more affluent voting Republican and the poor voting Democratic. In an age when income seems to matter more for most Americans, it seems to matter less for Jews.[1]

What do we mean when we assert that American Jews are politically liberal? First, Jews continue disproportionately to support the more liberal party in the United States, the Democrats. In the presidential election of 1984, 59 percent of Americans (and an even larger percentage of whites) voted for Ronald Reagan; 41 percent voted for Walter Mondale. The results were considered a landslide for Reagan. Among American Jews, however, the landslide went the other way: 68 percent of American Jews voted Democratic and only 32 percent voted Republican (Schneider 1985). The only other population groups to vote Democratic by such a large margin were blacks, the poor, and the unemployed. Most Jews thought it appropriate to vote Democratic even if doing so was not in their interest. The year after the election 69 percent of Jews in a national sample agreed that "even if Jews were sure Mondale would lose heavily, and that voting for him would hurt their political influence, it was still right for them to have voted for Mondale"; only 19 percent disagreed. Disproportionate Jewish support for the Democratic presidential candidate emerged clearly in 1988 as well: only 46 percent of the national electorate voted for Michael Dukakis, but according to exit polls around 68 percent of all Jews did.

Along with the Jewish attachment to the Democratic party and its liberal values there is an antipathy to conservatism, which Jews associate with indifference to humanitarian values. Elliot Abrams, assistant secretary of state under President Reagan, wrote about the "guilt over appearing 'conservative' and thus indifferent to injustice or poverty, and . . . the sentiment that Republicans aren't 'our kind of people'" (*Commentary* 1980, 16). The political scientist Werner Dannhauser sharpens the point: "I hesitate to become a Republican. Some of my reluctance is purely instinctual. I watch the national conventions on TV and am forever being forced to conclude that I just don't belong among those worthy folks. What is more, business is not my business and corporations are not my cup of tea" (*Commentary* 1980, 31).

The evidence that Jews remain liberal is not limited to their tendency to support Democrats over Republicans, and liberals over conservatives. Throughout the 1980s surveys showed that about twice as many Americans called themselves conservatives as called themselves liberals; among Jews the proportion was reversed in several surveys (1983, 1984, and 1988).

Democratic voting and liberal identification reflect a package of political and social attitudes. These fall into six overlapping areas, or dimensions of liberalism: (1) support for social welfare programs, (2) sympathy for minorities, (3) commitment to civil rights, (4) support for civil liberties, (5) extreme dedication to the separation of church and state, and (6) a nonmilitaristic, noninterventionist foreign policy. Jews are distinguished from other whites, particularly other upper-middle-income whites, in their avid support for social welfare programs. During the presidential campaign of 1988 between Dukakis and George Bush, Arnold Eisen not only placed concern for "social welfare" at the top of his political priorities but connected this concern with his understanding of the Jewish tradition:

> My vote goes to Dukakis. First, because my social agenda, being a Jew, is far closer to his. . . . It should be clear to all, after eight years of Reagan, that the current policy—which Bush has vowed to further—simply does not give a damn about the millions of Americans too weak to make their own way in our dog-eat-dog economic system. Fall by the wayside, and Bush is happy to leave you there. . . . Ask him about his economic policy, which blatantly ca-

ters to the rich, and he tells you that "when you cut capital gains you put people to work." This is not exactly the Jewish way. It is the way which has left thousands of people in this country homeless, left millions without decent medical care, and left tens of millions without ever buying their own home or getting a college education. Ugh. (1988, 154–55)

In 1985, 54 percent of Jews favored restoring "spending on many of the social welfare programs which have been cut back since 1981"; 32 percent disagreed. In parallel surveys of Jews and Gentiles conducted in 1988, most white non-Jews approved of cutting domestic spending to relieve the federal budget deficit; a plurality of Jews disapproved. Although Jews regard blacks as the most anti-Semitic and most anti-Israel of any major American population group, in 1985 47 percent of all Jews surveyed agreed that "American Jews should still support welfare and other programs which help mostly blacks"; 33 percent disagreed. Jewish liberalism also embraces a strong commitment to other minorities, to women, and to the poor and disadvantaged. Harold M. Shulweis, a Conservative rabbi, links his concern for minorities with his reading of the Bible:

Those who counsel Jews to distance themselves from the anguish of other peoples are ignorant of the Biblical, prophetic, rabbinic and Jewish philosophic traditions that mandate an active empathy towards the submerged communities of non-Jews. Those advisors do not appreciate the radical choice of the rabbinic tradition that selected the story of Hagar's banishment and God's protection of Ishmael, no favorite son of Israel, on the first day of the Jewish New Year. They have no ears for the Rabbi's reading of the Book of Jonah on the Day of Atonement in defense of Nineveh the enemies of the Jews. They do not understand the example of Abraham in defense of the non-Jewish citizens of Sodom and Gomorrah. (Shulweis 1988, 149)

Sympathy for minority groups can of course be attributed to self-interest. An America free of prejudice, an America tolerant of groups who are the object of as much discrimination as blacks are, is also an America that is safest for Jews. A similar argument can be made about women's rights, for the women's movement has championed issues that are most important for socially ambitious, professional, middle-class and upper-middle-class women, and Jewish women are overrepresented in these groups. Social welfare spending also directly benefits social service agencies (Jewish and others) and the many Jews who work for them. But just as surely, sympathy for improving the condition of blacks, women, the poor, and other minorities in American society reflects at least partly a generalized commitment to minorities. In the course of an interview with three Jewish writers for the *Village Voice,* Jack Newfield commented: "We all referred to the sense of Jews as victims, Jews as underdogs, in the sixties, and at least for me, of blacks as victims and blacks as underdogs. And I think that I felt very deeply the bond with blacks. . . . It was very frustrating that blacks who I was politically educated to feel allied with through victimization and underdogism were becoming vehemently anti-semitic" ("Pride, Prejudice, and Politics," 12). Newfield's colleague Ellen Willis voiced similar sentiments later in the same interview: "We're all forced to confront . . . the question of what is a Jew and what does this all mean. And to me the status of Jews as outsiders and as persecuted outsiders is at the core of what Judaism and Jewishness is all about. It's what all Jews—religious and secular, Zionist and non-Zionist, conservative and radical—have in common" (p. 17).

Jews distinguish themselves from other whites by the level of their support for black mayoral candidates, even when the black candidates' opponents are Jewish (Singer 1987). Such support may be strongest among more highly educated Jews living in affluent urban neighborhoods such as the Lakefront of Chicago, the Center City in Philadelphia, and the Upper West Side of New York, but it is not confined to them. In 1985, 67 percent of Jewish respondents disagreed with the statement "American Jews are making a mistake by supporting politically weaker groups as often as they do"; only 14 percent agreed. When the Equal Rights Amendment was a live issue in the early 1980s, it was supported by a higher proportion of Jewish men than of American women (Himmelfarb 1981, 28). In some conservative or even politically centrist precincts of America, the National Organization for Women (NOW) is seen as a shrill and strident institutional symbol of the feminist movement in the United States: in a national sample of non-Jewish whites in 1988, only slightly more respondents had favorable impressions of NOW than had unfavorable impressions (28 percent to 24 percent). But among Jews the comparable figures were 51 percent and 14 percent.

The impression that there has been a Jewish swing to the political right derives largely from the mixed and highly nuanced positions of major Jewish organizations on affirmative action programs, and the steadfast opposition to such programs among writers aligned with *Commentary.* And the impression has been reinforced by the coolness of Jews toward the most prominent black leader of the 1980s, Jesse Jackson: 59 percent of Jewish respondents in 1988 said they thought Jackson was anti-Semitic, and only 8 percent did not.[2] But this has not resulted in a reversal of support for blacks among most Jews. Despite the wariness and occasional hostility that have characterized the relations between blacks and Jews since the late 1960s, most Jews profess great sympathy for blacks and their political struggles. In 1988, 49 percent of American Jews said they had a generally favorable impression of the best-known black organization, the NAACP, and only 15 percent said they had a generally unfavorable impression.[3] Among non-Jewish whites the figures were 28 percent and 25 percent. In 1985 Jewish respondents were asked whether they agreed or disagreed with a series of statements: each began with the contention "Even though many Jews think that some black leaders have been anti-Semitic or anti-Israel" and ended with a suggestion of what American Jews should nevertheless continue to do. Eighty-eight percent said that Jews should "try to improve relations with the black community," 48 percent said they should "support special efforts to recruit and hire black workers" (33 percent disagreed), and 54 percent said they should "support special efforts to recruit and admit black students into colleges and professional schools" (29 percent disagreed).

Many observers believe Jews are sympathetic toward minorities because they see Jewry itself as a historically persecuted minority: "Jews, as a religious and ethnic minority, have for centuries experienced a deprivation of civil rights and are therefore keenly aware of how important it is that equality in civil rights be enjoyed by all minorities—religious, ethnic, or racial. This explains why, for most of the history of the NAACP and the Urban League, Jewish money played such a large role in keeping those institutions afloat. It also explains why so many individual Jews participated so energetically, over these past twenty years, in the civil-rights movement itself" (Kristol 1984, 23). In other words, Jewish consciousness leads to sympathy toward minorities. But the converse may also be true, at least in the minds of the actors. Some Jewish feminists and gay activists say their Jewish commitment is enhanced by their conception of themselves as oppressed minorities. In their view, such sentiments are central to what it means to be a Jew in modern America. Jewish liberal activists have long argued that their political marginality and the marginality of Jews are mutually reinforcing. It matters not whether gay consciousness, for example, really does reinforce Jewish consciousness; what matters is the construction of Jewish meaning in the minds of social and political nonconformists: homosexuals, feminists, civil libertarians. Their views further testify to the powerful belief of American Jews that as Jews they ought to be especially sympathetic to other minorities because the minority experience is central to their conception of Judaism.

Related to the sympathy of Jews for minorities but distinct from it is the third component of Jewish liberalism, commitment to civil rights. Jews have been active in the struggle against discrimination in housing, employment, and other areas. Even Jews who are no longer liberal, who are seen by themselves or by others as neoconservatives, say that they have remained faithful to the civil rights agenda, and that it is American liberalism that has abandoned its own principles.

One example is Morris Abram, chairman of the Conference of Presidents of Major Jewish Organizations in the 1980s and a civil rights lawyer in Atlanta in the 1960s:

It irks me that many who called me liberal in Georgia, particularly during my bitter fourteen-year battle for the principle of one man/one vote against the racially motivated county-unit voting system, now say that I have changed my colors. . . .

I have not changed my views on human equality or freedom one whit. By the accepted meaning of the term I am a liberal. . . .

At the core, the liberal and conservative traditions are at least distinguishable in that the liberal celebrates equality and freedom. . . .

Equality before the law, neutrality as to ethnicity, religion, or sex, were the proper goals of the advocates of equal opportunity. (*Commentary* 1980, 15)

In 1985, 90 percent of American Jews surveyed said they "support vigorous enforcement of civil rights and anti-discrimination laws."

A commitment to civil liberties is the fourth pillar of American Jewish liberalism. Jews have been disproportionately supportive of the American Civil Liberties Union, which in 1988 evoked a favorable impression from 33 percent of Jewish respondents (21 percent had an unfavorable impression). In contrast, among non-Jewish whites in a parallel survey, 14 percent had a favorable impression and 29 percent an unfavorable one. In the survey of American Jews of 1985, 86 percent agreed with this statement: "Whatever I may feel personally about nonconforming groups—like black activists, feminists, homosexuals, and radicals—I think Jews are much better off in an American society which can be truly open to and tolerant of groups such as these." And in 1988 Jews were far more likely than white non-Jews to agree that homosexuals "should have the same rights as other people" (85 percent to 57 percent). The political scientist Lawrence Fuchs stressed the protection of civil liberties in his endorsement of Dukakis in the presidential election of 1988: "There are a clear range of issues—I call them civic culture issues—on which it can be argued that what is good for the Jews is clearly good for the United States of America. By civic culture issues I mean mainly those public questions which concern the protection of the fundamental rights guaranteed by the First Amendment and those which concern the protection of the process of Constitutional Democratic government. . . . Jews have a particular interest in first amendment freedoms . . . for Jews in this country have equal rights with all the citizens because of the Constitutional protections of the First Amendment" (1988, 159–60).

Of all civil liberties issues, perhaps the most urgent to Jews is a clear separation of church and state. This fifth distinctive dimension of Jewish liberalism is the one where American Jewish attitudes are most at variance with those of the general public. For example, the public favors by a margin of 68 percent to 26 percent "an amendment to the U.S. Constitution that would allow prayer in the public schools" (Gallup Poll/Phi Delta Kappa 1988). In contrast, in the "Joint Program

Plan, 1987–1988," the annual combined platform of all the major Jewish community relations agencies, the highest "strategic goal" in church-state relations is to defeat "school prayer amendments to the Constitution, and any legislation that might permit religious practices in the public schools" (National Jewish Community Relations Advisory Council 1988, 42). A great majority of Americans favor prayer in public schools; but among the Jewish public in 1984 only 21 percent were in favor of even "a moment of silent meditation each day in the public schools" and 70 percent were opposed. Eighty-one percent of white non-Jews would permit a Hanukah menorah on public property, but only 37 percent of Jews would (55 percent would not), and only 16 percent of rabbis would (Williamsburg Charter Foundation 1988, table 31).

American Jews fear that the introduction of prayer or even the semblance of prayer in the public schools will make their children feel uncomfortable, as a Jewish minority in an environment that ostensibly is religiously neutral. Many Jewish parents recall their anxiety as children when they were compelled to sing or listen to Christmas carols in their schools. In 1988 white non-Jews favored a constitutional amendment to permit school prayer by a margin of 71 percent to 18 percent; Jews opposed it by a similar margin of 74 percent to 18 percent. Jews have also opposed strenuously most attempts to secure direct or indirect government funding for private schools (and therefore for parochial schools). Most Americans favor tax credits for private schools (by a margin of 51 percent to 45 percent, according to a poll conducted in 1983 by the *Los Angeles Times*), but Jews oppose such credits (by a margin of 63 percent to 29 percent in the survey of 1984). The Joint Program Plan of 1987–88 calls on organized Jewry to "oppose efforts to enact programs of educational vouchers, as well as efforts at the federal and state levels to enact tuition tax credit or deduction programs" (1987, 42).

The passionate opposition of Jews to any breach in the wall separating state and religion may stem from their fear that such a breach would emphasize the distinctiveness of Jews and their status as a non-Christian minority. But they are more likely to phrase their belief in positive terms, to insist that only strict separation of church and state protects non-Christian minorities. This may also help to explain their hostility to the Christian right. In 1984 only 7 percent of Jews said they were generally favorable toward the Rev. Jerry Falwell's group Moral Majority; 69 percent said they were generally unfavorable toward it. In addition, Jews are suspicious of all other groups with strong ethnic or religious loyalties, whom they suspect of anti-Semitic attitudes (see chapter 3). This too is probably a factor in Jewish hostility toward the Christian right. Finally, Jews associate their own liberties with modernization. The strength of public anti-Semitism in the West "was linked to the vitality of cultural and political anti-modernism" (Endelman 1986, 105), so that Christian fundamentalism immediately evokes images of anti-Semitism.

Conservative Jewish intellectuals have called on Jews to moderate their opposition to the Christian right because of its support of Israel. Despite these blandishments and notwithstanding this commitment to Israel, the Jewish public remains stalwart in opposing the Christian right. In 1985, 52 percent of Jews rejected the statement "Since the Christian Right has been very pro-Israel, American Jews should overlook their objections to the Christian Right's ideas about America, and work more closely with it to help Israel"; only 20 percent agreed with it. The concern of American Jews for Israel's security is broad and deep, but it seems that few allow this concern to affect their position on other issues, from relations with the Christian right to various aspects of foreign affairs, which constitute the sixth dimension of liberalism.

A "liberal" approach is more difficult to define for foreign policy than for domestic policy. Liberals in the last two decades have generally adopted a nonmilitaristic posture in a number of areas. Since the Vietnam War liberal politicians have resisted the use of military force as an instrument of foreign policy, as well as the buildup of American military strength. Conservatives tend to view the Soviet Union in a more negative light than most liberals do and are less averse to challenging it. Particularistic Jewish concerns would seem to militate against support for a liberal foreign policy. Irving Kristol expresses his disappointment that most Jews fail to make what he considers the logical leap from pro-Israelism and concern for Soviet Jewry to a more interventionist foreign policy:

If American Jews truly wish to be noninterventionist, they have to cease being so concerned with Israel, with Jews in the Soviet Union, or indeed with Jews anywhere else. To demand that an American government be interventionist exclusively on behalf of Jewish interests and none other—well, to state that demand is to reveal its absurdity. Yet most of our major Jewish organizations have ended up maneuvering themselves into exactly this position. They cannot even bring themselves openly to support the indispensable precondition for the exercise of American influence on behalf of Jewish interests in the world: a large and powerful military establishment that can, if necessary, fight and win dirty, little (or not so little) wars in faraway places. (1984, 27–28)

Kristol's description is accurate, even if one demurs from his prescription. It seems that Jews were disproportionately represented among the opponents of the Vietnam War; they even rebuffed unsubtle attempts by Israeli prime ministers to mute their opposition. In the survey of 1988 they supported cuts in defense spending more than other white Americans did, rich or poor (support among blacks for cuts was comparable). At the same time, Jews were not discernibly more hawkish or dovish than non-Jews toward the Soviet Union. In short, on issues of foreign policy and defense Jews range from centrist to mildly liberal.

Explaining Jewish Liberalism

That American Jews are liberals is beyond question. They typically offer three reasons to account for this: an adherence to values inherent in Judaism, a universalization of these values, and a recognition of Jewish interests. Scholars have suggested a fourth reason: the impact of history. At the heart of the historicist argument is the observation that contemporary Jewish liberalism originated in the Jews' encounter in the nineteenth century with European emancipation, and that the memories retained and the lessons learned from this continue to have a powerful influence over Jewish political thinking and behavior: "Emancipated Jews discovered that they could only remain free in a state where emancipation was general; they could only make their way in a society where careers were open to talents, discrimination was barred, private life and personal choice were protected. Which means that Jews could only remain free and make their way in a liberal state and a liberal society. . . . Jews were liberal, then, from self interest. But to say that is not to denigrate the emancipated Jew's commitment. Self-interest is a powerful root from which all sorts of idealism can grow" (Walzer 1986, 14).

In the struggle for their own emancipation and for an emancipated society in general, "Jews found that, with few exceptions, those who would deny them political rights represented the old order—the aristocracy, the military, the nationalists, the political Right, and above all the Church" (Dawidowicz 1985, 25). Because their political friends were often on the left and their adversaries often on the right, with some notable exceptions Jews joined the liberals and the liberal parties in pursuing the politics of emancipation in Western and Central Europe. According to the historicist argument, liberals advocated the rights of man, the liberty of the individual, freedom of conscience and of worship. Liberals upheld a political order that offered the Jews rights as citizens, security as a religious and communal group, and economic opportunity as individuals (Dawidowicz 1985, 25).

Of course not all politically active Jews today are aware of the history in the modern West of the Jewish alliance with the left; but the historicists assume that many Jews have learned some of the lessons of that history, if only vaguely, and internalized the idea that their friends are on the left, their enemies on the right. Events in the United States reinforced this: "Roosevelt fought the Nazis, Truman recognized Israel; the Democrats managed the cities, where Jews lived; the Republicans were isolationists. Over time, the association became self-sustaining; Jews came to positions of influence and power in the Democratic party, and enjoyed the fruits of their investment in that party" (Leonard Fein, *Commentary* 1980, 35). When Jews seek to explain their own liberal orientation they frequently submit that liberalism is inherent in the core values of the Jewish tradition. Michael Walzer's characterizations are typical: "Our ethos is leftist: because we remember that we were slaves in Egypt, because we remember the ghetto, the years of persecution, the pariah years. . . . We have learned, many of us, to part with our money in the name of justice. . . . It is a simple fact of our experience that . . . radical ideas come naturally" (*Commentary* 1980, 77).

The Reform movement has been the most outspoken in linking aspects of the liberal agenda to its interpretation of Judaism. Classical, nineteenth-century Reform in fact tried to expunge what it deemed the primitive elements of Judaism, elements that inhibited the integration of the Jews into the larger society and the adaptation of Judaism to the enlightened world. Among these were nationalistic, ritualistic, and legalistic elements of the Jewish tradition. As a result *Tikun Olam* (the

Jews' obligation to "repair the world"), or a commitment to "prophetic justice" (along with "ethical monotheism"), achieved more importance in Reform thinking than in any other modern Jewish movement. This generalization still applies. According to a leading Reform rabbi, "Our conviction [is] that somehow it is necessary for the public sector of society to intervene compassionately and protectively on behalf of the disadvantaged, the sick, the poor, those in whom the spark of divinity burns too dimly and who need the breath of compassion to fan that spark into full light. Freedom and social concern are values as Jewish as the Jewish belief in God. When any aspect of freedom is threatened, Jews have an obligation to protest as Jews. *Nothing could be more Jewishly elemental than this*" (Balfour Brickner, *Commentary* 1980, 25; italics added).

Albert Vorspan is the head of the Reform movement's Social Action Commission. His pamphlet "Reform Judaism and Social Action" illustrates the extent to which Reform leaders see liberal politics as intrinsically Jewish: "A commitment to social justice is inherent in Judaism. . . . Justice is by no means the end-all or be-all of Jewish teachings; but a Judaism *without* keen involvement in the struggle for human decency is a contradiction, a denial of the deepest elements of the Jewish spirit. . . . Social action is not politics or sociology or economics, though it involves all of them. It is of the essence of religion, certainly of the Jewish religion" (1983, 1–14).

It is not only Reform leaders who identify traditional Jewish values with liberalism or social action, even though they may be the most outspoken in doing so. Ted Mann, a member of a Conservative synagogue who has led several national Jewish organizations, has said that "the impulse to eliminate poverty and discrimination is an important part of the Jewish heritage." In 1985, 80 percent of a national sample of American Jews agreed with this statement: "Jewish values, as I understand them, teach us that we must make economic sacrifices for the poor"; only 11 percent disagreed. Earl Shorris's secular leftist polemic against Jewish neoconservatives is appropriately entitled *Jews without Mercy* (1982). Shorris says that mercy and compassion for the downtrodden have been essential values of the Jewish tradition, and that the neoconservatives of *Commentary* are in essence bad Jews for failing to exhibit these qualities. "According to this theory, Jews are liberals because their tradition predisposes them to value social justice and democracy:

the Jewish community of the Middle Ages was inherently democratic, and traditional philanthropy was a symbol of the Jewish commitment to the underprivileged" (Biale 1986, 196).

Not everyone agrees that the values of the Jewish tradition are inherently liberal.[4] Even some Jewish liberals demur. But apparently this is what many Jews believe, as is borne out by the survey of the *Los Angeles Times* and our own survey of 1988, in which 44 percent of all respondents agreed with the statement "Jewish values as I understand them teach me to be politically liberal" (31 percent disagreed). This last statement is especially demanding: it presupposes both that Jewish values teach liberalism, and that the respondent has learned their lessons. Presumably, some moderates and conservatives would feel obligated to disagree with this statement not because they reject the characterization of Jewish values as liberal, but because they have not adopted liberalism as a political orientation. And by a margin of 58 percent to 13 percent, Jews reject the idea that Jewish interests might lead a person to be politically conservative.

Some liberals have advanced a more sophisticated version of the argument about Jewish values. They contend that in traditional Judaism the values of compassion and justice focused primarily on one's fellow Jews, whereas in modern times Jews have universalized the tradition by extending these values to all mankind. Walzer, writing of Jewish communities before the emancipation, notes the wide "range of communal provision . . . [that] included systems of distribution of food and clothing, care for orphans and widows, dowries, hostels for travelers, ransom for captives, . . . public physicians and midwives, and perhaps above all, schools" (1986, 15).

Walzer suggests that the emancipation made the Jews transpose to the larger society of which they were now full members their conception of a caring community, what he calls a "participatory welfare state": "To some extent, the exilic view of justice [the view prevailing before the emancipation] has itself survived, outlasted emancipation and even transferred to the secular communities in which we now live. . . . The Jewish readiness to support the welfare state, to pay for it and to participate in it, expresses the same values transferred from our own to the larger community" (1986, 15).

For their part, conservatives largely agree with Walzer's analysis of how Jewish energies were universalized, even if they take a dim view of the outcome. They may view as excessive the concern for non-Jews who have suffered misfortune, or believe that support for the welfare state is a misguided denial of Jewish self-interest, but they recognize the profound connection between contemporary Jewish liberalism and traditional modes of communal organization and social thought.

The argument that liberalism is an extension of inherent Jewish values ignores the issue of material Jewish interests. But contemporary Jewish liberals do present additional arguments to demonstrate that these interests are compatible with the liberal program. The one most frequently advanced is that liberalism promotes the interests of Jews because they are members of a minority group. Reform Jewry's most important leader writes: "Liberalism . . . spurs us to create through the political process a society which is compassionate and open and respects . . . variety. This is precisely the kind of society which has always been safest for the Jew" (Alexander Schindler, *Commentary* 1980, 64). Leonard Fein sees Jewish safety flowing from domestic tranquility: "Jewish liberals still believe that Jews are safest where the social peace is stablest, and that the social peace is best assured by the politics of amelioration which has been the program of the moderate Left in the West for decades. . . . Jews do not expect to benefit directly from the welfare programs they endorse. . . . But they do expect that a politics of equity is both the right thing to do and the best defense against chaos, and it is chaos that Jews fear" (*Commentary* 1980, 35).

Most of America's Jews would agree with Fein. Fifty-five percent of our respondents in 1985 agreed that "one good reason for Jews to support government spending on social welfare programs is that, in the long run, they help avoid social unrest and upheaval"; only 32 percent disagreed. An even larger majority (86 percent) agreed that "bad economic times and major social unrest in the U.S. could easily lead to increased anti-semitism."

Jews are conscious that they are a minority that has suffered persecution (see chapter 3). This reinforces their sympathies with other minorities and their sense that it is in their interest to support liberalism, which Jews assume offers greater protection to minority groups than conservatism does. As an insecure minority, Jews have an interest in the strict enforcement of civil rights laws. As a cultural minority, they have an interest in the protection of civil liberties: the rights of assembly and expression of all, no matter how unpopular their views. And as a religious minority, they have an obvious interest in maintaining a high wall of separation between church and state, for they fear that its absence would permit the promotion of one religion over another, with obviously adverse consequences for non-Christian groups.

In general, Jews have a stake in maintaining a pluralist society and a government that refrains from advancing one moral vision or another. One political scientist offers a telling description of contemporary American liberalism, with obvious appeal to Jews as a minority group: "Communal conservatives . . . believe government should affirm moral and religious values. They want to ban abortion, restrict pornography, and restore prayer to public schools. . . . Like laissez-faire conservatives, liberals believe that government should be neutral on moral and religious questions. Rather than affirm in law a particular vision of the good life, liberals would leave individuals free to choose their values for themselves. They believe government should protect people's rights, not promote civic virtue. It should offer a framework of rights, neutral among ends, within which its citizens may pursue whatever values they happen to have" (Sandel 1988, 21–22). American Jews may believe that liberalism derives from Jewish values, from the universalization of Jewish values, from Jewish self-interest, or from some combination of the three. But it is clear to them in any event that behaving as a liberal means acting in fidelity to the Jewish tradition and with responsibility toward Jewish self-interest.

The Nonliberal Israeli

Most Israelis are probably not as liberal as most American Jews. But it is more significant that liberalism is not viewed by Israelis as a central component of their Judaism. Indeed the term *liberalism* itself has no Hebrew counterpart, and many of the elements that define a liberal orientation are missing from the Israeli political agenda. Some issues relevant to American Jewish liberalism are present in Israeli politics, especially those concerning civil liberties and the treatment of minorities. Along with basic conceptions about the equality of man, concern for such issues characterized the ideology and ideals of democratic socialism, an ideology shared by the political elite and a large part of the population before statehood and into the first few years of statehood. These values were conceived as central to the Jewish tradition. They found expression not only in the rhetoric and programs of secular Zionist socialism but in the ideology of Torah V'Avodah, the religious labor Zionist movement.[5] Even among these influential movements, however, one important strain in American Jewish liberalism was absent. Zionists of almost all persuasions tended to be collectivist rather than individualist. In keeping with the Jewish tradition, socialist ideology, the East European and North African backgrounds of the Jewish settlers, and the necessities arising from the struggle for independence, Israelis were far more sensitive to the rights of groups than the rights of individuals (see chapter 4).

It is difficult and probably pointless to compare Israeli and American Jewish attitudes in the six areas that define American liberalism (see above), for some are irrelevant to conditions in Israel and others have different implications in Israel. Israel is a welfare state, and public support for social welfare programs cuts across political boundaries. The level of support that virtually all Israeli parties offer for government intervention in the economy and welfare support for the poor places them to the left on the American political spectrum. But it is worth observing that whereas in the United States the benefits of government programs accrue mostly to non-Jews, in Israel they accrue to fellow Jews. Indeed some social security and welfare benefits are restricted to members of two groups: relatives of army veterans, and relatives of yeshiva students (who do not serve in the army). These two groups account for almost all the Jews in Israel, and they account for virtually none of its non-Jews.

The indifference of Israelis to the welfare of non-Jews is evident in the findings of a study on the condition of Israeli Arabs.[6] Forty percent of Arab families in Israel fall below the poverty line, and 26 percent live in extremely overcrowded conditions (compared with 11 percent of Jewish families). Forty-six percent of Arabs between the ages of thirteen and seventeen do not receive any education (compared with 6 percent of Jews). The mortality rate for Arab infants is double that for Jews, and only two of the 604 medical teams of the national health service operate in Arab settlements (*Hadashot,* 6 May 1988, p. 4).

Sympathy for minorities and support for civil rights are appreciably less noticeable among Israelis than among American Jews. Feminists and homosexuals in Israel compare their own lack of achievement with the more impressive record of their counterparts in American society, and protest their inferior status in Israeli society as well as the absence of legislation to ensure their rights. In view of the widespread Jewish support in American society for feminists and homosexuals, it is reasonable to assume that Israeli Jews are less liberal in this regard. After spending a year in Israel as a Fulbright scholar, the American psychologist Rhoda Kesler Unger noted that "equality of the sexes is not even on the Israeli agenda" (*Jerusalem Post,* Weekend Magazine, 14 April 1989, p. 17). The absence of a strong feminist movement in Israel is all the more striking in light of how much sexual discrimination has been documented (*Israel Social Science Research* 1987). In addition, the effort by at least some American Jewish feminists and homosexuals to associate their behavior and ideology with Judaism is absent in Israel.[7] On the contrary, homosexuals and perhaps most feminists assume that their demands place them in opposition to the Jewish tradition; their opponents certainly feel this way.

It is a deeply entrenched principle of liberalism in its American Jewish variety that people have the right to live their lives as they choose, with a minimum of interference or even guidance by government and society. But in most respects this principle is foreign to Israeli political culture. Israel's laws regarding marriage and divorce, censorship and pornography, and the use of drugs are far less permissive than American laws, and Israelis are inclined to make them less permissive still. In our survey of Israelis in 1986, 31 percent favored more government involvement and stricter law enforcement in such matters and 29 percent wanted less. Among American Jews only 11 percent favored more government involvement and stricter law enforcement, and 60 percent wanted less.

The differences between Israeli and American Jews are most apparent on issues of civil liberties (see chapter 4). Israelis are less sensitive to the private rights of the individual, including the rights of free speech and the press. This is also evident in levels of political tolerance. A comparison of Israelis and Americans based on the percentage who agreed with tolerant statements and disagreed with intolerant statements found Israelis significantly less tolerant than Americans (Shamir and Sullivan 1983). In another study, which compared support for unpopular minorities in Israel, New Zealand, and the United States, the authors concluded that Israelis were the least tolerant and that religiosity was the major variable distinguishing the tolerant from the intolerant (Sullivan et al. 1985). Because Jews are consistently rated the most tolerant of all American groups, the differences between them and Israeli Jews in regard to tolerance may be readily inferred.

Although it is difficult to compare the liberalism of Israeli Jews and American Jews because many of the measures of liberalism in American society seem inappropriate to Israel, it is certain that Israeli Jews are not liberals by the standards of liberal American Jews. This should come as no surprise. The causes of American Jewish liberalism are not altogether clear, but surely the minority status of Jews in American society, their sense of relative powerlessness, and their continuing fear of anti-Semitism help to explain their advocacy of individual and minority rights, their sympathy for the oppressed, and their support for the most extreme separation of religion and state. As the dominant group in a state of their own, Israeli Jews do not share these fears.

Further, because Israelis have a rather weak conception of state in the Western sense but a very strong conception of society as a community or extended family (see chapter 4), it seems appropriate for them to pass laws that restrict people's activities and provide for their moral guidance. The Israelis' collectivist heritage and the special threats to their existence as a group also weaken their commitment to liberal objectives. Because Israeli Jews are threatened from without, what strengthens the society as a whole serves the needs of the individual Jew. And toleration is not perceived in the same way in the two societies. Toleration in the United States means suffering others whose life style or values are different from one's own and whose threats are remote. Toleration in Israel is often perceived as suffering an enemy who threatens one's survival and whose threats are immediate.

Liberalism and the Meaning of Judaism in Israel

It is not surprising to find that Israelis see very little relationship between Judaism and liberalism. The Jewish tradition, the Zionist tradition, the memory of the Holocaust, and the perception of international isolation all reinforce a strong sense of group identity. In their perception of themselves Jews suffer neither from discriminatory laws nor from an oppressive state; they suffer from goyim. It matters not whether the goyim are the majority or the minority, whether they also are oppressed or oppress others. What matters in the Israeli Jewish perception is that liberalism—support for individual rights or for minorities in general—offers the Jews no protection.

That this idea is powerful is clear from the growing frequency and vigor with which some Israeli secularists have charged in recent years that liberalism and Judaism are incompatible. In the past those who espoused universalist and broadly humanitarian values, and even those who emphasized values of individual rights, tended to agree with American Jews that these values were not only consistent with the Jewish tradition but anchored in it. Zionist socialists sought to reinterpret the tradition in this vein, but by the 1950s it was clear that their ideology had relatively little appeal to the Israeli public.

Why do so few Israelis interpret Judaism as an expression of the "prophetic tradition" of moralistic, humane, liberal, and democratic values? Some Israelis do view Judaism in this light, even some who are faithful to traditional customs and ceremonies.[8] But by and large those who describe Judaism in these terms tend to deemphasize its halakhic components. And as we cannot stress too strongly, Israelis recognize that Judaism is also a religion, and that whatever else the Jewish religion may mean it is a system of law.

Another reason why the liberal, prophetic formulation attracts a minority of Israelis is that Jewish humanists have failed to articulate their version of Judaism in intellectually coherent terms. Secularists who still retain their links to the tradition tend to be rather defensive about their world view (see chapter 6). They often apologize for not being religious.[9] Perhaps as a reaction to the failure of Jewish secularism, one finds among a growing number of secularists a point of view that is not merely antireligious: it is a point of view according to which Judaism itself is the barrier to the development of a liberal, democratic state. In the Israeli context, many leftist secularists see Judaism as so inimical to liberal values that they have severed their own ties with it. Whereas their predecessors held that one could be a humanistic socialist and be Jewishly committed at the same time, intellectuals in this new circle are in effect walking away from the battle over the political meaning of Judaism. They view Judaism as so thoroughly conservative, nationalistic, and particularistic that it cannot be reformed. In their view the only hope for the Israeli liberal is the disestablishment of Judaism.

The Israeli political scientist Ze'ev Sternhall articulates this position in the pages of *Politika,* the journal of Ratz, the Citizens Rights Movement, perceived as the most antireligious of all Israeli parties (Sternhall 1987). Sternhall bewails the absence in Israel of Western democracy, which he defines as a system of government that places the individual rather than collective goals at the center of its concern. He says that the key problem is not "education for democracy," a subject of concern in the Israeli school curriculum since the election to the Knesset of Meir Kahane in 1984. It is rather "understanding the essence of democracy. And democracy is first and foremost the expression of the rights of humans to be masters of themselves. Democracy is the expression of man's recognition that all sources of political, social and moral authority inhere in man himself" (1987, 3). To Sternall, Israeli political culture rejects the basis of democratic thought—that "society and state exist in order to serve the individual . . . and are never ends in themselves" (1987, 3, 5). Sternhall traces Israel's collectivist culture to the Jewish tradition, among other elements. He maintains that even the nonreligious Zionists "never really freed themselves from the tradition of their father's home, and in one form or another they deferred to *Yisrael Saba*" (1987, 5).[10]

In the view of Sternhall and others like him, Israel needs urgently to overcome its inherently antidemocratic and antiliberal Jewish identity. This is a major theme in several articles that appeared in *Politika* in October 1987, in an issue devoted to the question "Who Is an Israeli?" The authors went beyond protesting the role of religion in Israel; they challenged the public role and influence of Judaism itself. Some attacked the law of return, which provides that Jews have the right to emigrate to Israel and benefit from automatic citizenship. Those who play a prominent role in the Ratz party share a universalist secularism that is highly antagonistic toward Judaism's public role. Secularists who still insist that Judaism is compatible with the values of democratic socialist Zionism, those we call "nationalist secularists," are especially prominent among the older leaders of Mapam, a left-wing Zionist party. Despite their continued antagonism to clericalism, nationalist secularists are increasingly constrained to defend Judaism against the charge that it is incompatible with liberalism.[11] There is a growing sense in Israel that not only liberalism in its individualist version is foreign to the Jewish tradition, but even liberalism as a set of egalitarian and humane imperatives.

This perception was hardly to be found a few decades ago, it is not found among all Israelis today, and it may not characterize most Israelis in the future. The Mapam leader Yair Tzaban referred to an "alliance of the heart" being forged "between secular Jews who are not alienated from the heritage of their people and religious Jews, faithful to the humanistic and democratic values of universal human culture" (Rash 1987, 130). But Tzaban's affirmation is more a hope for the future than a description of the present. The novelist Aharon Appelfeld, interviewed by the *Jerusalem Post,* was asked if Jews could do to others the kinds of inhuman things that were done to them. He replied: "I hope and believe not . . . You know there's a beautiful saying: 'More than the Jews have kept and protected the Sabbath, the Sabbath has kept and protected the Jews.' I take this to mean that as long as we're connected to our tradition, we're assured that we won't do such things as you're referring to. The tradition I believe is humanistic" (*Jerusalem Post,* Weekend Magazine, 27 November 1987, p. 4). But the interviewer then observes that Appelfeld knows his is fast becoming a minority position, under attack from both the religious right, which denies the humanistic values of the tradition, and the secular left, the members of which are "dangerously alienated from their fellow Jews in the Jewish state."

Our survey of the Israeli public demonstrates the close correspondence between secularity and left-wing political beliefs. We divided the population into four groups: the dati'im; those who report a high level of ritual observance but identify themselves as *masorati'im;* those who report a moderate level of religious observance; and those who report a low level of religious observance. Because the spectrum of liberalism incorporates a wide range of images, attitudes, and behavior, we used a number of indicators to measure it. First, we examined party affiliation. The religious parties in Israel arguably are highly conservative, which itself is evidence of the correspondence between religiosity and conservatism. But even when we eliminated from consideration respondents who said they supported religious parties (as well as the undecided), the association between religiosity and political conservatism remained quite marked. Those who identified with parties seen as left of center (Labour, Ratz, Mapam, and Shinui) accounted for only a fifth of the dati'im, for a third of the highly observant, for a majority of the moderately observant, and for three-quarters of the least observant. Had we reintroduced the religious parties into the analysis and regarded them as right-wing, the association would have been even more dramatic.

The relation of party to religiosity is not mere happenstance. It reflects the conservative political and social views of the more religious. We constructed an index of militarism on the Arab-Israeli conflict based on the level of agreement with a series of militaristic statements.[12] Agreement with these statements was highly correlated with religiosity. Fewer than a quarter of the dati'im opposed all the militaristic statements, as did just under a third of the highly observant, 40 percent of the moderately observant, and 60 percent of the least observant. In another domain, we asked respondents whether they favored laws restricting abortion and pornography, and protecting the rights of homosexuals.[13] Support for the conservative position on these questions rose with religiosity. Those taking a conservative stance on at least two of the items constituted only 12 percent of the least observant, a quarter of the moderately observant, more than 40 percent of the highly observant, and three-fifths of the dati'im. And as noted earlier, support for equal treatment of non-Jews (Arabs) in Israel also declines with religiosity.

Liberalism clearly declines as religious observance increases (except perhaps on economic matters). The more religiously traditional in both Israel and the United States are less politically and culturally liberal. Because it is these more traditional Jews who can claim greater authority than the more secular in defining the meaning of Judaism, they in effect advance the contention that Judaism is inherently antiliberal. Conversely, because the more liberal political sector is the more secular in belief and practice, and the more anticlerical politically, it advances the corollary that liberalism stands in opposition to the Jewish religion as it is practiced, if not to Judaism in principle.

The centrality of liberalism in the construction of American Judaism and its absence from Israeli Judaism should not surprise us. Many observers have noted that Americans historically have said they find their identity not in ethnic community or even in a shared historical experience, but in dedication to a value system.[14] "Dedication to the liberal creed" is considered at least by some to be fundamental to the cohesion of American society.[15] It is therefore not surprising that Jews should seek to root their Judaism in a set of values and that these are liberal values. Jewish liberalism "constructs positions that allow for full partic-ipation in American life without renunciation of a Jewish identity" (Biale 1986, 197).

American Jews are not only familistic but eager to affirm a particular ideology or value system that identifies Judaism and the Jewish people (see chapter 2). By defining Judaism as both centered on values and liberal in content, Jews maintain that their religion is highly compatible with Americanism. This is entirely consistent with our argument that American Jews have reformulated their Judaism in accordance with principles of universalism and moralism (see chapter 6). For by empha-sizing that Judaism is a system of shared values they deny the ethno-centricity of their heritage, by making Judaism accessible to those who share these values they universalize it, and by affirming the values as "liberal" they moralize them.

This formulation is not found in Israel, for a number of reasons. The Jewish tradition is not unambiguously liberal. In many important re-spects liberalism and traditional Judaism are incompatible. Without any specific pressure to reconstruct Judaism in the direction of liber-alism, Israelis retain greater fidelity to the tradition in this regard, as they do in most others. Second, it clearly is shared ethnicity and a shared set of religious symbols that cement Israeli society, not shared values. It is not politics that unite Israeli Jews but metapolitics. Politics, the conflict over the authoritative allocation of values, is what divides them. This is continually emphasized both by Israel's immediate ene-mies, who reject the Israelis because they are Jewish (regardless of how they interpret the content or meaning of their Judaism), and by Israel's friends, the United States in particular, who emphasize that Israel and the United States share a system of basic values, in which case it is ethnoreligion and not values that distinguishes the two societies.

Very few American Jews believe that liberalism is the sum and sub-stance of Judaism. Further, their own behavior demonstrates the con-tinued importance of ethnicity, of community, and of parochial respon-sibilities. American Jews are particularistic in their ethnic loyalties, but universalistic in the ideology or content they impute to Judaism (see chapter 2). Israeli Jews share the ethnic particularism but not the philo-sophical universalism of American Jews.

6 Religious Life

Judaism is a culture. Defining it in exclusively religious terms does an injustice to the breadth of its concerns and its capacity to evoke continued commitment from those who have no religious faith. Nevertheless religious faith, religious practice, and religious symbols lie at the heart of traditional Jewish culture. In this chapter we ask what particular reinterpretations Jews offer for the specifically religious tradition.

Religion among American Jews: Observance of Jewish Law

Jewish law, halakha, stands at the center of the religious tradition. Like Moslems, Jews always assumed that God was revealed to man through the law that was divinely ordained. Observance of the law was both the fulfillment of God's will and the path through which one might lead a virtuous life. Most American Jews no longer view the observance of halakha as central to Judaism. On the other hand, some forms of observance appear widespread. Most American Jews celebrate the three holiday seasons of Rosh Hashanah and Yom Kippur, Hanukah, and Passover. According to several recent studies, about two-thirds of American Jews say that they fast on Yom Kippur and even more say that they attend services at some point during the High Holidays (Cohen 1983c, 1988a; Tobin and Lipsman 1984; Wertheimer 1989). About four-fifths light Hanukah candles, and almost 90 percent say they attend a Passover seder. In different ways, these are all family events. Accordingly, parents of school-age children report higher rates of observance than average, whereas the unmarried and the childless report lower rates than average.

The population studies inform us about a variety of other practices that are less frequently observed. Well over a third of respondents report that Sabbath candles are lit in their homes on Friday evenings, and about a third say they attend synagogue services at times other than the High Holidays. About a third report buying meat only from kosher butchers, and about a quarter say they use separate sets of dishes at home for meat and dairy products. These practices also vary by family status: couples with children at home engage in them far more often than do the unmarried and the childless. Those who undertook the population studies did not enquire about the observance of such events in the life cycle as circumcision, bar mitzvah and bat mitzvah, marriage, divorce, and mourning. It is our impression that although these may not be observed with the attention to detail demanded by Jewish law, they are celebrated in one form or another. A study of Jews in Queens and Long Island, New York, demonstrated that the rate at which Jewish families became affiliated with a synagogue rose as their children approached the ages of twelve and thirteen and then fell (Cohen and Ritterband 1988). The peak rate of affiliation, 90 percent, was reached among families with children ten to twelve years old, suggesting that roughly 90 percent of all children celebrated their bar mitzvah or bat mitzvah in a synagogue. It seems fair to say that rabbis officiate at most weddings of Jews to Jews, that most baby boys are ritually circumcised, and that most American Jews ensure that their parents are buried in a Jewish cemetery and observe some period of mourning in a manner that at least recalls the halakhic mode of observance.

How are we to understand these data? What is it that Jews are doing when the members of an extended family gather to "celebrate" a seder or light Hanukah candles? And how do we explain that some forms of observance declined during the first two-thirds of this century while others did not? The answers to these questions may lie in part in the distinction between ceremony and ritual in American Jewish life.

Although the terms *ceremony* and *ritual* are used interchangeably in popular discourse, students of religion distinguish between them (Alexander 1987). According to some anthropologists, ritual is stylized, repetitive behavior that is explicitly religious; ceremony is social. In ceremony, aspects of the social and cosmological order find representation. Participation in the ceremony affirms the individual's membership in this order. More significantly, the ceremony reinforces the sense that the social order exists and that the individual is part of it.

All ritual may be a form of ceremony, but not all ceremony is ritual. Ritual not only involves "intentional bodily engagement" (Zeusse 1987, 406), which is necessarily more stylized than ceremonial behavior, but it is also believed to be efficacious. It is directed toward a particular goal and becomes among other things a mechanism for achieving the goal. Religious ritual connects the participant to some transcendent presence. It provides a bridge between man and God by engaging the participant in an act that God has commanded. It is perceived as efficacious, at the very least because it is pleasing to God or avoids God's displeasure. But to the religious adherent it is efficacious only when performed correctly.

All rituals in Judaism are *mitzvot* (commandments), though not all mitzvot are rituals in the sense that there is a detailed prescription of the manner in which they are to be performed. For example, although a Jew is commanded to give charity (*tzedakah*), and the giving of charity is certainly a mitzvah, charity is not given in a ritual manner. But halakha commands that before eating bread a Jew must recite a blessing, and before this blessing the hands must be washed and a blessing recited over the hand washing. Even the manner in which the hands are to be washed is prescribed: the kind of utensil used, the order in which the hands are washed, the number of times each hand is washed. The tendency among traditionalists has been to elaborate the mode of performing mitzvot, to render them less subjective and limit the options concerning the manner in which they are performed (Liebman 1983b). Within the Jewish tradition, questions are raised about whether people who perform a ritual in an improper manner have fulfilled their obligations. But indifference to the manner in which the ritual is performed is certainly inappropriate. It may render the blessing recited before the mitzvah a "superfluous blessing," which is itself sinful.

As Mary Douglas has observed, ritualism is the opposite of ethicism, which attributes primary importance to intention and devalues the precise manner in which an act is performed. "The move away from ritual is accompanied by a strong movement towards greater ethical sensitivity" (1973, 41). But Douglas's own study shows how ultimately self-defeating this movement may become. There can be little question that during the past two decades there has been an increase in ritual behavior among Orthodox Jews in the United States (Liebman 1988; Heilman and Cohen 1989), and at least until recently a decline in ritual behavior among the non-Orthodox,[1] who account for nearly 90 percent of American Jews.

On the other hand ceremonial behavior flourishes, especially among the non-Orthodox majority. This phenomenon is most noticeable within the Reform movement, which has embraced Jewish symbols and encourages its members to take part in ceremonial activity—often mistakenly called ritual. Reform temples are far richer in Jewish ceremony than they were in the past, in part because they attracted congregants of East European origin, a group with a less fervent commitment to classical Reform than their predecessors of German origin had. But ceremony should not be confused with ritual.

The Sabbath service in a Reform synagogue need not include reading from the Torah (the central point of the traditional Sabbath service), or may include the reading of only a few lines rather than the traditionally prescribed portion; but it will include a rather elaborate ceremony in which the Torah scrolls are taken out of the ark in which they are kept and returned to it. At a bar mitzvah ceremony in a Reform synagogue the rabbi may remove the Torah scroll from the ark and hand it to the parents of the boy whose bar mitzvah is being celebrated; the parents in turn hand the Torah to their son. The symbolic meaning is clear to all the congregants. In traditional Judaism, however, the Torah scrolls may be taken from the ark only to read from them. Jewish law is strict in proscribing other use of the scrolls, because of their special sanctity.

The ceremonial service need not be contrary to ritual for us to appreciate what is being celebrated and what is not. A good example is the recent flowering of *havdalah* services. To mark the close of the Sabbath, traditional law commands Jews to recite three blessings that distinguish the Sabbath from the rest of the week. The havdalah service, as performed by most Orthodox Jews, is recited immediately after the Saturday evening prayers conclude and takes no more than two or three minutes. Hardly a single Jewish meeting, conference, seminar, or other event in the United States that is held on the Sabbath fails to include the havdalah ceremony. Among the non-Orthodox this ceremony tends to be far more elaborate in such circumstances than among the

Orthodox. It may conclude with all those present forming a large circle, holding hands, singing together, and, quite often, kissing one another. Although few of the non-Orthodox perform havdalah in their own homes, they look forward to the ceremony when it is performed under Jewish organizational auspices. The ceremony may be performed in a ritually correct manner, but from a traditional point of view it is strange to conduct a havdalah service and yet omit the evening prayers that are supposed to precede it.

The popularity of the havdalah and the other ceremonies suggests a ceremonial renaissance among American Jews, one that would not have been foreseen by students of Jewish religious life in the United States a generation ago. These observers believed that the eventual assimilation of most American Jews was foretold by the steady decline in ritual and ceremonial behavior among them (the two forms of behavior were not distinguished). But we find that the situation is more complex. American Jews are not assimilating by abandoning Jewish ceremonials, nor are they substituting non-Jewish ritual for Jewish ritual. Instead they are transforming Jewish patterns of behavior (some might say they are also modernizing and Westernizing them), and in the process constructing new conceptions of Judaism. The emphasis on ceremony and the diminishing emphasis on ritual are an important part of the transformation. In addition, ceremony lends itself far more than ritual to reconstruction, and it is this reconstruction that is critical to understanding contemporary developments in the religious life of American Jews.

In his study of Jewish life in a wealthy suburb (first published in 1967), Marshall Sklare detected what is now perceived as a major trend in American Jewish life. As one of Sklare's respondents noted: "I feel Judaism is changing . . . Some people only think of religion in terms of ritual. I don't" (Sklare and Greenblum 1979, 77). How do Jews think of Judaism? We suggest that the tools through which American Jews are reconstructing that tradition are personalism and voluntarism on the one hand, and universalism and moralism on the other. The tools are all interrelated but are best discussed separately.

Examples of change in the Conservative movement are especially illuminating. The Reform movement is a conscious advocate of change that abounds in examples of personalism, voluntarism, universalism, and moralism (Furman 1987). Orthodoxy, numerically the smallest denomination in American Jewish life, consciously resists change, and examples of change among the Orthodox are more subtle and difficult to identify (although they do exist, especially among the modern Orthodox). But the Conservative movement is the centrist movement in American Jewish life, and its leaders insist that it is governed by Jewish law and faithful to the Jewish tradition; here the changes are visible and have the most significance for our argument.

Personalism and Voluntarism

Personalism is reflected in Sklare's observation that "the modern Jew selects from the vast storehouse of the past what is not only objectively possible for him to practice but subjectively possible for him to 'identify' with" (1979, 48). Sklare was referring to the performance of mitzvot, but personalism is imposed on all aspects of the religious tradition. Personalism is the tendency to transform and evaluate the tradition in terms of its utility or significance to the individual. "The best assurance of Jewish survival is the development of a community that offers its members opportunities for personal fulfillment not easily found elsewhere" (Cohen and Fein 1985, 88).

Voluntarism is the consequence of the absence or devaluation of mitzvah, of commandment. Rabbis, educators, and parents urge, encourage, and cajole others to perform certain acts of a ceremonial nature in part by reassuring them constantly that whatever they do is legitimate if it is what they choose to do. Personal choice is endowed with spiritual sanctity, and contrary to past tradition it is always considered more virtuous than performing an act out of a sense of obedience to God. Subtle distinctions exist between personalism and voluntarism, but the two are interrelated. The examples we offer here illustrate both these principles.

As it is transformed by personalism and voluntarism, prayer ceases to become a medium of communication between man and God. One writer asks, "How, practically, can Jewish prayer function to help one confront anger and utilize it for personal transformation and social change?" (Dekro 1984, 73). Here is a reconstruction of tradition intended to make it compatible with the needs of the individual Jew, which is not surprising given the emphasis on voluntarism. Personalism and voluntarism are incompatible with ritual—that is, specified, stylized behavior engaged in to obey God's command—but they are not incompatible with ceremonial. *Siddur Sim Shalom* (Harlow 1985), the new prayer book of the Conservative movement, offers alternative services or prayers for different occasions. Rabbinic spokesmen for the Conservative movement have maintained that each of their alternatives in the Conservative prayer book, unlike those in the Reform prayer book, has a basis in Jewish law. But the Union for Traditional Conservative Judaism, which represents the more traditional wing within the Conservative movement, has published a responsum (legal opinion of Jewish law) that concludes: "Although *Siddur Sim Shalom* may be used as a resource work, it should not be used for the purpose of fulfilling one's prayer obligations" (Union for Traditional Conservative Judaism 1986, 12). Among other reasons, this is because some of the alternative services are not those that the tradition prescribes. In any case, to offer the worshiper a choice reflects the spirit of voluntarism.

Temple Beth Ami, a Conservative synagogue in Reseda, California, is proud of its efforts to encourage "ritual observance" and has prepared a booklet on the topic that it has distributed to other Conservative congregations. The program was conceived and developed by a member of the faculty at the University of Judaism, the Conservative movement's rabbinical seminary and institution of higher education on the West coast. The synagogue program is built around a voluntary group patterned on the diet program sponsored by Weight Watchers. Each member of the group undertakes to perform certain "rituals" and report back to the monthly meeting of the group on his or her progress. Members fill out a twelve-month "goal sheet" in which "they should determine which rituals they would like to involve themselves in during the coming year. The members should understand that the goal of this program is not to make them become any more Jewish than what they will be confortable with" (Temple Beth Ami, n.d.). It is hard to imagine a traditional rabbi telling his followers that they should become no more Jewish than they will be comfortable with. It is also interesting that a number of the "rituals" in the booklet have no great significance in Jewish law, others are custom rather than mitzvot, and still others are probably contrary to Jewish law. Their functions (here we return to the theme of personalism) are to contribute to a sense of family harmony and personal fulfillment. For example, among the eighteen Sabbath rituals we find the following: playing shabbat music to set the mood, blessing one's children, blessing one's wife, blessing one's husband, having a special Shabbosdick meal, using a white tablecloth and good dishes, and singing Shabbat songs around the table.

Elements of personalism and moralism are found among Orthodox Jews as well, although they are less common, as a recent study of modern Orthodox Jews makes clear (Heilman and Cohen 1989). The study was based on a nonrandom sample of highly educated, Orthodox young adults in and around New York. (It is important to note that the sample reported higher levels of ritual observance than were found among the American Orthodox generally or among all Orthodox Jews living in the New York area.) The sample was divided into three groups according to levels of observance: the centrists (the largest group), the traditionalists (more observant), and the nominals (nominally Orthodox). The centrists were defined as those who identified themselves as Orthodox, maintained separate sets of dishes for meat and dairy products, never worked on the Sabbath, never turned on lights on the Sabbath, and fasted on Tisha B'Av.

Among the centrists—even among the centrist modern Orthodox— personalist and voluntarist criteria clearly influenced the choice of which rituals to observe. Centrists are aware of halakhic norms but often decide for themselves which rituals to observe. These are the rituals most widely ignored by centrists (and observed by virtually all traditionalists): to attend synagogue on late Saturday afternoons, to refrain from eating cold salads in nonkosher restaurants, for men to cover their heads "on the street," and for married women to immerse themselves monthly in a mikvah (lustral bath) and cover their heads in public. To attend synagogue for services on late Saturday afternoons often means having less time for socializing with one's family and friends. That centrists do not always attend synagogue at this time suggests an assertion of individual choice and a rejection of authority that one is unlikely to find among Orthodox Jews in Israel. The wife's monthly immersion in a mikvah about twelve days after the beginning of her menstrual cycle is a precondition for sexual intercourse, according to Jewish law. This ritual has a high priority in halakha; we suspect that it is ignored by many centrists not only because of the self-restraint it demands from the married couple but because it imposes an outside authority on relationships that the modern world views as particularly personal and a matter of choice. The covering of one's head and the observance of dietary laws visibly distinguish Orthodox Jews from the rest of society on the one hand, while categorizing them on the other: these observances depersonalize them in the eyes of others. Moreover, if one cannot even eat cold salads in a nonkosher restaurant, one's social and professional associations are severely limited.

In keeping with our understanding of personalism and voluntarism, we would expect that among non-Orthodox American Jews the definition of who is a Jew and the boundaries between Jew and non-Jew would become increasingly flexible. In accord with these principles, Jews would be defined socially by the public as those who simply choose to call themselves Jews.[2] A notable step in this direction was the recent decision by the Reform movement to define as Jewish a person whose mother was Gentile but whose father was Jewish (provided that the person affirm a Jewish identity by means of one or more public actions). This decision, of which 59 percent of American Jews approved (Cohen 1988c), simply formalized practices that existed for years in many Reform synagogues, if not most. It can be attributed to the rising number of mixed marriages (the marriage of a Jew and a non-Jew when neither partner converts to the other's religion) and, no less important, to the desire of many mixed couples to affiliate with a synagogue and bring up their children within a Jewish framework, particularly under Reform auspices. In other words, Jews married to non-Jews (who may remain believing Christians) now proposed to normalize the Jewish status of their children; some Jewish spouses even sought to have legitimacy accorded by the Jewish religion to their Christian partners. More than half the nonconverts in a study of conversion "felt that one could be part of the Jewish people and community without undergoing a formal conversion process" (Mayer and Avgar 1987, 9).

This point is brought home in articles by converts to Judaism who remain married to non-Jews, a condition facilitated by an increasingly tolerant Jewish community. Thus, a potential convert to Judaism writes: "Chanuka and Christmas will probably both be observed, simply because the family ties my husband associates with the mid-winter holiday are too significant to abandon" (Richards 1987, 41). Another says: "I am very fortunate because my husband supports my decision to convert to Judaism . . . His main concern was that I might expect him to convert also, or that the rabbi might expect it. [Apparently the rabbi did not.] Tom is a very spiritual person and I had no expectations that he would have to take the same journey. I knew that we could still share much of Judaism as a couple and as a family" (Anderson 1987, 42–43). Later, a description of her synagogue: "At Beth Shalom there are many non-Jewish spouses and so there is a great deal of concern that these non-Jewish family members feel accepted and a part of the community. Our religious school also is very supportive of the children who have a non-Jewish parent or relative and every effort is made to make those children feel that they belong" (1987, 43). And most telling: "I refuse to let my religious choice cause strife in my family. I made a personal religious choice and if I expect people to honor my choice then I must honor theirs" (1987, 44). Or, according to another writer: "As for synagogue and community involvement, I do not see a need for the gentile spouse to feel excluded. While there are definite honors from which one would be excluded, there are plenty of meaningful opportunities to involve the non-Jew in synagogue life and congregations should do that. Though these people may not be Jewish, that does not mean they do not want our synagogue and organizational activities to be successful. Because their families are involved, they do want to see us reach our goals" (Haber 1987, 51).

A recent book entitled *Raising Your Jewish Christian Child: Wise Choices for Interfaith Parents* (Gruzen 1987) is advertised as telling "how to give your children the best of both heritages" and urges readers to "act now to enrich your children's spiritual lives. This year's holidays can be the richest, most harmonious ones your family has ever celebrated" (*Commentary* 84 [September 1987]: 78).

Even when published by a large, commercial house, a book on this topic is only a straw in the wind. It is somewhat more significant that the advertisement appears in *Commentary,* published by the American Jewish Committee, a major Jewish organization. Our point is not merely that many American Jews are failing to act in accord with ancient Jewish law. It is rather that they are choosing to modify and remake the very norms that underlie the practices. In so doing they express the principles of voluntarism (choice) and personalism (giving the choices personal meaning). American Jews find this spirit of innovation commonplace and totally legitimate. Our impression is that even secular Israelis view all this as Jewishly inauthentic and as another indication of American Jewish assimilation. In Israel there is less license, less le-

gitimacy, and less institutional support accorded to attempts to modify or choose among traditional norms in line with personal needs and
interests.

Universalism and Moralism

Universalism is the idea that the Jewish tradition has a
message for all people, not only for Jews, and that Judaism is open to
the messages of other traditions and cultures. Further, Judaism is con-
strued as being open to non-Jews, who may develop a variety of partial
affiliations with the Jewish people. *Moralism* is also a term borrowed
from Sklare, who defines it as the idea that "religious man is distinguished not by his observance of rituals but rather by the scrupulous-
ness of his ethical behavior" (Sklare and Greenblum 1979, 89). Recently, American Jewish life has continued to invoke the term *ritual,*
but often the ritual is converted to the ceremonial, and its meaning reinterpreted in moralistic terms. Jewish symbols are retained in their
particularistic form, but the referent or meaning is explained as a moral
or ethical imperative. Because ethics are generally viewed as universal,
examples of universalism and moralism tend to overlap. The Conservative movement's new prayer book, *Siddur Sim Shalom* (Harlow 1985),
includes among its selected readings a statement entitled "Why I Am a
Jew" by Edmund Fleg (1874–1963), the modernized French Jew who
affirmed his Jewishness only in mid-life. One of his reasons for being a
Jew is that "the promise of Judaism is a universal promise." At a recent
Conservative convention this statement by Fleg was read aloud, and a
selection entitled "The Essence of Judaism" (author unknown) was
read immediately before the *Sh'ma,* a central point in the religious service. "The Essence of Judaism" begins by affirming that Jews are united
by a bond four thousand years old that has "sensitized the Jewish individual to the needs of the group" and continues: "From one group to
one humanity has been our goal. From our early teachings came the
ideas of a society where individuals will treat each other with dignity
and respect. These ideas are the essence of Judaism" (Harlow 1985). In
other words, the essence of Judaism is contained in three ideas: group
needs (that is, Jewish needs), the dissolution of the group into one humanity, and the treatment of all individuals with dignity and respect.
Universalism is also illustrated in a newspaper article by a Conser-

vative rabbi on the topic of galut, or golus (see chapters 3 and 4). According to the rabbi, "While *golus* is a Jewish word it is not only a Jewish issue. It is a human issue as well. *Golus* in 1986 is children going to
sleep hungry night after night. It is approximately 30 armed conflicts
raging around the globe. It is the continuing deterioration of our habi-
tat and ecosystem . . . And most alarmingly, it is thousands of nuclear
warheads ready at this moment to annihilate us all" (cited in Liebman
1988).

Another illustration of universalism is the reformulation of Jewish
holidays and celebrations to diminish their Jewishly particularistic meaning and infuse them with meaning for all humanity. Some holidays lend
themselves to this kind of transformation. Passover, for example, the
holiday commemorating the Jewish exodus from Egypt, easily trans-
forms itself into a holiday with the universal message of freedom. In the
1960s Jewish civil rights activists developed the "freedom seder," where
non-Jews, blacks in particular, were invited to join in a seder ceremony.
The ritual was reorganized to focus on aspects of freedom present in
the traditional ceremony, and new symbols were introduced. The holiday that seems least amenable to this kind of universalizing is Tisha
B'Av, the midsummer fast day that commemorates the destruction of
the Temple—that is, the exile of the Jews and the calamities that later
befell them and are peculiar to them. Most American Jews do not observe Tisha B'Av. But in an effort to revive Jewish ceremonial, some
Conservative and Reform synagogues have sought to infuse this holiday
as well with contemporary meaning. In one northeastern city all the
Conservative and Reform synagogues cooperate in sponsoring a Tisha
B'Av service in a Conservative synagogue. According to the chairman
of the evening, a leader of the Conservative synagogue, "Originally the
observance of Tisha B'Av recalled only the destruction of the Holy
Temple," but now it also commemorates other calamities. The chairman concluded the service as follows: "This year, in honor of the 100th
anniversary of Miss Liberty, special recognition will be included of our
great debt to the United States of America for the opportunity that this
country has given our people" (cited in Liebman 1988).

In a sophisticated and carefully balanced discussion of biblical particularism and universalism, Jon D. Levinson makes the following statement, which is very relevant to our concerns:

For Jews in the post-Enlightenment West, where ideas of human equality and democratic government hold sway, there is a temptation to stress the instrumental dimension of Jewish chosenness and to deny or ignore the self-sufficient dimension. We are sometimes told that the "chosen people" means the "choosing people," as if passive and active participles were not opposite in meaning. Judaism is presented as a commitment to some rather amorphous "Jewish values," which, on inspection, turn out to be *universal* values, in which Jews and gentiles alike ought to believe. Covenant, if it is mentioned at all, appears only as the basis for a warm, meaningful community life. The fact that the Covenant distinguishes sharply between insiders and outsiders—although both are God's—is ignored.

In large measure, such attitudes are dictated by the exigencies of living as a minority in a mixed society with a high degree of openness. It is simply not prudent to affirm a distinctiveness of ultimate significance based on heredity, and what is not prudent to express publicly often loses credibility, becoming peripheral or taboo even in private discourse. In addition, the contemporary theology in question represents a cognitive surrender to a Kantian theory of ethics in which morality entails universalizability: if the behavior cannot be advocated for everyone, it cannot be moral. On Kantian principles, Jewish ethics—a norm for one group only—is a contradiction in terms. Hence the common substitution of ethics for Torah. "Ethics," writes Michael Wyschogrod, "is the Judaism of the assimilated." (1985, 12)

One illustration of the moralistic trend in Judaism is offered by Arthur Waskow, formerly executive director of the Shalom Center, which is situated at the Reconstructionist Rabbinical College but has a board of directors and advisory council that include three Orthodox rabbis. Here for example is an excerpt from a recent fund-raising letter:

Across the US, Jews will celebrate the harvest festival of Sukkot from October 17 to 25 as *Sukkat Shalom*—the Shelter of Peace. The fragile Sukkah, open to wind and rain, is the exact opposite of a fallout shelter or of a "laser shield." It symbolizes that in the nuclear age, all of us live in a vulnerable Sukkah. *Our only real shelter is making peace.*

The theme of Sukkat Shalom is *"From Harvest Booth to Voting Booth."* Urge your congregation or Jewish group to press your members of Congress *to end all nuclear testing.*

Rosh Hashanah is the birthday of the world. As the new year turns and returns, *let us look our children and all the world's children in the eye and say—*

"We did our best to choose life for you and us this Rosh Hashanah!" (all italics in original)

The letter concludes "Shalom and shanah tovah" (a good year) and is signed by Arthur Waskow.

Universalism and moralism are not confined to the Jewish left. In his book *Sacred Survival,* Jonathan Woocher demonstrates how moralism is a basic component of what he calls the "civil religion" of American Jews, though what he actually describes is the civil religion of the Jewish communal leadership. He quotes one Jewish leader: "Charity and working for social justice—*Tzedakah* and *Mitzvos*—are not options for Jews. They have the force of articles of faith. They are duties and requirements" (Woocher 1986, 85). It is notable that Woocher translates *mitzvah* and *tzedakah* as "working for social justice." But this is a commonplace among American Jewish leaders. As another says, "For us, social justice—*Tzedakah* in its full meaning—has always been indivisible—for all" (1986, 86). And still another says: "It has always been Jewish doctrine that social justice cannot be limited to Jews alone; Jews are dedicated to social justice for all mankind. 'Love the stranger as thyself,' the Bible taught" (1986, 86). This citation is taken out of context, and confers a meaning on the passage that biblical scholars would find somewhat forced.

Woocher points out that in the conception of American Jews or at least in that of their leaders, as long as Jews remain a people committed to these values "Jewish survival is not a chauvinistic conceit but a requisite for the continued fulfillment of the Jewish role as an exemplar of human values" (1986, 87). Even the modern Orthodox of the United States demonstrate an inclination toward moralism and a rejection of unqualified ritualism. In a study by Heilman and Cohen (1989), respondents were asked whether "one should give alms because the Torah commands it or because it's the kind thing to do." A slim majority of the most traditional Orthodox in the sample cited the Torah exclusively, but almost half said both reasons were important. In contrast, three-quarters of the less traditional Orthodox (centrists) rejected exclusive reliance on the Torah; two-thirds relied on both the Torah and the dictates of human kindness. This sample of modern Orthodox Jews, a group more observant than most Orthodox Jews in America, felt compelled to draw on universalism and moralism to legitimate an act explicitly commanded by the Torah. The traditionalists felt fewer compunctions about relying exclusively on the Torah: they provided the kind of response that we suspect would be typical of most Israeli Orthodox.

Overtones of personalism mix with a universalism of style in the following report of a Purim celebration at a Conservative synagogue in Connecticut. According to the rabbi, "The Hebrew text will be wrapped around with song, dance and narrative in musical revue format—a folk art pageant involving the entire congregation . . . We present Esther in this way in order to bring out its ever-current as well as its ancient meaning . . . A point like this is brought out through the songs of such composers as Spike Jones; Cole Porter and George Landry, late voodoo chief of New Orelans" (*Connecticut Jewish Ledger,* 12 March 1987, p. 13). A more explicit example of the transformation of Purim in moralistic terms is its celebration at Congregation B'nai Jacob, the largest Conservative synagogue in the New Haven area. The congregation printed a pamphlet called "Purim Service" for its members, which is read aloud instead of the biblical story of Esther. It is an abbreviated version, almost entirely in English, organized in the form of responsive readings. What is especially striking when one contrasts the transformed version with the Biblical story is the excising of any violence. Haman is not hanged on a gallows. Instead, "When the King found out that Haman plotted against the people of Esther, the Queen, he removed him from office and appointed Mordekhai in his place." The moral of the story is formulated as follows: "Our story is important because it is about people who had courage and who risked their lives to help others. That's what we celebrate on Purim."

Traditional sources of course lend other interpretations to Purim. The Jewish tradition accords to the holiday a variety of meanings. Some interpretations encompass a comic dimension, which the modernized version loses entirely. But a common denominator in all the traditional interpretations is the persistence and wickedness of anti-Semites bent on destroying the Jews, and the role of divine Providence in frustrating their evil intent.

Universalism emerges again in the study by Heilman and Cohen of modern Orthodox Jews, in which almost all traditionalists (92 percent) agreed with the traditional view expressed in the Torah and reinforced by rabbinic authorities and social custom that "homosexuality is wrong." Any deviation from this proposition can be attributed only to a kind of amoral universalism—a nonjudgmental acceptance of homosexuality as a personal choice or condition. It is noteworthy that only two-thirds of the centrists in the survey condemned homosexuality, and this finding is supported by other surveys.[3] Our impression, buttressed by the survey data on Israeli attitudes toward homosexuality, is that very few Israeli Orthodox would take such a relaxed, nonjudgmental view of homosexuality.

Other evidence of the universalism of American Orthodox Jews is found in their attitudes toward friendship with non-Jews. Most traditionalists in Heilman's and Cohen's study rejected the idea that "an Orthodox Jew can be close friends with non-Jews," but more than two-thirds of the centrists accepted it. In contrast, we speculate that few Israeli Orthodox could imagine having a Gentile as a close friend. Almost all of the Orthodox (98 percent) as well as almost all the non-Orthodox in our survey of American Jews in 1986 agreed with this statement: "As Jews we should be concerned about all people and not just Jews." By comparison, this universalist sentiment was espoused by fewer than two-thirds of the Israelis, secular or religious. It would therefore appear that a universalist construction of the Jewish tradition has taken place even among Orthodox Jews in the United States, despite the resistance to this tendency among the Orthodox elite.

We do not suggest that personalism, voluntarism, universalism, and moralism are entirely new, much less that they are alien to Judaism. They certainly can be found within the tradition itself. But they now have become major dimensions or instruments through which American Jews interpret and transform the Jewish tradition.[4]

Religion in Israel and Observance of Jewish Law

Proportionately more Israelis than Americans observe almost any given Jewish ritual. The most complete report on the ritual observance of Israelis was published in 1979 and is based on data collected a few years earlier (Ben-Meir and Kedem 1979). By combining this study with our own survey of the Israeli population in 1986 we find the following levels of observance for some key rituals (in percent):

Takes part in a seder	99
Lights Hanukah candles	88
Buys only kosher meat	79
Fasts on Yom Kippur	74
Lights Sabbath candles and recites a blessing in the home	53
Separates milk and meat dishes	44
Hears kiddush on Friday night	38
Attends Sabbath services at least once a month	30
Prays every Sabbath	23
Goes to mikvah regularly (wives only)	14

Although the level of ritual observance is higher among Israelis, it is not clear whether this difference is substantial. To ascertain whether it is or not, it is useful to compare middle-aged Israelis (forty to sixty-four years old) with American Jews of the same age group, for it is in middle age that ritual practice in both societies peaks. For all four rituals in the surveys—the lighting of Hanukah candles, fasting on Yom Kippur, having two sets of dishes, and attending Sabbath services at least monthly—the Israeli rates exceed the American rates, sometimes considerably. The differences range from eight percentage points for lighting Hanukah candles to twenty-five for keeping kosher dishes.

These differences are not entirely attributable to the higher proportion of Orthodox in the Israeli population. We compared the American Orthodox with Israelis who defined themselves as dati, the American Conservatives with Israelis who defined themselves as masorati (traditional), and Reform Jews with Israelis who defined themselves as *hiloni* (secular).[5] The comparisons point up some interesting differences between Israeli and American Jews. In the United States but not in Israel a noticeable segment of Orthodoxy is relatively nonobservant. For ex-

ample, in our American sample almost a fifth of those who defined
themselves as Orthodox did not report that they kept separate dishes
for meat and dairy products; virtually all the Israeli Orthodox did. The
masorati Israeli was more observant than the Conservative American
Jew on all our measures of observance. The most marked difference
was in the keeping of separate dishes, a basic requirement of a kosher
home: only a quarter of Conservative Jews reported that they did, compared with 57 percent of masorati Israelis. The patterns of observance
of hiloni Israelis and Reform American Jews were similar. In each
group a large majority lit Hanukah candles, a narrow majority fasted on
Yom Kippur, and very few attended services often (more did among
the Americans) or had two sets of dishes (more did among the Israelis).

These results together show that Israelis are more observant than
American Jews partly because the Israeli population has a higher proportion of Orthodox Jews: the gap in religious observance between
Americans and Israelis diminishes when the two populations are compared according to their religious orientation. But controlling for this
orientation does not erase the gap entirely: at least for the more traditional groups, the Orthodox and Conservative in the United States and
the dati'im and masorati'im in Israel, Israelis are more observant than
their American counterparts.

One reason for this discrepancy is that Israeli society simply lends
more social support, significance, and legitimacy to Jewish ritual practice than American society does. Not only are there proportionately
more Orthodox in Israel, but for those who choose to practice traditional observances these practices celebrate their relationship with the
larger (Israeli Jewish) society, and they probably take place in the context
of a more cohesive and intensive traditional community, which is capable
of applying social sanctions with greater reliability and effectiveness. To
some extent self-identification as dati or Orthodox, masorati or Conservative, reflects a certain basic orientation to the tradition. Apparently the
ritual standards or consequences of such identification are higher in
Israel than in the United States.

Is there a direction in which the Israeli interpretation of the tradition
is moving? Can we point to certain principles, as we did among American Jews, that provide the tools through which Israeli Jews are reconstructing the meaning and practice of Judaism? It would be neat and
reassuring if we could find that these principles were the reverse of the

American Jewish principles—if we observed that Israeli Judaism were being reconstructed in accordance with collectivism rather than personalism, involuntarism rather than voluntarism, particularism rather than universalism, ritualism rather than moralism. There are some grounds for arguing that this is taking place in one segment of the population. But to do so would be misleading, because it would overlook other, equally important developments in other segments. The picture is in fact rather complex, and we find it impossible to arrive at a simple summary statement.

Slightly fewer than 20 percent of Israeli Jews say they are religious (dati, which in the Israeli lexicon is equivalent to Orthodox), roughly 45 percent say they are secular, and 35 percent say they are traditional. The last category is rather amorphous, and respondents who place themselves in it are probably uncomfortable in defining themselves as religious or secular. They are uncomfortable with the religious label because they do not observe most traditional rituals; they are aware that they violate many religious commandments. But at the same time they are uncomfortable in defining themselves as secular, because they do feel a strong attachment to many of the customs and laws of the tradition.

The percentage of dati Jews has remained constant over the last twenty years. The percentage of those who define themselves as traditional has declined slightly, and the percentage of those who define themselves as secular has increased slightly. Consequently, if by secularism we refer to a way of life, to an absence of religious observance, then secularism in Israel is on the rise. It is widely conceded that there is more overt violation of the Sabbath in both private and public life than there was twenty or thirty years ago. But secularism as a way of life must be distinguished from secularism as an ideology. And as an ideology, as an affirmation of one particular mode of Jewish living and one way of understanding what Judaism means, as a sharp critique of Jewish religiosity and the life of halakha, secularism has lost much of the vitality and support that it once enjoyed.

Secularism need not be antireligious. The founders of Israel were heirs to a secular Zionist tradition that was anticlerical but only in some respects antireligious. Its orientation was strongly Jewish; in its efforts to co-opt Jewish symbols for its purposes it inevitably reinforced aspects of the Jewish tradition.[6] Its antireligious inclinations, a partial leg-

acy of its internationalist socialist orientation, was primarily a consequence of its efforts to redefine Judaism and to form the character of
the new Jew (*Hebrew* was the preferred term). But antagonism toward
religion was blurred by an ambivalent commitment to the Jewish tradition, and the tradition is in turn so overlaid with religious elements that
it is virtually impossible to separate the two.[7]

With the declaration of statehood, political leaders sought to unite
Israelis around the symbols of the state and its institutions, the army in
particular. They selectively drew on ideas and symbols from the Jewish
tradition that would serve these purposes. But in the late 1960s, and
with increasing intensity after the Yom Kippur war of 1973, the political
elite no longer sought to use religion in this way, and religious symbols
penetrated the society less selectively. In a response to the growing authority of religious symbols and leaders, political leaders sought to
demonstrate their personal fidelity to the tradition and the compatibil-
ity of the state with the tradition. Religion and state became increasingly inseparable in the cultural as well as the political sense, severely
undermining the legitimacy of secularist ideologies.

Israeli Jews are no more religious now than they were before the
1970s, but secularism as an ideology that reinterprets the Jewish tradition in purely national or social terms elicits little support. As the writer
Amos Oz puts it, secularists have become defensive about their stance.
They stutter before the Orthodox, saying, "You are of course more
Jewish, but we're also okay, aren't we, even though not at your level?"
(cited in Eisen 1986, 133). As religious symbols have penetrated society
over the last twnety years, a new civil religion has emerged. Four religious developments in Israeli society can be distinguished.[8]

Religious Triumphalism: From Haredim to Religious Zionists

Although religious (Orthodox) Jews represent an esti-
mated 20 percent of the Jewish population in Israel, their importance in
defining the meaning of Judaism outweighs their numbers. In part because of the decline of Zionist socialism and other secular interpretations of Judaism, the religious interpretation of Judaism has become
increasingly normative. Religious spokesmen have become the authoritative interpreters of Judaism, at least for the masses of Israeli Jews.

The new, more traditionally oriented civil religion has helped to instill confidence in the religious segment of the population. Religious parties have more political influence than they enjoyed in the past, because of the developments already mentioned and because of a coincidence of voting patterns. Paradoxically, the political influence of religious voters may continue to grow even if the vote for religious parties declines. Indeed the decline since 1977 in the vote for the National Religious Party, the party of religious Zionism, suggests that religious Zionist voters no longer feel that they require the party to protect their interests, and vote increasingly for nonreligious parties. For their part, these parties are increasingly likely to nominate religious candidates and compete for the votes of the religious public. On the other hand, in the elections of 1988 the haredi parties increased their vote substantially;[9] most of the increase came from religiously traditional but socially discontented voters. That these voters were able to express their discontent in a vote for the haredi parties indicates the growing legitimacy of religion in Israeli public life.

Another reason for the confidence of the religious public is the mistaken popular belief that the proportion of religious Jews within the population is growing. The confidence of the religious Jews is reflected in the following passage, taken from an interview with a haredi Jew in Jerusalem. We quote it at some length because we feel that it accurately portrays the mentality of at least one important segment of the religious camp:

Why do you think Ben-Gurion agreed to exempt yeshiva students from his army? From an abundance of love of Torah? No! He thought to himself: let us leave them alone because whatever happens, they will disappear . . . At the most a small group in B'nai B'rak [a suburb of Tel Aviv, large parts of which constitute a haredi enclave] or Mea Sha'arim [an exclusively haredi neighborhood in Jerusalem] will remain.

That is what he thought to himself. But see for yourself, God denied him his wish. Among the secularists there is a wife and child, and maybe a dog (he laughs), in every family. And among us, without an evil eye, . . . our neighborhoods are expanding more and more. . . . Look how many *ba'alei t'shuvah* there are round here. A little longer, with God's help, and Jerusalem will look like

B'nai B'rak. For more than fifty years the Zionists ruled here, now the time for Jewish rule has come. First of all, at least in Jerusalem. Among us, the children want to live near their parents and thus we continue to expand.

We want to see a Jewish street. Without Sabbath desecration, without non-kosher food, without exaggerated permissiveness, without pornographic advertisements on bus stops. And this is coming to pass, thank God.

At this point the interviewer interrupts and says, "But you are arousing the secular public against you." The respondent replies:

Ridiculous. Just as we know that Esau hates Jacob [i.e., the Gentiles hate the Jews] so the ignorant hate the learned [i.e., the secular hate the religious]. The Gemara [the major text of oral law] has already told us this . . . in Pesachim, page 49. Look for yourself, did you ever learn Gemara? No? Well, here's what it says there. The hatred of the ignorant toward the learned is greater than the hatred of idol worshipers to Jews, and their wives even more. You know Shula Aloni [Shulamit Aloni is a member of the Knesset and the leader of the Citizens Rights party, often perceived as the most antireligious of all parties]. Isn't it true? I told you, everything is already written in the Gemara. If they didn't need to negotiate with us they would kill us. (Rosenberg 1987, 10–11)

This triumphalism is reflected in the readiness of many haredim to demonstrate publicly and sometimes violently against the opening of movie houses and coffee shops on the Sabbath, against certain types of archaeological excavations, and against advertisements they consider pornographic.

The Orthodox in Israel are far from monolithic. Deep divisions and bitter conflicts separate the haredim from religious Zionists. Within each camp are subgroups that have so much animosity toward one another (at least among the *haredim*) that violence sometimes breaks out. Further, the standard division of Orthodox Israelis into the haredim and the religious Zionists is complicated by the growing religious and political strength of Sephardi Jewry, which does not fit neatly into either camp.[10]

It is probably more helpful to think of religious Jewry as ranged along a continuum. At one end Judaism is understood as hostile toward the state of Israel, toward modern culture, and toward nonreligious Jews. The Judaism at the other end sees the establishment of the state of Israel as signaling the beginning of divine redemption. It affirms much of modern culture (though not all) and commands Jews to love and to cooperate with fellow Jews, even if they are secularists. Our concern is however not with the organizational or political divisions among the Orthodox, but rather with whether we can point to evolving conceptions of Judaism that are common to all the Orthodox in Israel. We think that such conceptions are developing, although a minority in the religious sector certainly seeks to interpret Judaism in a different light. In the mainstream of Israeli Orthodoxy one will find conceptions that are the mirror image of those found among American Jews, including many Orthodox Jews in the United States. Personalism is the exception to this generalization. Like Americans, Israelis—even Orthodox Israelis—have absorbed elements of personalism. The opposite of personalism is to interpret the tradition without regard to its relevance or meaning for the individual. We find no such tendency among Israelis. Efforts on the part of the religious sector to attract *ba'alei t'shuvah* (penitents) have sensitized its leaders to the need to reformulate Judaism in terms that speak to the personal needs of the individual (Danzger 1989).

Personalism has therefore come to characterize both American and Israeli constructions of Judaism. It is of course not an entirely new element in the Jewish tradition. Hasidism, the Jewish movement that developed in eastern Europe in the mid-eighteenth century, was notable for its emphasis on the "redemption of the individual's soul rather than that of the nation or the cosmos as a whole." Hasidism sought mystical contact with God, "usually attained while praying but also achieved when a person is working for his livelihood or engaged in any other physical activity" (Dan 1987, 207). (In contrast, some might argue that the tendency of today's Hasidic communities to demand and enforce religious conformism actually runs counter to the demands of personalism.) Personalism has emerged as a major tendency among all religious groups, even the religious ultranationalists, who generally emphasize collective rather than individual concerns. An article in *Nekudah,* a publication sponsored by the Jewish settlements on the West Bank and

Gaza, notes that "posing 'personal' ideals can fill the spiritual vacuum that results from organized movements." The author observes that renewing the "creativity of Gush Emunim depends on the ability of the individual to express and fulfill his individuality" (Moses 1987, 25).

Religious Jews in Israel eschew the voluntarism we found among American Jews, even that of the modern Orthodox who pick and choose the elements of Jewish law that they observe. The major thrust of contemporary religious formulations is to interpret Judaism so as to enhance the role of halakha and the authority of the rabbis who rule on the details of halakha, thus diminishing the element of subjectivity, choice, and personal interpretation (Liebman 1983b; Friedman 1987). This tendency embraces a number of currents. The law is defined as rigid and very precise in its demands; it leaves no room for subjective interpretation. In addition, the law is increasingly interpreted as strict, imposing ever greater burdens on its adherents.

Laws of feminine modesty are a good example. No Israeli Orthodox rabbi would now define the appropriate dress for women as something that depends on the environment, the circumstances, or contemporary norms. Instead rabbis decree precisely which parts of the body must be covered according to Jewish law. At one time sleeves covering the upper part of the arms, or skirts extending below the knees, were considered sufficiently modest. Now one increasingly finds stricter norms: sleeves below the elbow if not to the wrist, skirts to the ankles, and stockings. This not only reflects internal tendencies in Israeli Orthodoxy, but perhaps indirectly parallels developments in the increasingly fundamentalist Moslem Middle East.

Universalism, a central component in the American Jewish understanding of Judaism that extends to many Orthodox,[11] is deliberately rejected by mainstream Orthodoxy in Israel. The triumph of Jewish particularism is evident with regard to relations between Jews and non-Jews (see chapter 3) and to conceptions of state and territory (see chapter 4). It seems that everything is viewed through a Jewish prism and judged from a Jewish perspective.

The rise of particularism has implications for the interpretation of "moralism" as well. Emphasis on law (and ritual) means less of an emphasis on the centrality of ethics. But religious Jews in Israel have also redefined the very term *morality* in particularistic rather than universalistic terms. According to the rabbi who helped to introduce extremist education in the religious Zionist school system, Jews are en-joined to maintain themselves in isolation from other peoples. Foreign culture in particular is anathema when its standards are used to criticize Jews (Liebman 1985, 46). "Between the Torah of Israel and atheist hu-manism there is no connection"; there is no place in Judaism for "a humanistic attitude in determining responses to hostile behavior of the Arab population" (p. 46). According to a leader of Jewish settlers on the West Bank, "Jewish national morality is distinct from universal mo-rality. Notions of universal or absolute justice may be good for Finland or Australia but not here, not with us" (p. 46).

A rabbi of some prominence wrote to his pupil on the problem of killing unarmed women and children during a war: "Even though the rule, 'If someone comes to kill you, you may kill him first,' applies also to a Jew . . . this is true only if there is a suspicion that [the Jew] has come to kill you. But the *Goy* in time of war . . . is always to be judged as coming to kill you unless it is clear that he has no evil intention. It is this rule that determines 'purity of arms' according to *halakha* and not the Gentile sense that is now accepted in the Israeli Defense Forces, an interpretation that to our regret has resulted in the loss of more than a few [Jewish] lives" (*Niv Hamidrashia* 1974, 31). This diminishing em-phasis on universal standards of morality extends to areas other than the Jewish-Arab dispute. For example, the chief rabbi of Ramat-Gan decries the practice of childless Israeli couples of adopting Brazilian children and then having them undergo conversion. He says that such children will be brought up as Israelis but that not all of them will iden-tify with the Jews. "After all, it is clear that children inherit characteris-tics from their parents." The rabbi cites sacred texts as evidence that non-Jews are not blessed with the same quality of mercy as the Jews are, but on the contrary are cruel by their very nature (*Hatzofeh,* 20 June 1988, p. 4).

The Moderate Religious Camp

In addition to the central tendencies of the religious population of Israel there are contrary tendencies. At its outset reli-gious Zionism conceived of Judaism in far more voluntaristic, univer-salistic, and moralistic terms than it does today. Not all religious Zionists have attuned themselves to the new, particularistic tendencies. Several developments have in fact provoked a moderate counterreaction. Among these are the growth of religious extremism, particularly the excesses associated with nationalism and chauvinism; the activity of the Jewish underground, and its justification of acts of terror against non-Jews, ostensibly based on halakhah; and the election of Meir Kahane to the Knesset in 1984, and the recognition that large numbers of religious Jews, youth in particular, were sympathetic to his ideas if not his movement. In the last few years the news media, dominated by radical secularists and nourished by religious chauvinists, have projected an image of the Jewish religion as antagonistic to liberal democratic values. This too has invited a religious response of some sort.

Religious moderation is espoused by at least two recently formed organizations (Oz V'Shalom–Netivot Shalom and Neemanei Torah V'Avodah), one new periodical (*Emdah*), an older periodical (*Petachim*), and a new political party (Meimad). One also finds religious moderates in the Masorti movement (the Conservative movement in Israel) and even among Reform leaders, although most of the Reform associate themselves at least for political purposes with the national or universal secularists.[12] The religious moderates are strongly Zionist and affirm the religious significance of the state of Israel. "We see army service as no less a *mitzvah* than Sabbath observance," one religious moderate says (quoted in *Jerusalem Post Magazine,* 4 December 1987, p. 13). But this is true of the ultranationalist religious Zionists as well. What distinguishes the religious moderates is their opposition to other prevailing currents in Israeli religious life. There is only a little inclination to favor greater voluntarism and subjectivity in religious interpretation. They place greater emphasis on the virtues of secular education and the ethical imperatives of the Jewish tradition in their relations with non-Jews. The religious moderates have a relatively dovish orientation in foreign policy, characterized among other things by a willingness to surrender territory in return for peace.

According to Yehezkel Cohen, a leading spokesman for the religious moderates, those he represents are divided from the rest of the Israeli religious world by "a deeply philosophic question—whether to emphasize those *mitzvot* directed towards divine service or those guiding relations with one's fellows" (*Jerusalem Post Magazine,* 4 December 1987, p. 6). Most of the efforts in the last few years to mitigate tensions between the secular and the religious have come from the ranks of these religious Jews. Their point of view is a minority position within the religious camp, certainly among its elite. It is possible that many religious Jews from the rank and file have some sympathy for their position, although there is little evidence for this. And it is only in the last three or four years that the position of the religious moderates has found expression in print, in public lectures, and organizational forums. Although the political party allied with the religious moderates, Meimad, received only about sixteen thousand votes in the elections to the Knesset in 1988, not quite enough to win a seat, its positions may yet prove important in defining how Israeli Jews interpret their religious tradition.

Secular Nationalism: Three Variations

The secular interpretation of Judaism most widespread today attributes central importance to the state and the land of Israel and interprets the tradition in nationalist terms. This is particularly true of secularists who are sympathetic to the political right. They see religious Jews as their political allies and accord great deference to the religious tradition. Their conceptions of Judaism may more properly be termed a mood or an identity than an ideology. Of all the other interpretations of Judaism discussed here theirs is most lacking in anything like systematic articulation, although this has not diminished its popularity. The reason it lacks clear articulation may be that its proponents are so sympathetic to traditional religious conceptions of Judaism that they are reluctant to pose an alternative. Further, their ideas about state and land are reinforced by those of the religious Zionists (see chapter 4).

This camp includes a disproportionate number of Sephardi Jews, among them the bulk of those who define themselves as masorati'im (traditional in their religious orientation). But it includes also some who define themselves as hiloni (secular). Ariel Sharon, the favorite political leader of the ultranationalists, is secular rather than traditional. He is quoted as having said, "I am proud to be a Jew but sorry that I am not religious" (*Ma'ariv,* Weekend Supplement, 10 March 1986, p. 12). Whether he was expressing what he really believes or merely being politically expedient, the statement reflects the deference of the secular right toward religion.

As divisions between doves and hawks have deepened in the last few years, it has been suggested increasingly that fidelity to religion and loyalty to the state are associated. Thus a circular to principals of religious schools from the Religious Division in the Ministry of Education (a unit controlled by religious nationalists) reminded the principals that Jewish traitors came from the anti-religious left of the Israeli political map and not from the ranks of the religious. And a columnist for the religious Zionist daily newspaper discusses "the Israeli left, sections of which betrayed the State and associated themselves with the PLO." The writer notes that "leftism" is correlated with disorganized family life, divorce, and "unofficial marriages" (marriages not conducted in accordance with Jewish law; *Hatzofeh,* 27 June 1968, p. 3).

It is not surprising that religious spokesmen should emphasize the association between religion and patriotism. What is surprising is that secular leaders do so as well. For example Prime Minister Yitzhak Shamir, leader of the Likud party, is quoted as having said: "The left today is not what it once was. In the past, social and economic issues were its major concern. Today, its concern is zealousness for political surrender and, on the other hand, war against religion. It is only natural that someone whose stance is opposed to the Land of Israel will also oppose the Torah of Israel" (*Ma'ariv,* 20 December 1987, p. 6). But not all those who subscribe to a nationalist secular position are ultranationalists and political rightists, nor are those who conceive of Judaism in secular terms and attach central importance to the state and the land of Israel in their interpretation of the Jewish tradition. One can distinguish two additional variations of nationalist secularism that are not necessarily associated with the right and in practice tend to be associated with figures on the left.

One variation is a kind of residual secular nationalism from the Zionist socialist period. It is intensely Jewish and seeks to permeate Israeli public life with its conceptions of the Jewish tradition. These conceptions are primarily moralistic, though not devoid of a strong element of Jewish particularism that is marked by loyalty to Jewish culture, the Jewish people, and the Jewish state. Peculiarly enough, adherents of this brand of secular nationalism are wary of separating religion and state; they defend Judaism against the charge that it is incompatible with liberalism. A good example of this line of thought is Yehoshua Rash's criticism of Joseph Agassi (see note 11 to chapter 5).

Abba Kovner represented this type of secular nationalism. Kovner, who died in 1987, was a heroic figure in Israeli society. Leader of the Jewish underground in the Vilna ghetto, educational officer in Israel's War of Independence, member of a kibbutz, renowned author and poet, Kovner personified to many Israel's moral conscience. His position in Israeli society somewhat resembled that of Elie Wiesel in the United States, although he never acquired quite the prominence among Israelis that Wiesel has achieved among American Jews. According to Kovner, Israel is a Jewish society in which secularists suffer from ignorance of their own tradition and "need the religious in order that they may have roots" (1987, 283). On the other hand the religious (apparently he was referring to the haredim) are insufficiently sensitive to the collective concerns of the Jewish people. Kovner was frightened by the rise of antireligious secularism that he associated with a rise in individualism and a decline in concern for the Jewish community. He said that those who built the land, even if they were called secularists, did not "cast off the yoke" (a rabbinic metaphor that refers to the "yoke of Torah"). Kovner admitted that Israelis are engaged in a search for roots, but he added that they are also engaged in "a search for foreign gods . . . that is the essence of the crises of the generation raised in the state that is called secular" (1987, 283). In Kovner's understanding of Judaism the religious and communal elements merge, and commitment to both is necessary for the sake of national survival. Both are encompassed in Kovner's conception of Jewish commitment, and it becomes painfully obvious how such a conception is irrelevant to the libertarian concerns that other secularists affirm as primary (see below).

Eliezer Schweid is another writer who represents this line of thinking. Like Kovner he is concerned about the growing tensions between secular and religious Jews in Israel, because he fears the consequence of a purely secular culture devoid of Jewish elements.

The secular lifestyle in this generation has become more individualistic and centered around the values of egotistical self-fulfillment . . . The mass expression of this ethos in the street and the entertainment centers and the media are superficial, coarse, and permissive, and the message they emit is a powerful stimulant to the impulses. These constitute sources of satisfaction and pleasure of a kind but they are of doubtful compensation for the growing sense . . . that Israeli culture has been emptied of values, that it is hollow, imitative, and shallow, that its distinctive character has been lost and what remains is a pale imitation; that society's highest values, even if they are still esteemed by some . . . do not serve to guide the people. (Schweid 1988, 14)

This strand of Jewish secularism attracts relatively few Israelis. It finds continuing expression in the works of some intellectuals, older ones in particular, but it is beset by difficulties. The most serious is its inability to provide an alternative to religion, not as an ideology or belief system but as a way of life. To ask that it do this is of course to ask that it become a quasi-religion rather than a secular ideology, something that makes its own adherents uneasy. The forms of secular nationalism we have described are neither ideologies nor programs but mechanisms for rationalizing and legitimating a non-Orthodox or non-believing Jew's continued allegiance to traditional Jewish folkways and practice of these folkways.

This legitimation is least characteristic of the third and final variant of secular nationalism, one that really overlaps with secular universalism (see below). The adherents of this variant seek to redefine Judaism as a synonym of Israeli culture. Judaism is what Israelis do, for Israelis live in a Jewish state. This position is especially popular among those who are reluctant or not yet ready to sever their nominal ties to the Jewish tradition, but unwilling to acknowledge that the tradition has any compelling quality. For example, the popular author A. B. Yehoshua defines Judaism in national and antireligious terms. He argues that it is necessary to change the definition of the Jews by weakening the religious element of their religion and strengthening the national element. According to Yehoshua, a Jew is someone who sees the state of Israel as his or her state or land; and the spirit of religion must be weakened so that new sources of authority may be found (Yehoshua 1984). The Israeli is "the Jew (religious or secular) who lives a total Jewish existence whose identifying characteristics are land, language and an independent social environment" (p. 126). Whatever Israelis do is by definition Jewish. According to Yehoshua's formulation, non-Jews in Israel are entitled to full civil rights but will always remain strangers in a Jewish country.

Secular Universalism: More Mobilized, More Assertive

The religious triumphalists and right-wing secular nationalists have generated a backlash among some secularists and led to the growth of antireligious tendencies that border on hostility toward Judaism in general. In the last two or three years secular Jews have staged several demonstrations against the demands of the religious. Some have endeavored to overturn status quo agreements on the closing of places of entertainment on the Sabbath, and some of these efforts have succeeded. (In Israel the term *status quo* is applied to informal agreements among political leaders to maintain long-standing practices regarding public observance of the Sabbath and other Jewish holidays—practices that are often inconsistent.) For the first time in recent memory antireligious elements have initiated incidents of violence, including the desecration and burning of synagogues—although everyone attributes these acts to a mere handful of extremists.

Secular universalists reserve a special hostility toward the religious establishment. They see the Orthodox leaders as narrow-minded, intolerant, and ignorant, eager to impose their peculiar, antiquated views of Judaism on the entire Israeli population. Some Israelis who are certainly not antireligious, let alone hostile to Judaism (including some leaders of Reform Judaism), have aligned themselves with the secular universalists because they also harbor intense resentment toward the religious establishment. The result is a growing sentiment for privatizing Judaism and eliminating its collective, political, and public aspects. The secular universalists have become increasingly outspoken in recent years, and their political influence within the Israeli left seems to be growing. They are characteristically Ashkenazi, second-generation Israelis who see themselves as the figurative and literal heirs of the pioneers and founders of Israel, the natural elite of the society. But since the rise of the Likud in 1977 to political dominance the political leadership of the secular universalists has passed to others, and there is a growing unease among them that those who ought by virtue of ethnicity as well as ideology to lead no longer do. This may account more than anything for the frustration of the secular universalists, and one cannot dismiss the possibility that their attacks on religion are really sublimated attacks on Israel's new social order and political hierarchy.

For many years the secular universalists nurtured their grievances in relative silence. Their views are widely shared in literary, artistic, and some academic circles, especially at Tel-Aviv University. They found expression in works of fiction that contained apocalyptic visions of an Israel ruled by rabbis who resembled Ayatollah Khomeini. These views were also disseminated in the mass media but especially in the theater, which in Israel is the special province of the radical left. Nonetheless, the circle of people influenced by these views was relatively small.

The problem of the universalist secularists was that they had no banner, no ideological position that would mold a consensus and confer legitimacy on their position. After all, even the leaders of the Labour party sought to co-opt religious symbols when they were in power. The penetration of religious symbols into society began before 1977 and accelerated only after the victory of the Likud. The major institutions of the state—the schools and the army—had long since adopted the position that the Jewish tradition was a major value in Israeli society and that the good citizen was the one who adhered to it most closely. The state had in fact provided nationalist legitimation to the religious segment of the population. If one wanted to oppose religion, not to mention Judaism, one was opposing major values of Israeli society.

The situation changed somewhat in the mid-1980s. The secularists found a banner under which they could challenge the growth of religion in the name of Israeli values—the banner of democracy. Israelis have long complained of religious coercion. But for many secularists, the absence of movies or coffee houses or busses on the Sabbath is seen more as an inconvenience than as a matter of conscience. The election of Meir Kahane to the Knesset in 1984 and the growth of overt racism in Israeli society provided new opportunities for the secular universalists. It allowed them to argue that the growth of religion was an indication of a deep malaise in Israeli society, a challenge to Israel's liberal democratic system itself. Signs pointed to the spread of authoritarian sympathies, and survey research indicated that a large segment of the public was prepared to deny the Arabs their basic democratic rights. The secularists have tied these tendencies to violent street demonstrations by the haredim, the abuse of Arab rights by some religious Jewish settlers on the West Bank, demands by religious leaders for stricter censorship of the arts, literature, and the theater, the violation of rights of privacy, laws requiring that businesses close on the Sabbath, and other forms of "religious coercion." They have portrayed religion and to some extent Judaism itself as a threat to Israeli democracy.

There are a number of indications of a renewed aggressiveness on the part of the secularists. Even a member of the editorial board of the *Jerusalem Post* urged secularists to take to the streets (for they have no other choice), in a fight "that the secular population should not fear [because] it needs a good dose of consciousness-raising" (*Jerusalem Post,* 4 December 1987, p. 10). Until then those who opposed the behavior of religious Jews or were critical of what they termed religious coercion or the aggressive posture of the religious were likely to distinguish haredim from religious Zionists and to blame the haredim for what they did not like, even where the distinctions were unjustified. Those who attacked the haredim were likely to preface their attacks by exempting the religious Zionists, or religious moderates. In many cases this is no longer true. In recent years one has increasingly heard charges against religious Jews in general when the reference could have been limited to the haredim. One has also heard it charged that the more religious the society, the less democratic it will be, and even the inference that the more Jewish the society, the less democratic it will be.[13]

Meanwhile, overt antagonism to religion or to any connection between religion and the state continues to grow among some segments of Israeli society. It remains to be seen what consequences this will have for the construction of Israeli Judaism, if any.

Although Israeli Jews are sharply divided over the significance of the Jewish tradition, there is less disagreement over its interpretation than might be expected. And it is especially important that almost all interpretations of the Jewish tradition stress its public aspect. Although Israelis disagree over whether religion and state ought to be separate, those who do believe in separation do not advance a "private" conception of Judaism that is especially relevant to them. The debate over separation of religion and state does not occur in Israel as it did in some Protestant countries, where religious adherents were found on both sides of the issue. Most of those who favor the privatization of Judaism, who would restrict it to the home rather than the street, feel this way because they find public Judaism bothersome and oppressive. They take it for granted that the Orthodox interpretation of Judaism is authoritative, and it is this interpretation from which they wish to escape.

In the American Jewish interpretation of Judaism, the personalistic and voluntaristic elements in particular have served as instruments in refashioning Judaism so that it carries a message or meaning for individual Jews in their personal lives. The Orthodox argue that this message is not "authentically" Jewish. They view much of American Judaism as a distortion of the "real" tradition anyway, as catering to the weakness of the individual rather than demanding that the individual respond to the demands of God. Even if one acknowledges the justice of this critique, many American Jews nonetheless believe that Judaism speaks to them as individuals, that it has something to say about cycles of life and cycles of the year, about joy and tragedy, about sin and redemption.

Judaism has personal meaning for religious Jews in Israel as well. But for the nonreligious, especially for the secular, the explicit message of authentic Judaic leaders is almost exclusively confined to public life. It is about the state (either for it or against it), about which territories belong to the land of Israel, about the obligation of Jews to live in the land of Israel, about one's responsibilities to other Jews and the nature of relations between Jews and non-Jews. It is also about what public life ought to be like on the Sabbath or holidays. But it is rather irrelevant to the individual's "spiritual" or transcendent concerns.[14]

Certainly this perception of the predominantly public nature of Judaism by the nonreligious may stem from their own ignorance or rejection of the Jewish tradition. But this observation is also beside the point. The very perception of Judaism as having major relevance for the public sphere tells us about how Judaism in Israel has been projected by Orthodox spokesmen, and because there are no serious alternative projections, about what Judaism means to the Israeli Jew.[15]

7 Are Two Judaisms Emerging?

American and Israeli conceptions of Judaism have salient differences. Each culture has reinterpreted in its own way the premodern Jewish tradition that is common to both, and the reinterpretations diverge sufficiently to warrant their being called new constructions of Judaism. There are three plausible explanations for these divergences: the American and Israeli constructions of Judaism may represent different levels of commitment, they may reflect different population characteristics, or they may be due to different structural and environmental conditions.

The Major Points of Difference

We would do well to recall the principal ways in which American and Israeli conceptions of Judaism differ. Both American and Israeli Jews construct their sense of what it means to be a Jew from the common perspective of historical familism. In each society Jews see themselves as part of an extended family, with a common descent and destiny and a special obligation and responsibility toward one another. In addition they use the memory of their collective past to draw lessons about the present. These lessons inform their understanding of Jewish symbols and influence their behavior as Jews. Nevertheless, even though the two groups have a common cultural heritage, each has reinterpreted the heritage differently.

On the one hand are certain symbols and motifs of the past that Israelis have seen fit to emphasize as well as reinterpret. For example, the significance of the land of Israel and the concept of galut have been

157

central to the Judaism of most Israelis but are virtually ignored by American Jews. To most Israelis (secular and religious alike), the land has a sacredness that few American Jews appreciate. Other motifs, such as Jewish obligations and responsibility toward non-Jews, have been reinterpreted and expanded by American Jews and virtually ignored by Israelis. Conceptions of the Gentile and of relations between Jew and Gentile have undergone major transformations in the American Jewish construction of Judaism.

Among Israelis new interpretations are also evident, but they play a very different role in explaining reality. The state of Israel, a new Jewish symbol, is central to both Israeli and American Jews, but it has far more power and meaning for Israelis; for them it is a pervasive symbol, intertwined with many other dimensions of Judaism. For example, the state plays a critical role in Israeli conceptions of anti-Semitism, as a bulwark against assimilation, and in the Israeli reinterpretation of the notion of redemption. American Jews evince considerable interest in Israel, one that centers on their anxious concern for Israel's security. Israel clearly dominates the public arena of American Jewish life. But for the most part the concern of American Jews for Israel and their interest in its culture and politics do not impinge on other aspects of American Jewish identity, or on how American Jews understand the basic components of Judaism.

There are marked differences in how American and Israeli Jews have refashioned aspects of their religious life. Even among the more traditionally inclined Orthodox, the distinguishing characteristics of the religious life of American Jews can be conveniently summarized as personalism, voluntarism, moralism, and universalism. These refer to the manner in which American Jews interact with their tradition. They have selectively retained ideas and customs, especially the ethical principles that have universal application and a moral dimension or can be interpreted in a universalist fashion, and reshaped these and others to give them more personal meaning.

In many respects the Israeli conceptions have developed in a contrary direction. Religion in Israel is very much a public affair. The idea of personal religious innovation, so common among American Jews, is underdeveloped and far less legitimate in Israel. Even though the majority of Israelis are non-Orthodox, they tend to regard Orthodox spokesmen as the most authoritative interpreters of Judaism. Rather than expand on the universalist side of the Jewish tradition, Israelis generally and the Orthodox especially have chosen to emphasize the separateness and distinctiveness of Jews, and the special obligations that Jews have toward one another rather than toward Gentiles. And Israeli Judaism remains decidedly more ritualistic and less moralistic than its American counterpart. The ritualism of Israeli Jews is manifest not only in their more frequent observance of ritual (in contrast to American Jewish ceremonialism) but also in the very definition of what is obligatory and appropriate in Jewish practice. Even secular Israeli Jews believe that there is a proper, authoritative (that is, Jewishly legal) way to observe Jewish law and custom. The tendency of American rabbis to find embedded in ritual observance a morality that carries personal meaning is less prevalent among Israeli religious authorities.

This is of course a very brief summary of the differences between American and Israeli Judaism. But it suffices to introduce the central question of this concluding chapter: do these differences point to the emergence of two distinct variations of Judaism, perhaps even to two different Judaisms?

First Explanation: Levels of Commitment

The first problem to be resolved is whether the differences between Israeli and American Jews are differences of degree or of essence. Do they derive primarily from the Israelis' apparently greater commitment and faithfulness to the Jewish tradition (assuming that such a tradition can be identified), or are the differences primarily the result of different interpretations of what it means to be a Jew, with each side no less faithful than the other to its version of Judaism? If the former is true, then the question of how two constructions of Judaism emerged may be trivial, for as American Jews become increasingly estranged from the tradition their conceptions of Judaism will appear progressively less compelling to fewer people.

The two possibilities are not mutually exclusive. American Judaism and Israeli Judaism may be different in part because Americans are typically "less Jewish," and in part because the Judaically committed in each country practice and believe in a qualitatively different religion. We believe that Israelis on the whole are "better" Jews by our own standards of what it means to be a good Jew—standards that even most

Jews in the United States would accept. A number of studies have demonstrated a wide measure of agreement among American Jews on what criteria define a good Jew, and we believe that most Israelis would agree with many of these criteria. They include certain standards of religious observance, association with other Jews (both formal and informal), concern for Israel and the welfare of other Jews, and a knowledge of Judaism or Jewish culture. Israelis score higher on all these measures. Does this putative gap in Jewish commitment and involvement account for the different construction of Judaism among Israeli and American Jews?

On its face the answer would seem to be no. After all, Israelis and American Jews differ not only with respect to certain attitudinal and behavioral measures, but also on how they conceive of Judaism and on what symbols and myths speak to their condition and mobilize their energy and attention. (On the other hand, one may argue that the myths and symbols that are conceived as central to Judaism are themselves a function of the strength of Jewish commitment.)

A look at the early development of German Reform Judaism helps bring this point into sharp relief. It is fair to say that Jewish law was the backbone of Jewish life before the emancipation. It was around this law that the institutions of the social order had to be organized.[1] Reform Judaism, which arose in nineteenth-century Germany, denied the binding nature of Jewish law. Classical Reform theology taught that the essence of Judaism lay in the teachings of the prophets rather than in halakha. Seen through the lens of classical Reform, the prophetic model of Judaism meant that Jews were obliged to conduct themselves according to standards of ethics and morality prevailing in the Western world and that they were free of ritual obligations (such as observing the Sabbath and maintaining dietary laws) and of the obligation to study sacred text.

Was classical Reform Judaism posing an alternative model of Judaism in its day, or was it legitimating the estrangement of the Jew from Judaism? We suspect that both explanations are correct, or that the first may be correct for some Reform Jews and the second correct for others. German Reform leaders who first proposed the model of "prophetic Judaism" in the nineteenth century as an alternative to the halakhic model may have been no less Jewishly committed than the traditionalists. But at the same time many other German Jews were increasingly estranged from Judaism and more willing to embrace non-Jewish culture and society; this group had an elective affinity for the Reform model. The process may also operate in reverse: those who develop new models of Judaism may do so because they seek to legitimate their growing estrangement from the tradition, but their models may be embraced by other Jews who seek an understanding or interpretation that permits them to embrace the "tradition"—and that speaks in Jewish terms to a reality and a moral vision that they view as appropriate.

Second Explanation: Population Characteristics

Education, ethnicity, and religiosity differentiate Israelis with regard to every conception of Judaism covered in this book. Generally the less educated, the Sephardim, and the more religious hold views that are closer to traditional conceptions of Judaism; the more educated, the Ashkenazim, and the secular deviate further from these traditional conceptions. Population characteristics may account for many of the differences between American and Israeli Jews outlined above and detailed in the preceding chapters: if more "modern" Israelis have more "modern" Jewish attitudes and beliefs, perhaps the basic reason American Jews are different from Israelis is that they are more "modern" than Israelis. And if this is so, then as Israelis increasingly undergo modernization the differences should disappear.

Part of the basis for this argument is that Jewish immigrants to the United States and Israel arrived at different times, from different places, and with different conceptions of Judaism. Even if Israel and America had exerted the same influence on Jews and their Judaism, the demographic differences between the two communities would have led to substantial religious differences. This sort of reasoning is often used to explain why Canadian Jewry is apparently so much more Jewishly involved and committed than American Jewry, which is much larger. Observers note that a much greater proportion of Canadian Jews are European immigrants who fled from the Nazis around World War II. Their closer roots to the rich Jewish life of the European past ostensibly explain why Canadian Jews may be more ritually observant and communally cohesive than their American counterparts. (Those who look to structural or environmental factors to explain the differences might focus on Canadian culture and governmental policy, which support religious and ethnic communities more than in the United States, or on the weaker legitimacy accorded to internal religious diversity in Canada.)

The three characteristics we have identified as most critical for explaining intersocietal Judaic differences—religiosity, ethnic origin, and higher education—share two crucial statistical properties. First, the proportions of Jews who are Orthodox, Sephardi, and well educated are far different in Israel and in the United States. Second, all three dimensions differentiate Israeli Jewry internally, and both Orthodoxy and education differentiate American Jewry internally (the number of American Sephardim is too small for ethnicity to have any appreciable impact on measures of Jewish identity, involvement, or belief). For a characteristic to be able to explain the differences between the two cultures, it would need to have both properties (it would have to distinguish between American and Israeli Jews, and it would have to be associated with one or more measures of Jewish identity). Some characteristics have one property but not the other. For example, family status differentiates Jews within the United States and Israel, but there is no pronounced difference between American and Israeli Jews who are married and have children (the family status with the highest level of Jewish involvement on many measures). Affluence or income is also an inadequate explanation: American Jews have a far higher income than Israelis, but sheer wealth and access to material goods do not differentiate Jews internally in either society. American Jews are older than Israeli Jews, but in each country older age is if anything associated with a more traditional approach to Judaism. On the basis of age distribution we might expect a more modern orientation in Israel; but of course our evidence generally points in the opposite direction.

Orthodoxy, ethnicity, and education therefore seem the most prominent of the few axes of social differentiation that meet all the statistical requirements. There may be others, but none of the more common social background factors seem to hold as much potential as these three. Fortunately, two of the three variables can be eliminated because they are explained by the third. Religiosity is the most critical variable by far. The educated Israelis differ from the less educated and the Ashkenazim from the Sephardim largely because a greater proportion of the Sephardim and the less educated are close to the religious tradition: once religion is taken into account, the differences between Sephardim and Ashkenazim and between well educated and less educated diminish considerably and in some cases disappear. Among American Jews, education generally has minor effects on most relevant variables, and the impact of denominational affiliation is far greater. This being the case, it may appear that we can simplify our analysis merely by comparing American and Israeli Jews who have analogous levels of religiosity (dati and Orthodox, masorati and Conservative, hiloni and Reform). The key question is whether the Israeli construction of Judaism differs from the American one because more Israeli Jews than American Jews are religious.

This effort to simplify the analysis must be qualified. In the years surrounding its formation in 1948, Israel experienced huge migrations of Jews from Europe and from North Africa and Asia. A disproportionate number of these immigrants were religious, and many others were deferential toward the religious tradition, though not strictly observant of Jewish law. Most of these Jews, Sephardim from Africa and Asia in particular, were unaware of any alternatives to the Orthodox model of the tradition. Nothing in their experience compared to European-American Reform or Conservative American Judaism. To the extent that they were sympathetic to the tradition, the new immigrants never challenged the Orthodox claim to exclusive legitimacy in interpreting the meaning of Judaism.

Informal estimates suggest that a disproportionate number of newcomers from the West since 1973 have been Orthodox (some believe half or more have been). The number of these immigrants is not significant; there are so few that they barely affect the proportion of religious Jews within the Israeli population. But because they have high status, and because their presence is symbolically important to Israelis, that they are disproportionately Orthodox reinforces the equation of Orthodoxy and authentic Judaism.

The proportion of Orthodox Jews in the United States is much lower than in Israel. About 10 percent of American Jews call themselves Orthodox, or roughly half as many as those who call themselves dati in Israel. No less important is that the Orthodox in the United States enjoy no monopoly on the interpretation of the religious tradition. Orthodox conceptions of Judaism are far less powerful in the United States than in Israel and make far less of an impression on the non-Orthodox. Differences between Israeli and American Jews that appear to be due to differences in religiosity may therefore be attributable not merely to the proportion of traditionally inclined Jews in the total Jewish population but also to Israeli Orthodoxy's greater influence on the non-Orthodox.

It is simplistic to argue that the differences between Israeli and American Jews are attributable to the larger number of Orthodox Jews (or other traditional Jews) in the Israeli Jewish population. How does this explain the major differences between the Israelis who are not dati and the American non-Orthodox, or between the Israeli dati and the American Orthodox? The two religious communities have much in common, but they are also distinguishable from each other by many of the same issues that distinguish non-Orthodox Israeli Jews from their American counterparts (see chapter 6).

According to a more sophisticated version of the argument based on population characteristics, the differences between Israeli and American Jews derive not only from the proportion of American Orthodox and Israeli dati'im, but from the greater influence exerted on the Jewish culture of Israel by Orthodoxy. This argument is subject to the same objection as the preceding one: even if it is sound, the differences do not necessarily stem from social characteristics of the population but are perhaps general cultural differences. The origin of the differences may be tied to the influence of the dati conceptions on Israeli society and their lack of influence on American Judaism, but the extent of their influence may be the result of structural and environmental factors: Israelis may have an elective affinity for ideas that originate in Orthodox conceptions of Judaism by virtue of the structural and environmental conditions under which they live; on the other hand American Jews may reject or ignore these same conceptions and develop others because of the structural and environmental conditions under which they live. There is no way to prove or disprove this assertion, but we can subject it to one kind of test. For it to be an accurate explanation, the following conditions would have to hold: first, American Orthodox and Israeli Orthodox would need to agree substantially on what is normatively Jewish; second, the Israeli non-Orthodox would need to act in greater measure than the American non-Orthodox do in ways that approximated the Orthodox standard; and third, other explanations for why the Israelis behave like the Orthodox would need to be refuted.

It is clear with regard to many of the Judaic conceptions treated earlier that these conditions do not hold. A case can be made for the normative unity of Orthodoxy, but still one can recall the clearly observable differences between American and Israeli Orthodox Jews. In particular, the Israelis' emphasis on the state and land of Israel is understandably more a part of secular Israeli Judaism than it is a part of American Orthodox Judaism. With regard to the behavior of the non-Orthodox Israeli, there are instances where they resemble the Orthodox more closely than non-Orthodox American Jews do, but also a few instances where they are more distant from Orthodox norms than non-Orthodox Americans are. For example, secular Israelis (as distinct from religious or traditional Israelis) are more particularist, coming closer than American Jews to the Orthodox world view. But they are just as ritually inactive as Reform Jews in the United States. Moreover, non-Orthodox Israeli respondents place less emphasis on their ties to the Jewish people than comparable Americans do. In the extent to which they see themselves as part of a worldwide Jewish people, the American non-Orthodox more closely resemble the Orthodox than the Israeli non-Orthodox do.

Finally, there may be another explanation for why the Israeli non-Orthodox in some ways resemble the Orthodox more closely than their American counterparts do: the influence of structure and environment. This explanation strikes us as being at least as plausible as the explanation that Israelis behave the way they do because of Orthodox influence. Alternatively, structure and environment may reinforce the influence of Orthodoxy: for example, the particularism of Israelis can be explained by Jewish social density and the perpetual Arab threat (see below), but it is probably reinforced by the influence that Orthodoxy exerts on the larger society.

Third Explanation: Structure and Environment

A central argument throughout this book is that structural or environmental conditions are important in accounting for differences between Israeli and American constructions or interpretations of Judaism. "World views change as a consequence of material or historical change," according to Clifford Geertz.[2] But as Geertz also notes, this is something of an oversimplification. Can we identify which environmental and structural differences are most influential? We can only speculate, but several differences do appear more important. These can be understood at two levels: as the sum of interrelationships that circumscribe the members of each community, and as the general environment that leads people in different communities to perceive reality in different ways.

First, Israeli Jews live entirely among other Jews. Most Jews in America report that at least one of their closest friends is a Gentile and that most of their neighbors are non-Jewish (Cohen 1984). Further, roughly a third of American Jews who married in recent years took non-Jewish spouses, which means that many American Jews—no one knows exactly how many—have at least one non-Jew in their family. The effect of confining one's social interaction to Jews alone, as opposed to interacting with at least some Gentiles, becomes clear when American Jews in heavily Jewish social networks are compared with Jews in less Jewishly dense networks. Those with more Jewish friends and neighbors report higher levels of ritual observance, more traditional religious identification, lower levels of political liberalism, greater anxiety about anti-Semitism, greater attachment to Israel, and, most notably, greater commitment to Jewish familism (Cohen 1984). The causal order is of course impossible to establish. We can never be sure whether the density of Jewish social networks stimulates these tendencies or whether these tendencies generate greater Jewish exclusivity in the choice of spouses, friends, and neighbors. But it is reasonable to assume that living among strongly Jewish networks stimulates or at least helps maintain phenomena of Jewish identity.

It is reasonable to assume that a dense Jewish network leads to more Jewishly parochial conceptions. This process has a twofold effect: not only do Israelis view the world around them differently from the way American Jews do because as individuals they are exposed to denser or more exclusively Jewish networks, but Jewish density also affects their general culture. The immediate referent of the Israeli is a Jew. Indeed the very term *Jew* is used colloquially as a synonym for "person." For example, an Israeli might say, "I was sitting next to a Jew (*yehudi*) on the bus." The word *Jew* in this phrase has no particular meaning. It simply designates another person. (Yiddish speakers use the word *yid* in the same fashion.) If the person on the bus had been an Arab, the whole context of the story would surely change.

The insensitivity to the presence of Gentiles in Israeli society was obvious in the election campaign of 1988. Israeli Arabs watch Israeli television broadcasts, and according to some surveys they do so more intensely than Jews do. Nevertheless, the election broadcasts sponsored by the various Jewish parties were not only geared exclusively to the Jewish voter but seemed sure to alienate Arab voters. Parties of the right could perhaps afford to be indifferent to the Arab voter; it is more surprising that the Labour party, which was eager to attract Arab voters, ran a television campaign that was extremely offensive to Arabs. Advertisements for Labour showed pictures of Arab babies and contrasted the high Arab birthrate with the low Jewish birthrate. The intention was to justify territorial concessions by Israel that would reduce the number of Arabs living under Israeli control. But the advertisements were so blatantly racist that Labour allowed a response from the Israeli Communist party, which is largely Arab: the Communists showed excerpts from Labour's broadcast and then had an Arab declare, "I studied Bialik [the greatest national Hebrew poet] in school. Does the Labour party really think I can't understand Hebrew?"

We do not believe that Labour intended to appeal to Jewish Israelis who are racists: these voters had better options than Labour (more right-wing options). Nor was Labour indifferent to the Arab voter, for it ran a separate campaign in the Arab sector on which it spent large sums of money. But in preparing campaign material for the general population, Labour simply took it for granted that the general population is composed exclusively of Jews, as most Israelis did until recently. By contrast, American Jews and the Anglo-Jewish press are aware that what they say to Jews—can be heard and read by non-Jews. Even when speaking to general Israeli audiences (which in theory include non-Jews as well as Jews), Israelis speak as though what they say will be heard only by other Jews. In both cases we believe the process is unconscious—an example of how the density of the networks indirectly influences the general culture and the perceptions that are conveyed through it.

Although both Israeli and American Jews feel personally threatened by non-Jews, they agree that the threat of Arabs to Israelis is far more palpable and serious than the anti-Semitism that threatens American Jews. The classic responses of a community under siege and mobilized to defend itself include heightened levels of solidarity and greater antagonism toward outsiders and dissenters. Undoubtedly the Israeli-Arab conflict has contributed to the Israeli Jews' sense of Jewish famil-ism, Jewish particularism, antagonism toward non-Jews and fear of them, and cultural chauvinism. This also operates directly on the per-ceptions of the Israeli Jew and indirectly through Israeli culture.

Israelis confront a physical threat primarily from outside their state, but American Jews feel the insecurity of being a minority living in a multiethnic democracy. They seek to protect themselves by combating prejudice, discrimination, and poverty, and by supporting the strict en-forcement of civil rights, the protection of civil liberties, and the sepa-ration of church and state. All this amounts to the domestic liberal agenda; not only has their concern for Jewish interests made liberals of many American Jews, but their liberalism has become incorporated into their very definition of what a good Jew ought to feel and believe.

In opposition to what may be called the minority consciousness of American Jews, Israeli Jews evince a majoritarian consciousness. As the majority in their society, as the "owners" of the state apparatus, and as a group faced with physical dangers from belligerent outsiders, Israelis have little reason to adopt a liberal political posture akin to that of American Jews. They have even less reason to incorporate the prin-ciples of American liberalism into their definition of what it means to be a "good Jew." And because Israel is both a Jewish state and a Jewish society, Judaism and the protection of Jewish interests are at least in theory an important component of public policy.

American Jews live in a society of religious voluntarism. Not only can people freely choose with which religious body to affiliate and how to interpret their affiliation, but they can freely choose not to affiliate at all. No coercive state power is brought to bear on these choices. One consequence of this freedom is the emergence of non-Orthodox Jewish denominations led by rabbis and lay leaders, who offer alternative models of Jewish authenticity and compete for the allegiance of Ameri-can Jews. America's religious pluralism is also expressed in the univer-sal right of people to interpret their religion as they see fit: intra-religious differences are tolerated as well as interreligious differences. Americans expect that the various religious groupings will generate a variety of interpretations, schools of thought, and institutions. None of these conditions exist in Israel. There are no alternative religious for-mulations to Orthodoxy, no need for different religious groupings to compete for the allegiance of the religious consumer, and no expectations about variant interpretations of the tradition. This helps explain why the nonreligious population is not especially upset by the monopoly on Jewish religious authenticity that the state grants to the Orthodox.

As a voluntarist religious group, American Jews have needed to construct a large infrastructure of voluntary organizations: schools, synagogues, philanthropic organizations, defense agencies, periodicals, hospitals, old age homes, summer camps, and fraternal organizations. Similar agencies exist in Israel, but most are under government auspices or are heavily subsidized by public funds. As a result (or at least as a corollary), American Jews have attached great imortance to voluntarism as an aspect of Jewish life, whereas Israelis are more likely to stress the role of centralized and coercive institutions in protecting Jewish interests, the expression of Judaism, and the articulation of Jewish meaning. This is not simply a matter of each society reinterpreting Judaism to suit its own interests; that is too crude a way of explaining how religious interpretations develop. Rather, world views, religious world views in particular, take shape in a process of interaction between traditional conceptions of reality and changing material conditions. It is true that the world views must conform to reality; but reality is defined through the perception of world views.

To take one example, the threats of the PLO to Israeli security evoke images of the Nazis for many Israelis, and Arafat evokes the image of Hitler.[3] Because these images are linked to the Holocaust, they summon a whole set of associated symbols. These then serve to define the reality of who the Israelis' enemies are (as the Israelis perceive it), of their enemies' irrevocable hatred of the Jew (they have no instrumental goal but seek only the destruction of the Jews, which makes negotiation pointless), of the likely reaction of the nations of the world (they will do nothing to help the Jews), and of the only response to this type of hostility (Jewish or Israeli power). This imagery may be consistent with reality, but perceptions of reality are not simply a function of one's material conditions: because the material conditions may be understood through perceptions of reality, in some respects the perceptions shape the conditions. When the perceptions are legitimated religiously, when they appeal to a religious tradition that affirms the inherent hatred of the Gentile for the Jew ("Esau hates Jacob"), then the perceptions are reinforced and the religious tradition is paradoxically confirmed.

The process is circular. But as Geertz points out, "Religion, considered as a human phenomenon, is always like that. It draws its persuasiveness out of a reality it itself defines" (1971, 39).

American Jews have the same set of images about the nature of the Gentile and the threats to Israeli and Jewish security; all are linked to the symbol of the Holocaust and rooted in the religious tradition. But these images are neither as pervasive as in Israel nor as deeply rooted, and they must compete with other images and models of reality that also derive from Jewish conceptions. The English rabbi Jonathan Sacks, principal of Jews College, has pointed to these other images in his assessment of how English Jews reacted to the criticism that Israel received for its conduct during the war in Lebanon. Sacks distinguishes two types of English Jews on the basis of how they reacted to the criticism (we believe that this distinction is also applicable to Israeli and American Jews). When the British press attacked Israel for its savage treatment of the Arabs, some Jews responded by seeing the established Gentile world as again venting its anti-Semitism, in this case symbolized by Israel. Because the attacks were seen as signaling a campaign of anti-Semitism, they strengthened Jewish solidarity and the belief that a community unfairly attacked by a more powerful enemy is by definition morally superior. Sacks says that this is the typical response of the more traditionally oriented Jew; we suggest that it is the response of the typical Israeli as well.

The second type of response is based in Jewish universalism, according to which Israel has a mandate to be "a light unto the nations," an exemplary people, a "kingdom of priests and a holy people." To the universalist the Gentile cannot be inherently evil or even anti-Semitic; otherwise, there would be no need for the Jew to act in exemplary fashion. If the world press accuses Israeli soldiers of engaging in torture, senseless beating, imprisonment without trial, and wanton destruction of civilian property when they suppress the intifada, then these charges must be considered. And if they are true, Israel does not deserve defense in the name of the Jewish tradition but condemnation. This is how the leaders of the Reform establishment responded to the charges against Israel, at least in the United States.

After the Israeli invasion of Lebanon in 1982, the editor of *Moment,* Leonard Fein, made a similar point, albeit in sermonic fashion:

There are two kinds of Jews in the world.

There is the kind of Jew who detests war and violence, who believes that fighting is not "the Jewish way," who willingly accepts that Jews have their own and higher standards of behavior. And not just that we have them, but that those standards are our lifeblood, are what we are all about.

And there is the kind of Jew who thinks we have been passive long enough, who is convinced that it is time for us to strike back at our enemies, to reject once and for all the role of victim, who willingly accepts that Jews cannot afford to depend on favors, that we must be tough and strong.

And the trouble is, most of us are both kinds of Jew. (1982, 13)

We agree with Fein's last point. Most Jews are both kinds of Jew in Israel, and even more so in the diaspora, among leaders and the masses alike.

Finally, in explaining differences between Israeli and American Jewish conceptions, one must consider the tendency of religion to sacralize life. Religion imposes its meaning on its environment. It draws connections between ultimate reality (God, or in our case the Jewish tradition) and the immediate circumstances in which Jews find themselves (religiously serious Jews in particular). The Jew living in the state of Israel in the land of Israel is likely to impose religious meaning on this environment, especially when this meaning is not artificially contrived but rooted in themes embodied in the Jewish tradition. Similarly, American Jews tend to attribute less meaning to these conceptions and greater meaning to aspects of the tradition that speak to the need for Jew and Gentile to live together in harmony.

This book focuses on the differences between American and Israeli Judaism, but the differences must not be overstated. Jews in both countries observe many of the same holidays, rituals, and ceremonies, respond to many of the same symbols, retell many of the same myths. Having explained why structural or environmental differences have led American and Israeli Jews to different interpretations of Judaism, perhaps it is appropriate to consider why a common basis persists. There are a number of reasons, some particular to the nature of Judaism and the condition of American and Israeli Jews, and some relating to the general nature of religion.

First, Jews in both Israel and the United States (as well as in all other parts of the world) share a belief in their common peoplehood—the myth of common descent, common destiny, and a strong sense of mutual responsibility.

Second, both Israeli and American Jews not only affirm a common past in nominal terms but continue to share much in that past. They share a set of symbols that are reflected in liturgy and ritual. They may not celebrate the symbols in the same manner—some may transform the ritual into ceremony, or the liturgy may be revised and rewritten and the symbolic referents transformed—but the basic symbols remain the same. If one asked a liberal Protestant and a Reform Jew in the United States what their religion demanded of them, there would doubtless be less difference between them than between an American Reform Jew and an Israeli dati who answered the same question. It is fair to say that the Reform Jew's image of God is closer to that of the liberal Protestant than to that of the Orthodox Jew. But the symbols of the Jew and the Christian are different; and symbol is more important than referent in defining a religious tradition.

Third, the differences between Israeli and American Jews are moderated by the unimportance to some Jews of aspects of Judaism that are important to others. Political scientists have noted that the model advanced by civics textbooks of a citizenry that is active, concerned, and issue-oriented would threaten the very fabric of society if it were carried to an extreme. Societies are often held together by the very indifference and muddleheadedness that advocates of good government bemoan. Similarly, the differences between American and Israeli Jews may not result in outright rupture so long as ideologies remain confused and members of one society remain ignorant of the Judaism of the other. Each society interprets the other society and culture in its own terms. The ignorance of American Jews about the Israeli construction of Judaism is not entirely without benefit, but it will become a problem if some American Jews suddenly awake to the differences and have no background for appreciating their basis.

The fourth point is related to the third. Most Israeli Jews are interested in the question of what Judaism means, and almost all have some implicit understanding of the tradition, but not all of them exhibit the same intensity of concern. This is even more true of American Jews. And it is among the least committed that one finds the greatest differences between Israeli and American Jews, with respect to attachment to the land and state of Israel (greater among Israelis) and to worldwide Jewish peoplehood (greater among American Jews). Paradoxically, the integrity of Judaism may be maintained in part by the lack of interest that the least committed have in its reconstruction. In this respect, the integrity of Judaism is threatened as well as reassured by the rise in the status of American Jews, which makes it attractive to be Jewish, and by the ethnic revival and the need of less traditional segments of American Jewry to find a Jewish formulation for their continued attachment to Judaism.

Fifth, Israeli and American Jews are linked not only by their Jewish formulations and conceptions but by their enemies. Each community takes as an article of faith that an attack on one is the same as an attack on the other. The two communities are also linked by ties of family. More than one-third of each community reports having family members in the other. Along with the continuing exchange of visitors and leaders between the two communities, these family ties mean that each side is at least vaguely aware of the new Jewish conceptions emerging in the other, and at least slightly influenced by them. Even more important than the exchange of leaders is the constant exchange of Judaic scholars between Israel and the United States. There are hardly any Judaic scholars in the United States of any prominence who have not spent months or more in Israel over the course of many visits. To the best of our knowledge, there is no Judaic scholar in Israel who has not visited the United States at least once to attend a Judaic conference, give a lecture at an American university, or otherwise take part in the life of the American Jewish community. These are the people who articulate the different conceptions that have emerged in Israel and the United States. Their articulation is critical to the formulation of these different conceptions, because the formulation is to a great extent mediated and transferred by their writings, which are in turn influenced by developments in communities that are not the scholars' own.

Finally, culture in general and religious culture in particular develop slowly. Religious culture is predicated on a belief in ultimate truths; selfconscious change undermines the belief. However far it may have wandered from its immediate traditions, it is not surprising that Judaism in both Israel and the United States should be recognizable as a single religious culture anchored in the same tradition. Leonard Binder, describing Islam from the perspective of Clifford Geertz, notes that it "is not the selfsame phenomenon in every historical context. Historical circumstances contrive to lead human beings to understand the Islamic world view in significantly different ways. . . . Muslims have not been bound by the text of the Qur'an, but neither have they freely interpreted the text in accordance with individual inclination. While Islam has not, in fact, been a single religious phenomenon as some orientalists would have it, neither has it varied so as to defy the tyranny of the disciplined discourse of Anthropology" (Binder 1988, 98).

This is a good characterization of the differences we have found between Israeli and American Judaism. These are noteworthy differences, but there are hardly two Judaisms, certainly not at this stage.

A Final Word

Not only have two Judaisms failed to emerge, but we do not see the possibility of their emergence in the near future. That Israeli Jews and American Jews interpret the tradition in significantly different ways is not only to be expected, but is in many respects healthy. It indicates the liveliness of the tradition, its importance for its adherents, and its transformative capacity under a variety of conditions. It would be foolish to believe that such a development is without dangers. Yet it is not the dangers of divergence that are our immediate concern but the content of the different conceptions. In this final word, we make no effort to conceal our own preferences.

We are unhappy with major aspects of both the Israeli and the American conceptions of Judaism. To simplify grossly our analysis, we find that most Jews in America have reinterpreted the tradition in overly universalist and cosmopolitan terms, leaving too little of what is especially Jewish and faithful to the tradition. Their reinterpretation has yielded too much authority to the surrounding culture and left its adherents with too little of a usable past. On the other hand, the Israeli conception is too particularistic and parochial for our tastes. We have reservations about its fidelity to the tradition, though it is probably more faithful to the tradition than the universalist conception. But we are troubled more by its concern for Jews to the exclusion of non-Jews, and we find tragic its use of the tradition to legitimate discrimination against non-Jews. It is much the poorer for failing to develop non-Orthodox models of Jewish authenticity, for failing to extend adequately the meaning of Judaism to the personal domain, and for failing to engage and adapt for Jewish purposes non-Jewish cultural elements.

Each conception would be enriched by elements of the other. And it is in the hope that our work may have contributed something to this mutual enrichment that we conclude.

Notes

Chapter 1: Introduction

1. For the case of Christianity see Pelikan 1985.

2. David Biale (1986), among others, has maintained that the powerlessness of the Jews between the time the Temple was destroyed and the modern era has been exaggerated. Although this is undoubtedly true, it is perhaps more important that the Jews retained a self-image of powerlessness.

3. See for example Barnai 1987 and Wasserman 1987.

4. For more details see Cohen 1987a.

5. For further details see Zemach 1986.

Chapter 2: Historical Familism

1. An elaborate discussion of the transformation and transvaluation of traditional holidays is found in Liebman and Don-Yehiya 1983a.

2. The *yishuv* was a particularly rich period for the development of Israeli Jewish mythology. The myths of the yishuv have receded in importance in the last few years because of the shift in the center of political gravity in Israel and the growing importance of Sephardi Jews, who refuse to recognize the yishuv as Israel's most heroic period.

3. This is a fairly powerful statement, more demanding of respondents than something like the statement "All Jews are like a family."

4. To our knowledge, there are no comparable survey data on other white American ethnic groups. Our observation on Italian- and Irish-Americans is based in part on conversations with Richard Alba, a sociologist who specializes in survey research of white American ethnic groups.

5. Some indirect evidence in support of the inference that Israelis are less open to non-Orthodox conversions is found in the results of simultaneous surveys conducted in 1983 (Cohen 1983b; Smith 1983, 28).

6. See for example Kimmerling 1985 and Liebman 1985.

7. We defined as deeply committed to Jewish peoplehood those respondents who agreed that they saw the Jewish people as an extension of their families and who said that being Jewish was important to them inasmuch as it provided them with a tie to other Jews.

Chapter 3: Ethnocentrism and Anti-Semitism

1. Tobin (1988) summarizes the evidence that the fear among American Jews of anti-Semitism is pervasive and argues that the fear is justified. He believes that surveys of non-Jews showing sharp declines in anti-Semitism are mistaken. We find Tobin's analysis unconvincing. To us the widespread perception among Jews of anti-Semitism says little about the objective presence of anti-Semitism and more about the character of their Jewish identity.

2. On the debate over whether anti-Semitism was a significant factor in the American past see Sarna 1986.

3. Moore (1986) suggests that the very definition of Jews as outsiders facilitated their Americanization. Further, their condition of being in American society and culture but not of it, a condition shared by Catholics and a few other groups, was one to which mainline Protestants became accustomed.

4. According to the National Conference on Soviet Jewry, New York.

5. We measured perceived anti-Semitism by combining measures of agreement with two statements: "Anti-Semitism in America is currently not a serious problem for American Jews"; and "Virtually all positions of influence in America are open to Jews." The index of Jewish familism combined appropriately scored responses to three statements and one question: "As Jews, we have special moral and ethical obligations"; "As a Jew, I have a special responsibility to help other Jews"; "I see the Jewish people as an extension of my family"; and "How close do you feel to other Jews?" (very close, fairly close, or not very close).

6. The national data are not much different. In our national survey of 1986, 42 percent of American Jews said they would be upset if their child married a non-Jew, but 40 percent said they would not be (18 percent were not sure). Our survey in 1988 had almost identical results: 40 percent said they would be upset if their child married a non-Jew, 47 percent said they would not be. This survey also posed an additional question, in response to which 32 percent of all Jews said they would be upset if their child married a Hasidic Jew: almost as many Jews are disturbed by what they consider excessive traditionalism as are disturbed by potential assimilation. (But it should be noted that these responses do not measure the depth of unhappiness at the two kinds of marriages.)

7. The best discussion of Zionist ideology is found in Arthur Hertzberg's introductory essay to *The Zionist Idea* (1959). The historical context in which Zionist thought evolved is described in Vital 1975.

8. But see also Eisen (1986), who believes that the Zionist transformed the metaphysical meaning of the conception as well.

9. Don-Yehiya cites the Israeli author A. B. Yehoshua, who continues to regard the world in these terms. But his view is the exception.

10. These and similar derogatory comments about Arabs are cited in Sivan 1988, 208.

Chapter 4: Land, State, and Diaspora

1. The English-language literature on the Canaanite movement is sparse. But see Kurzweil 1953, Diamond 1986, and Shavit 1987.

2. See for example Domb 1958 and Seltzer 1970.

3. This quotation and the two that follow are given in English and Hebrew in Liebman 1985.

4. See also Yonathan Shapiro (1977), who makes a similar point.

5. Virtually every history of the state of Israel treats Ben-Gurion and his conception of statism. Works that seem particularly useful in this respect include Elon 1971, Avi Hai 1974, and Teveth 1988.

6. For a description of such a ceremony see Wisse 1987.

7. The statement was issued on 4 November 1985, reprinted in *Davar,* 22 November 1985, and translated in International Center for Peace in the Middle East, *Israel Press Briefs,* no. 40 (December 1985): 17.

8. See Liebman 1973, Cohen 1983c, Woocher 1986, and almost every other book written since 1967 about contemporary American Jews.

9. For a variety of examples see Liebman 1985.

10. *Midstream* is the English-language publication of the Herzl Institute, an agency of the World Zionist Organization.

Chapter 5: Liberalism and Judaism

1. Controlling for education and higher income does diminish the liberalism measured among Jews (Cohen 1984, 1989). Part of the reason why wealthy Jews are more liberal than equally wealthy non-Jews is that wealthy Jews are more likely to have a college and graduate education and to have used this education to achieve their high income. Higher education predisposes them to political liberalism in terms of political and social attitudes, although it bears little relation to partisan identification or voting.

2. Comparable results were obtained in response to a similar question in 1984 (Cohen 1984).

3. The results in 1984 were 54 percent favorable and 12 percent unfavorable (Cohen 1984).

4. The assumption is challenged in Liebman 1973.

5. See Sachar 1976 for summary treatment and references to the vast literature on the topic.

6. See *The Condition and Status of the Arabs in Israel,* a report submitted to the International Center for Peace in the Middle East by Henry Rosenfeld. The report was funded by the Ford Foundation and its major findings were widely quoted in the Israeli press. See for example *Jerusalem Post,* 5 May 1988. See also Semyonov and Lewin-Epstein 1987.

7. One example is the Jewish activity on Shabbat at the National March on Washington for Lesbian and Gay Rights in October 1987, an event reported with sympathy and enthusiasm by Felman (1988); or see Parfitt 1988.

8. On the Zionist thinker Ahad Ha'am, who advocated this interpretation, and his Judaic conceptions see Eisen 1986, 69–80.

9. See for example Julius 1987.

10. The term *Yisrael saba* (Grandfather Israel) invokes the image of the traditional Jew and Judaism. It is employed by religious and secularist spokesmen precisely because it invokes the Jewish tradition in general rather than the religious Jew specifically. Sternhall blames secularist leaders themselves, such as Ya'acov Hazan, the grand old man of the left-wing party Mapam, who attributed the growth of *yeridah* among kibbutz members to their lack of Jewish education.

11. One such effort was the publication in 1987 of a series of essays by Sifryat Poalim, the publishing house of the Kibbutz Artzi of Hashomer Hatzair, the dominant group within Mapam (see chapter 6). In an introduction written on behalf of the publishers, Zvi Ra'anan notes that the essays are presented as part of the movement's "historical-national mission" to "provide spiritual legitimation to Jewish secularism." An article by the editor, Yehoshua Rash, criticizes the philosopher Joseph Agassi's book *Between Religion and Nationality,* which is written in the universalist secularist vein. Rash charges that Agassi refuses to distinguish between clericalism and Jewish culture and abandons any hope for a liberal democratic humane Judaism. He calls Agassi a hellenist and cites with approval Shulamit Har-Even's dictum that religion need not be separated from the state, only from policy formation. See Rash 1987.

12. We asked respondents if they agreed or disagreed with the following statements: "Israel should agree to negotiations with the PLO if this organization recognizes Israel and refrains from terror"; "Palestinians have a right to a state on the West Bank and the Gaza Strip so long as it does not constitute a threat to the State of Israel"; "All things considered, the peace treaty with Egypt was bad for Israel"; and "Israel should not conduct talks with the Jordanians with respect to returning parts of the West Bank even if the Jordanians agree to recognize Israel and express a readiness to sign a peace treaty." A militaristic attitude was defined by agreement with the first two statements and disagreement with the last two.

13. We asked, "Would you be interested in Israel enacting laws that would: Prohibit schools from refusing to accept homosexual teachers? Prohibit the sale of pornography? Prohibit abortions except in special cases?" Nonliberalism was defined as opposition to the first question and support for the second and third.

14. See for example Gleason 1982.

15. See Ash 1984, 3.

Chapter 6: Religious Life

1. Whether this decline has continued is hard to ascertain. On the one hand, the great majority of American Jews are indifferent to core conceptions of halakha. Few

take seriously the notions of a transcendent external authority and of the submission of one's will to this authority. In the absence of such a conception, the celebration of Jewish rites cannot be described in our terminology as ritual behavior. On the other hand, recent surveys attest to stability in levels of observance over the last decade (Cohen 1983c, 1987a, 1988a). But these surveys contain no information about how Jews understand their religious practices, be they ceremonial or ritual in character. Because in our view ritual practice combines performance with a certain consciousness or intent, the available evidence simply cannot determine trends in ritual, quasi-ritual, or ceremonial observance.

2. In accordance with the same principle, an individual can also choose whether he or she will recognize another person as a Jew. In one sense, personalism and voluntarism therefore permit the Orthodox a certain latitude. But the context is so clearly contrary to the assumptions of a religious world view that it can hardly satisfy them. Further, personalism and voluntarism are never extended to their logical extreme: to do so would destroy the Jewish community (or any other) and is therefore inconsistent with other Jewish values discussed in earlier chapters.

3. For example, national samples of Jews and non-Jews were asked in 1988 whether homosexuals should have the same rights as other people. The small number of Orthodox respondents, though clearly less "liberal" on this issue than the non-Orthodox Jews, were just as liberal as secular white Christians and far more so than religious white Protestants or Catholics. Although 84 percent of all Jews supported the rights of homosexuals, 66 percent of the Orthodox did: this is similar to the percentage of nonreligious Christians who supported homosexual rights, slightly higher than that of Catholics who attended Mass regularly, and a good deal higher than the 38 percent of Protestants who called themselves "born again."

4. Many of these patterns are also to be found among non-Jews. See for example Dinges 1987, esp. 143–44, on the reasons for opposition to change in the liturgy (in our terms, movement from ritual to ceremonialism).

5. We omitted from the analysis American Jews who defined themselves as "just Jewish" (nondenominational), for it is among these Jews that one finds the largest number of Jews in mixed marriages and unaffiliated Jews, who one might argue are marginal to American Jewish society. The rates of practice among nondenominational Jews are indeed somewhat lower than those of Reform Jews, though not much lower. To demonstrate more conclusively that American Jews are less traditional than Israeli Jews, who by definition are part of Israeli society, we compared Israeli secularists with American Reform Jews.

6. For a description of the early development of secular Zionism and its ambivalence toward the Jewish tradition see Luz 1988.

7. This discussion relies on the detailed consideration of the development of religious tendencies in Israeli public life found in Liebman and Don-Yehiya 1983a and 1983b.

8. In our discussion we rely more heavily on ideological affirmations and elitist formulations than we did in our discussion of Jewish religious life in the United States. The primary reason is that in Israel, where virtually everything within the

culture is of Jewish relevance, people of all shades of opinion express themselves on Jewish matters, and it is fairly simple to select statements that speak directly to issues of concern to our study. In America those who address these concerns represent a very select category of Jew, and may in addition be sensitive to what the non-Jew will hear. It stands to reason that the full gamut of conceptions concerning what it means to be a Jew will not find explicit ideological expression in the United States. This is especially true for conceptions that are farthest removed from the tradition and that may have the least legitimacy in ideological terms. These expressions must be inferred from a variety of sources, as we attempted to do in our section on the religious life of American Jews.

The same point can be made somewhat differently. The gap between the conceptions to which Jews claim fealty and their actual behavior or beliefs is far wider in the United States than in Israel. This is an important phenomenon that deserves more extensive treatment. It helps to explain our confidence that the ideological affirmations of the Israeli cultural elite more accurately measure the conceptions of the average Israeli than the formulations of the Jewish American elites measure the conceptions of the average American Jew.

9. *Haredi* (plural *haredim*) literally means pietist and refers to the ultrareligious (estimated at around 5 percent of Israeli Jews), who are hostile to modernity and deny that any special sanctity should be accorded to the state of Israel. Some haredim are overtly hostile to the state: they either vote for the more extreme religious parties or refuse to vote at all.

10. For a typology of religious Jewry in Israel see Deshen 1978a and 1987b. On the haredim see Friedman 1986. On religious Zionists see Fishman 1982. For the distinctions between types of religious Jews and their attitudes toward the state of Israel see Liebman and Don-Yehiya 1985, 57–78.

11. Even among those American Orthodox who have not embraced universalism in their interpretation of the tradition, and these include the majority of the Orthodox elite, the principle is not explicitly denied. It is rejected only by inference.

12. On the differences between Conservative and Reform Jews in Israel with respect to their political allies see Tabory (forthcoming).

13. See for example the journal *Israeli Democracy,* published by the Institute for Diaspora-Israeli Relations of Tel-Aviv University.

14. This observation does not apply to the masses of Jews who came from North Africa. Large numbers of Sephardi Jews, who constitute the bulk of the traditional (masorati) segment of the population, did find Judaism, Jewish ritual and belief, and the charisma of their religious leaders relevant to their private lives, personal hopes, and individual struggles. This community is however in rapid decline. The most significant observation to be made about Sephardi Jewry is that as its religious elite has confronted the challenge of modernity it has resorted to the same instruments as Ashkenazi Jewry did two centuries ago: scripturalism, substituting the authority of the rabbinical leader for that of the father and the family, greater stringency in the interpretation of Jewish law, and greater stress on ritualism and less on

ethicism. But the leader's charisma has not declined in importance: in more rigorously religious circles it too has been strengthened.

15. As might be expected, the resistance on the part of some secularists to religion and religious rituals leaves them with a void that they must fill. Even if they define themselves as nonreligious, most people have a need to celebrate events in the life cycle and to find a place in their lives for spiritual concerns. The early kibbutzim devoted great effort to this enterprise. The best description and discussion are found in Lilker 1982. Urban secularists have by now developed their own rituals, as those who have attended secular weddings and even secular bar mitzvahs attest. Other secular institutions that provide alternative sources of meaning are no different in Israel from what they are in other Western societies. This subject merits more intensive study.

Chapter 7: Are Two Judaisms Emerging?

1. See Max Wiener's classic study *Judische Religion in Zeitalter der Emanzipation,* translated into Hebrew and published by Mossad Bialik in 1974 under the title *Hadat Hayehudit Bitkufat Haemantzipatzia.* Also see Meyer 1988.

2. As cited in Binder 1988.

3. On the specific use of this imagery see Liebman and Don-Yehiya 1983a. On the first day of Prime Minister Shamir's visit to the United States in April 1989, a member of his party gave an informal press briefing. According to *Ma'ariv* (5 April 1989) he said: "Nothing will convince Shamir to change his mind about the PLO. From his point of view Hitler is the symbol of the Holocaust of the past and Arafat symbolizes the Holocaust of the future."

References

Alba, Richard D., and Gwen Moore. 1982. "Ethnicity in the American Elite." *American Sociological Review* 47, no. 3 (June): 373–83.

Alexander, Bobby C. 1987. "Ceremony." *The Encyclopedia of Religion,* 3: 179–83. New York: Macmillan.

Amitay, Yossi. 1988. *The United Workers' Party (Mapam), 1948–1954.* Tel-Aviv: Tcherikover. In Hebrew.

Anderson, Anne. 1987. "My Support Is Real—So Are My Memories." *Sh'ma* 17 (23 January): 42–44.

Appelfeld, Aharon. 1987. Interview. *Jerusalem Post Magazine,* 27 November, p. 4.

Ash, Timothy. 1984. Review of Michael Howard, *War and the Liberal Conscience. New York Review of Books,* 22 November, p. 3.

Avi-Hai, Avraham. 1974. *Ben-Gurion: State Builder.* New York: John Wiley and Sons.

Avruch, Kevin. 1981. *American Immigrants in Israel: Social Identities and Change.* Chicago: University of Chicago Press.

Axelrod, Morris, Floyd Fowler, and Arnold Gurin. 1967. *A Community Survey for Long-Range Planning: A Study of the Jewish Population of Greater Boston.* Boston: Combined Jewish Philanthropies of Greater Boston.

Barnai, Jacob. 1987. "Trends in the Historiography of the Medieval and Early Modern Period of the Jewish Community in Eretz-Israel." *Cathedra* 42 (January): 87–120.

Ben-Meir, Yehudah, and Peri Kedem. 1979. "A Measure of Religiosity for the Jewish Population of Israel." *Megamot* 24: 353–62. In Hebrew.

Biale, David. 1986. *Power and Powerlessness in Jewish History.* New York: Schocken.

Binder, Leonard. 1988. *Islamic Liberalism: A Critique of Development Ideologies.* Chicago: University of Chicago Press.

Breakstone, David. 1988. "Woeful Neglect of the Vital Centre." *Jerusalem Post,* 29 July, p. 11.

Clark, Wayne. 1949. "Portrait of the Mythical Gentile." *Commentary* 7, no. 6 (June): 546–49.

Cohen, Steven M. 1982. "What American Jews Believe." *Moment* (July): 23–27.

———. 1983a. "The 1981–2 National Survey of American Jews." *American Jewish Year Book,* 89–110. New York: American Jewish Committee.

———. 1983b. "Attitudes of American Jews toward Israel and Israelis." New York: American Jewish Committee. Offset.

————. 1983c. *American Modernity and Jewish Identity.* New York and London: Methuen.

————. 1984. "The Political Attitudes of American Jews." New York: American Jewish Committee. Offset.

————. 1985. "From Romantic Idealists to Loving Realists: The Changing Place of Israel in the Consciousness of American Jews." In *Survey of Jewish Affairs 1985,* ed. William Frankel, 169–82. London: Associated University Presses.

————. 1986. "Outreach to the Marginally Affiliated: Evidence and Implications for Policymakers in Jewish Education." *Journal of Jewish Communal Service* 62, no. 2 (Winter): 147–57.

————. 1987a. "Ties and Tensions: The 1986 Survey of American Jewish Attitudes toward Israel and Israelis." New York: American Jewish Committee. Offset.

————. 1987b. "Reason for Optimism." In *The Quality of American Jewish Life: Two Views,* by Steven M. Cohen and Charles Liebman. New York: American Jewish Committee.

————. 1988a. *American Assimilation or Jewish Revival?* Bloomington: Indiana University Press.

————. 1988b. "Are Reform Jews Abandoning Israel?" *Reform Judaism* (Spring), 4–5, 24.

————. 1988c. "Unity and Polarization in Judaism Today: The Attitudes of American and Israeli Jews." New York: American Jewish Committee. Offset.

————. 1989. *The Political Attitudes of American Jews, 1988: A National Survey in Comparative Perspective.* New York: American Jewish Committee.

Cohen, Steven M., and Leonard J. Fein. 1985. "From Integration to Survival: American Jewish Anxieties in Transition." *Annals of the American Academy of Political and Social Science,* no. 480 (July): 75–88.

Cohen, Steven M., and Paul Ritterband. 1988. "The Utilization of Jewish Communal Services in Queens and Long Island." New York: United Jewish Appeal/ Federation of Jewish Philanthropies. Manuscript.

Cohen, Steven, and Susan Wall. 1987. "Recruiting and Retaining Senior Personnel in Jewish Education: A Focus Group Study in North America." Jerusalem: Jewish Education Committee of the Jewish Agency. Photocopied.

Commentary. 1980. "Liberalism." Special issue.

Congregation B'nai Jacob. N.d. *Purim Service.* Woodbridge, Conn.: Congregation B'nai Jacob. Mimeographed.

Conner, Walker. 1986. "The Impact of Homelands upon Diasporas." In *Modern Diasporas in International Politics,* ed. Gabriel Sheffer, 16–45. London: Croom and Helm.

Cuddihy, John Murray. 1974. *The Ordeal of Civility: Freud, Marx, Lévi-Strauss and the Jewish Struggle with Modernity.* New York: Basic Books.

Dan, Joseph. 1987. "Hasidism." *Encyclopedia of Religion,* 6: 203–11. New York: Macmillan.

Danzger, Herbert. 1989. *Returning to Tradition.* New Haven: Yale University Press.

Dashefsky, Arnold. 1989. "Determinants of Jewish Charitable Giving: Incentives and Barriers." In *American Pluralism and the Jewish Community,* ed. Seymour Martin Lipset. New Brunswick, N.J.: Transaction.

Dawidowicz, Lucy. 1985. "Politics, the Jews and the '84 Election." *Commentary,* February, 25–30.

Dekro, Jeffrey. 1984. "Prayer and Anger." *Response,* no. 46 (Spring): 63–77.

Deshen, Shlomo. 1978a. "Israeli Judaism: Introduction to the Major Patterns." *International Journal of Middle Eastern Studies* 9: 141–69.

———. 1978b. "Two Trends in Israeli Orthodoxy." *Judaism* 27 (Autumn): 397–409.

Diamond, James. 1986. *Homeland or Holy Land? The "Canaanite Critique of Israel."* Bloomington: Indiana University Press.

Dinges, William. 1987. "Ritual Conflict as Social Conflict: Liturgical Reform in the Roman Catholic Church." *Sociological Analysis* 48 (Summer): 138–57.

Domb, Yerachmiel. 1958. *The Transformation.* London: Hamadpis.

Don-Yehiya, Eliezer. 1988. "Festivals and Political Culture: Independence-Day Celebrations." *Jerusalem Quarterly,* no. 45 (Winter): 61–84.

———. Forthcoming. "Galut in Zionist Ideology and Israeli Society." In *State and Diaspora: The State of Israel and Jewish Diaspora: Ideological and Political Perspectives,* ed. Eliezer Don-Yehiya. Ramat Gan: Bar-Ilan University Press.

Douglas, Mary. 1973. *Natural Symbols.* New York: Random House, Vintage.

Eisen, Arnold. 1983. *The Chosen People in America.* Bloomington: Indiana University Press.

———. 1986. *Galut: Modern Jewish Reflection on Homelessness and Homecoming.* Bloomington: Indiana University Press.

———. 1988. "Shall We Resort to One-Issue Voting?" *Sh'ma* 18, no. 360 (28 October): 154–55.

Elazar, Daniel J., ed. 1983. *Kinship and Consent: The Jewish Political Tradition and Its Contemporary Uses.* Washington: University Press of America.

Elon, Amos. 1971. *The Israelis: Founders and Sons.* New York: Holt, Rinehart and Winston.

Endelman, Todd M. 1986. "Comparative Perspectives on Modern Anti-Semitism in the West." In *History and Hate: The Dimensions of Anti-Semitism,* ed. David Berger. Philadelphia: Jewish Publication Society.

Fein, Leonard J. 1982. "Days of Awe." *Moment* (September), 13–18.

———. 1988. *Where Are We? The Inner Life of America's Jews.* New York: Harper and Row.

Felman, Jyl Lynn. 1988. "For Love and for Life, We're Not Going Back." *Tikkun* 3 (January–February): 64–65.

Fishman, Aryeh. 1982. "'Torah and Labor': The Radicalization of Religion within a National Framework." *Studies in Zionism,* no. 6 (Autumn): 255–71.

Friedman, Menachem. 1986. "Haredim Confront the Modern City." In *Studies in Contemporary Jewry,* ed. Peter Y. Medding, 2: 74–96. Bloomington: Indiana University Press.

————. 1987. "Life Tradition and Book Tradition in the Development of Ultra-Orthodox Judaism." In *Judaism Viewed from Within and from Without,* ed. Harvey Goldberg, 235–55. Albany: State University of New York Press.

Fuchs, Lawrence. 1988. "Old Values and the Present Election." *Sh'ma* 18, no. 360 (28 October): 159–60.

Furman, Frida Kerner. 1987. *Beyond Yiddishkeit: The Struggle for Jewish Identity in a Reform Synagogue.* Albany: State University of New York Press.

Gallup Poll/Phi Delta Kappa. 1988. Survey of 10–13 April 1987. Reported in *PRRC Emerging Trends* 10, no. 1 (January).

Geertz, Clifford. 1971. *Islam Observed.* Chicago: University of Chicago Press, Phoenix.

————. 1973. "Religion as a Cultural System." In *The Interpretation of Cultures.* New York: Basic Books.

Gerber, Jane. 1986. "Anti-Semitism and the Muslim World." In *History and Hate: The Dimension of Anti-Semitism,* ed. David Berger, 73–93. Philadelphia: Jewish Publication Society.

Gleason, Philip. 1982. "American Identity and Americanization." In *Dimensions of Ethnicity.* A Series of Selections from the Harvard Encyclopedia of American Ethic Groups. Cambridge: Harvard University Press.

Greilsammer, Ilan. 1988. "Cohabitation: French and Israeli Style." *Jerusalem Quarterly,* no. 48 (Autumn).

Gruzen, Lee F. 1987. *Raising Your Jewish Christian Child: Wise Choices for Interfaith Parents.* New York: Dodd, Mead.

Haber, Sharon. 1987. "Gaining a Faith but Not Losing My Family." *Sh'ma* 17, no. 329 (6 February): 49–51.

Halpern, Ben. 1987. "Reactions to Anti-Semitism in Modern Jewish History." In *Living with Anti-Semitism,* ed. Jehuda Reinharz, 3–15. Hanover, N.H.: University Press of New England.

Hammond, Phillip E. 1988. "Religion and the Persistence of Identity." *Journal for the Scientific Study of Religion* 27 (March): 1–11.

Harlow, Jules, ed. 1985. *Siddur Sim Shalom: A Prayerbook for Shabbat Festivals and Weekdays.* New York: Rabbinical Assembly/United Synagogue of America.

Heilman, Samuel C., and Steven M. Cohen. 1986. "Ritual Variation among Modern Orthodox Jews in the United States." *Studies in Contemporary Jewry,* 2: 164–87. Bloomington: Indiana University Press.

————. 1989. *Cosmopolitans and Parochials: The Many Faces of Orthodox Jews in America.* Chicago: University of Chicago Press.

Herman, Simon. 1988. *Jewish Identity: A Social Psychological Perspective.* New ed. New Brunswick, N.J.: Transaction.

Hertzberg, Arthur. 1959. *The Zionist Idea.* Garden City, N.Y.: Doubleday.

Himmelfarb, Milton. 1981. "Are Jews Becoming Republican?" *Commentary* (August): 27–31.

Israel, Sherry. 1987. *Boston's Jewish Community: The 1985 CJP Demographic Study.* Boston: Combined Jewish Philanthropies of Greater Boston.

Israel Social Science Research. 1987. "Women in Israel." Vol. 5, nos. 1–2.

Jewish Theological Seminary. 1988. *Emet V'Emunah: Statement of Principles of Conservative Judaism.* New York: Jewish Theological Seminary.

Julius, Raphael. 1987. "Secularism Fighting for Its Life." *Kivunim,* no. 37 (November): 159–64. In Hebrew.

Kadushin, Charles. 1974. *The American Intellectual Elite.* Boston: Little, Brown.

Katz, Jacob. 1961. *Exclusiveness and Tolerance: Jewish-Gentile Relations in Medieval and Modern Times.* New York: Schocken.

———. 1979. "The Historical Image of Rabbi Zvi Hirsch Kalischer." In *Jewish Nationalism: Essays and Studies,* 285–307. Jerusalem: Zionist Library of the World Zionist Organization. In Hebrew.

Katz, Shaul. 1985. "The Israeli-Teacher Guide: The Emergence and Perpetuation of a Role." *Annals of Tourism Research* 12: 49–72.

Kimmerling, Baruch. 1985. "Between the Primordial and the Civil Definitions of the Collective Identity: *Eretz Israel* or the State of Israel?" In *Comparative Social Dynamics: Essays in Honor of S. N. Eisenstadt,* ed. Erik Cohen, Moshe Lissak, and Uri Almagor, 262–83. Boulder: Westview.

Kohn, Hans. 1944. *The Idea of Nationalism.* New York: Collier.

Kook, Zvi Yehudah. 1978. "The Sanctity of the Holy People in the Holy Land." In *Religious Zionism and the State,* ed. Yosef Tirosh, 140–46. Jerusalem: World Zionist Organization. In Hebrew.

Kovner, Abba. 1987. "Controversy: A Foundation Stone in Israeli Culture." In *Regard and Revere, Renew without Fear: The Secular Jew and His Heritage,* ed. Yehoshua Rash. Tel-Aviv: Sifriat Poalim. In Hebrew.

Kristol, Irving. 1984. "The Political Dilemma of American Jews." *Commentary* (July): 23–29.

Kurzweil, Baruch. 1953. "The New 'Canaanites' in Israel." *Judaism* 2 (January): 3–15.

Levinson, Jon D. 1985. *Jewish Perspectives: The Universal Horizon of Biblical Particularism.* New York: American Jewish Committee.

Lewellen, Ted C. 1983. *Political Anthropology.* South Hadley, Mass.: Bergin and Garvey.

Liebman, Charles S. 1973. *The Ambivalent American Jew.* Philadelphia: Jewish Publication Society.

———. 1981. "American Jews and the 'Modern Mind.'" *Midstream* 27 (April): 8–12.

———. 1983a. "Attitudes toward Jewish-Gentile Relations in the Jewish Tradition and Contemporary Israel." Cape Town: Kaplan Centre for Jewish Studies and Research, University of Cape Town. Pamphlet.

———. 1983b. "Extremism as a Religious Norm." *Journal for the Scientific Study of Religion* 22 (March): 75–86.

———. 1985. "Jewish Ultra-Nationalism in Israel: Converging Strands." In *Survey of Jewish Affairs, 1985,* ed. William Frankel, 28–50. London: Associated University Presses.

———. 1988. *Deceptive Images: Toward the Transformation of American Judaism.* New Brunswick, N.J.: Transaction.

———. 1990. "Ritual, Ceremony and the Reconstruction of Judaism in the United States." *Studies in Contemporary Jewry: An Annual.* Vol. 6, ed. Ezra Mendelson. New York: Oxford University Press. Forthcoming.

Liebman, Charles S., and Eliezer Don-Yehiya. 1983a. *Civil Religion in Israel: Traditional Judaism and Political Culture in the Jewish State.* Berkeley: University of California Press.

———. 1983b. "The Dilemma of Reconciling Traditional Culture and Political Needs: Civil Religion in Israel." *Comparative Politics* 16: 53–66.

———. 1985. *Religion and Politics in Israel.* Bloomington: Indiana University Press.

Lilker, Shalom. 1982. *Kibbutz Judaism: A New Tradition in the Making.* New York: Herzl.

Los Angeles Times. 1988. "Los Angeles Times Poll Number 149: Israel and the Palestinians." 25–31 March, 4–7 April.

Luz, Ehud. 1987. "Spiritual and Anti-Spiritual Trends in Zionism." *Jewish Spirituality: From the Sixteenth-Century Revival to the Present.* New York: Crossroad.

———. *Parallels Meet.* 1988. Philadelphia: Jewish Publication Society.

Matthiessen, Peter. 1984. *Indian Country.* New York: Viking.

Mayer, Egon, and Amy Avgar. 1987. *Conversion among the Intermarried.* New York: American Jewish Committee.

Medding, Peter Y. 1987. "Segmented Ethnicity and the New Jewish Politics." In *Studies in Contemporary Jewry.* Vol. 3, ed. Ezra Mendelsohn. New York and Oxford: Oxford University Press.

Meyer, Michael A. 1986. "Comments on the Last Chapter of Y. H. Yerushalmi's *Zakhor.*" *AJS Newsletter,* no. 36 (Autumn): 14–16.

———. 1988. *Response to Modernity: A History of the Reform Movement in Judaism.* New York and Oxford: Oxford University Press.

Milson, Menahem. 1986. "How Not to Occupy the West Bank." *Commentary* 81 (April): 15–22.

Moore, R. Laurence. 1986. *Religious Outsiders and the Making of Americans.* New York: Oxford University Press.

Moses, Zvi. 1987. "On Behalf of the Individual Ideal." *Nekudah,* no. 116 (December): 25.

National Jewish Community Relations Advisory Council. 1987. *Joint Program Plan for Jewish Community Relations, 1987–88.* New York: National Jewish Community Relations Advisory Council.

Nehorai, Michael. 1987. "Education outside the Boundaries." *Emdah,* no. 18 (August): 6.

Parfitt, Tudor. 1988. "A Gay Tribe of Israel." *Present Tense* 15 (March–April): 40–43.

Pelikan, Jaroslav. 1985. *Jesus through the Centuries: His Place in the History of Culture.* New Haven: Yale University Press.

Prager, Dennis, and Joseph Telushkin. 1983. *Why the Jews? The Reason for Anti-Semitism.* New York: Simon and Schuster.

Present Tense 14 (July–August 1987), inside front cover.

"Pride, Prejudice, and Politics: Jewish Jews on the American Left." *Response* 43 (Autumn 1982): 3–40.

Rash, Yehoshua. 1987. "Left, Right, Religion: The Political View." In *Regard and Revere, Renew without Fear: The Secular Jew and His Heritage,* 194–209. Tel-Aviv: Sifriat Poalim. In Hebrew.

Rash, Yehoshua, ed. 1987. *Regard and Revere, Renew without Fear: The Secular Jew and His Heritage.* Tel-Aviv: Sifriat Poalim. In Hebrew.

Richards, Amy. 1987. "I Wish to Be a Jew: My Husband Doesn't." *Sh'ma* 17, no. 326 (23 January): 41.

Roiphe, Anne. 1981. *Generation without Memory.* New York: Linden Press/ Simon and Schuster.

Rosenberg, Yehoshua. 1987. "Exile in Jerusalem." *Emdah* (June): 9–12.

Rosman, M. J. 1986. "Jewish Perceptions of Insecurity and Powerlessness in 16th–18th Century Poland." *Polin* 1: 19–27.

Sachar, Howard. 1976. *A History of Israel.* New York: Alfred A. Knopf.

Sacks, Jonathan. Forthcoming. "Religious and National Identity: British Jewry and the State of Israel." In *State and Diaspora,* ed. Eliezer Don-Yehiya. Ramat-Gan: Bar-Ilan University Press.

Sarna, Jonathan D. 1986. "American Anti-Semitism." In *History and Hate: The Dimensions of Anti-Semitism,* ed. David Berger, 115–28. Philadelphia: Jewish Publication Society.

Sandel, Michael J. 1988. "Democrats and Community: A Public Philosophy for American Liberalism." *New Republic,* 22 February, pp. 20–23.

Schneider, William. 1985. "The Jewish Vote in 1984: Elements in a Controversy." *Public Opinion,* December–January, pp. 18 ff.

Schulweis, Harold M. 1988. "Jackson, Jews, and Justice." *Sh'ma* 18, no. 359 (14 October): 148–49.

Schweid, Eliezer. 1985. *The Land of Israel.* Rutherford, N.J.: Associated University Presses.

———. 1987. "Land of Israel." In *Contemporary Jewish Religious Thought,* ed. Arthur Cohen and Paul Mendes-Flohr, 535–41. New York: Charles Scribner's Sons.

———. 1988. "Relations between Religious and Secular Jews in the State of Israel: An Academic Appraisal." Trans. in *L'Eylah,* March, pp. 11–15.

Seltzer, Michael, ed. 1970. *Zionism Reconsidered.* New York: Macmillan.

Semyonov, Moshe, and Noah Lewin-Epstein. 1987. *Hewers of Wood and Drawers of Water.* Ithaca: ILR Press, Cornell University.

Shamir, Michal, and John Sullivan. 1983. "The Political Context of Tolerance: The United States and Israel." *American Political Science Review* 77: 911–28.

Shapiro, Anita. 1984. *Berl: The Biography of a Socialist Zionist.* London: Cambridge University Press.

Shapiro, Yonathan. 1977. *Democracy in Israel.* Tel-Aviv: Massada. In Hebrew.

Shavit, Ya'acov. 1987. *The New Hebrew Nation: An Israeli Heresy and Fantasy.* London: Frank Cass.

Shorris, Earl, 1982. *Jews without Mercy: A Lament.* Garden City, N.Y.: Anchor.

Shprinzak, Ehud. 1986. *Every Man Whatsoever Is Right in His Own Eyes: Illegalism in Israeli Society.* Tel-Aviv: Sifriat Poalim. In Hebrew.

Singer, David. 1987. "American Jews as Voters: The 1986 Elections." New York: American Jewish Committee. Pamphlet.

Sivan, Emmanuel. 1988. *Arab Political Myths.* Tel-Aviv: Am Oved. In Hebrew.

Sklare, Marshall, and Joseph Greenblum. 1979. *Jewish Identity on the Suburban Frontier.* 2d ed.

Skowronek, Stephen. 1982. *Building a New American State.* Cambridge: Cambridge University Press.

Smith, Anthony D. 1983. "Ethnic Identity and World Order." *Millennium* 12 (April): 149–61.

Smith, Hanoch. 1983. "Attitudes of Israelis towards America and American Jews." New York: American Jewish Committee, 1983. Offset.

Smooha, Sammy. 1989. *Arabs and Jews in Israel.* Volume 1, *Conflicting and Shared Attitudes in a Divided Society.* Boulder: Westview.

Snyder, Charles. 1958. "Culture and Jewish Sobriety: The Ingroup-Outgroup Factor." In *The Jews: Social Patterns of an American Group,* ed. Marshall Sklare, 560–94. New York: Free Press.

Sternhall, Ze'ev. 1987. "The Battle for Intellectual Control." *Politika,* no. 18 (December): 2–5. In Hebrew.

Strassman, Gavriel. 1985. "Embarrassing Topics." *Ma'ariv,* 10 February, p. 10.

Sullivan, John, Michal Shamir, Patrick Walsh, and Nigel Roberts. 1985. *Political Tolerance in Context: Support for Unpopular Minorities in Israel, New Zealand and the United States.* Boulder: Westview.

Supplementary Prayer Book Guardian of Israel. 1986. Los Angeles: United Synagogue of America, Pacific Southwest Region.

Tabory, Ephraim. Forthcoming. "The Identity Dilemma of Non-Orthodox Religious Movements: Reform and Conservative Judaism in Israel."

Tal, Uriel. 1986. "Contemporary Hermeneutics and Self-Views on the Relationship between State and Land." In *The Land of Israel: Jewish Perspectives,* ed. Lawrence Hoffman. Notre Dame: University of Notre Dame Press.

Temple Beth Ami. N.d. *Hevrat Mitzvot Program.* Reseda, Calif.: Temple Beth Ami. Mimeographed.

Teveth, Shabtai. 1988. *Ben-Gurion: The Burning Ground, 1886–1948.* Boston: Houghton Mifflin.

Tivnan, Edward. 1987. *The Lobby: Jewish Political Power and American Foreign Policy.* New York: Simon and Schuster.

Tobin, Gary. 1988. *Jewish Perceptions of Anti-Semitism.* New York: Plenum.

Tobin, Gary, and Julie Lipsman. 1984. "A Compendium of Jewish Demographic Studies." In *Perspectives in Jewish Population Research,* ed. Steven M. Cohen, Jonathan Woocher, and Bruce Phillips. Boulder: Westview.

Union for Traditional Conservative Judaism. 1986. *Tomeikh kaHalakhah: Response of the Panel of Halakhic Inquiry.* New York: Union for Traditional Conservative Judaism.

Vital, David. 1975. *The Origins of Zionism.* Oxford: Oxford University Press.

Vorspan, Albert. 1983. "Reform Judaism and Social Action." New York: Union of American Hebrew Congregations.

Walzer, Michael. 1986. "Is Liberalism (Still) Good for the Jews?" *Moment,* March, pp. 13–16.

Wasserman, Henry. 1987. "Notes on Jewish Historiography in the State of Israel in Light of H. H. Ben-Sasson: Continuity and Change." *Kivunim,* no. 34 (February): 101–15. In Hebrew.

Wertheimer, Jack. 1989. "Recent Trends in American Judaism." *American Jewish Year Book* 89: 63–162.

Wiener, Max. 1974. *Judische Religion in Zeitalter der Emanzipation.* Hebrew trans. as *Hadat Hayehudit Bitkufat Haemantzipatzia.* Jerusalem: Mossad Bialik.

Williamsburg Charter Foundation. 1988. *The Williamsburg Charter Survey on Religion and Public Life.* Washington: Williamsburg Charter Foundation.

Wisse, Ruth. 1987. "Israel: A House Divided." *Commentary* 84 (September): 33–38.

Woocher, Jonathan. 1986. *Sacred Survival.* Bloomington: Indiana University Press.

Yehoshua, Abraham B. 1984. *Between Right and Right.* Jerusalem: Schocken. In Hebrew.

Yerushalmi, Yosef. 1982. *Zakhor.* Seattle: University of Washington Press.

Zborowski, Mark, and Elizabeth Herzog. 1952. *Life Is with People: The Culture of the Shtetl.* New York: Schocken.

Zemach, Mina. 1987. "Israelis' Attitudes towards Judaism, American Jewry, Zionism and the Israel-Arab Conflict: The 1986 Survey of Israeli Jews." New York: American Jewish Committee.

Zeusse, Evan M. 1987. "Ritual." *The Encyclopedia of Religion,* 12: 405–22. New York: Macmillan.

Index

Abortion, 121
Abraham, 60
Abram, Morris, 105
Abrams, Elliot, 101
Adoption, 147
Affirmative action, 100, 104
Affluence, 162, 179*n*1
Agassi, Joseph, 151, 180*n*11
Aliyah. See Resettlement
Am Yisrael, 74
American Civil Liberties Union, 106
American-Israel Public Affairs
  Committee, 41
American Jewish Committee, 11, 43
American Jewish Congress, 43
American Jews, 1; social status of,
  6–7; pragmatism of, 9–10; as
  minority, 30; commitment to Israel,
  84–88. *See also* Anti-Semitism;
  Judaism; Liberalism; *and other
  individual concepts*
Anti-Defamation League, 43
Anti-Semitism, 6, 31–34, 167;
  American Jews' perceptions
  of, 7, 40–45, 178*n*2; in Jewish
  consciousness, 36–40; private
  function of, 45–50; changing
  attitudes, 54–57; Israeli Jews'
  perceptions of, 58–59, 61–62;
  American and Israeli views
  compared, 63–66
Appelfeld, Aharon, 31, 120
Arab dispute, 147
Arabs, 23, 24, 61; Israeli view of, 62,
  65, 70–71; civil rights of, 79–81,
  155; terrorism against, 82; Israeli
  indifference to, 115–16, 121,
  167–70; threat of, 165

Arafat, Yasser, 169
Archaeology, 69, 144
Arian, Asher, 62
Ascription, 17
Ashkenazi Jews, 3, 17; view of statism,
  80, 81, 83; view of galut, 92;
  attitudes of, 153–54, 161, 162–63;
  response to modernity, 182*n*4
Assimilation, 1, 55, 56, 133; Israeli
  view of, 89, 91–92, 96
Authoritarianism, 154–55
Avruch, Kevin, 21, 22

Bar Kokhba revolt, 68
Bar mitzvah, 124
Baron, Salo, 31
Bat mitzvah, 124
Bathing. *See Mikvah*
Begin, Menachem, 61, 83–84
Ben-Ari, Uri, 90
Ben Bezalel, Rabbi Judah Loew, 59
Ben-Gurion, David, 16, 29, 58, 81, 82
Between Religion and Nationality
  (Agassi), 180*n*11
Binder, Leonard, 174
Blacks, 16, 44, 48, 134; Jewish support
  for, 100, 102, 103–04
Blau, Rav Amram, 24–25
Brandeis, Louis, 93
British mandate, 16, 76
Burg, Joseph, 24
Bush, George, 101–02

Camp David accords, 16
Canaanite movement, 70–71
Canadian Jews, 161–62
Catholics, 48
Censorship, 116

Ceremony, 124–27, 133, 159

Change, notion of, 3, 4, 5

Chauvinism, 148, 168

"Chosen people" concept, 26–28, 36–37

Christian Right, 107–08

Christianity, Jewish views of, 37–38, 39, 42, 43, 46

Christmas, 15, 47

"Christmas Comes to a Jewish Home" (Roiphe), 47

Church and state, separation of, 101, 106–07, 114, 155–56, 168

Citizens Rights Movement, 119

Civil liberties, 101, 106, 113, 114, 116, 168

Civil rights, 16, 44, 101, 105, 115–16, 168

Clark, Wayne, 50, 51

Classical Reform theology, 160

Cohen, Steven M., 11, 137, 138

Cohen, Yehezkel, 148

Collectivism, 115, 117, 119, 141

Commentary, 100, 104, 111, 132

Commitment to Judaism, 1–2, 12, 13, 29, 55, 71, 159–61

Common ancestry, myth of, 13, 14

Communitarians, 75, 82

Community, Israeli perception of, 75–76. *See also* State of Israel

Consent, 17

Conservative Judaism, 26, 85–86, 97, 99, 100, 120–21; changes in, 127–28

Converts to Christianity, 45–46

Converts to Judaism, 23, 24–26, 131–32

Cossacks, 33

Council of Jewish Settlements, 82

Courts, 78

Crusaders, 33

Cuddihy, John Murray, 20

Culture, Judaism as, 3–4, 8, 13, 173–74

"Culture-based solidarity," 13

Dannhauser, Werner, 101

Dati'im, 80, 120, 121, 139, 140. *See also* Orthodox Jews

Dayan, Moshe, 70

Defense spending, 109

Democracy, 119, 154

Democratic party, 100–101

Deutsch, Helene, 20

Diaspora Jews, 1; Israeli view of, 8, 96; anti-Semitism and, 61–62, 63; symbol of Israel to, 85–86. *See also* Exile

Dietary laws, 124, 130–31

Dishes, for meat and dairy, 130, 139, 140

Distinctive Jewish Name samples, 12

Divorce, 116

Douglas, Mary, 125–26

Drug abuse, 116

Dukakis, Michael, 100, 101–02, 106

East European Jews, 38–39

Eban, Abba, 40, 82

Education, 2–3, 41, 92, 115; influence of, 83, 161–63; extremist, 147; liberalism and, 179*n*1

Eichmann, Adolf, 33

Eisen, Arnold, 10, 26, 89, 93, 101

Emdah (periodical), 148

Emet V'Emunah: Statement of Principles of Conservative Judaism, 85–86

Environment, 165–71

Equal Rights Amendment, 103

Equality, 97

Eretz Yisrael, 91, 171, 173; significance of, 68–74, 157–58

Erev Shabbat, 91

"Essence of Judaism, The" (anon.), 133

Ethicism, 125, 133

Ethiopian Jews, 63

Ethnic community of Jews, 13

Ethnicity, 79, 154; effects of, 161, 162–63

Ethnocentrism, 122; anti-Semitism

and, 36–40; of American Jews,
40–45, 54; in Zionist ideology,
60–62
European emancipation, 109
European Jews, 6–7, 48
Exile, 35–36, 96, 157–58; and
homecoming, 10; and redemption,
57, 58, 88–89; anti-Semitism and,
61–62; Israeli perceptions of,
88–92; defined, 89–93; American
Jews' perceptions of, 93–95
Extremism, 146–47, 148

Falwell, Jerry, 43, 107–08
Familism, 13, 14, 157; among
American Jews, 17–21, 26–30;
among Israeli Jews, 21–26, 29–
30, 168
Family, as metaphor, 51–52
Fein, Leonard, 28, 110, 113, 170–71
Feminism. *See* Women's rights
Fleg, Edmund, 133
"Forbes 400," 41
Foreign policy, 108–09
Formality, 20–21, 78
Fuchs, Lawrence, 106
Fundamentalist Protestants, 48
Fund raising, 1, 32, 33, 43, 45, 84

Galut. *See* Exile
Galut (Eisen), 10
Geertz, Clifford, 3, 165–66, 170, 174
Gefen, Yonatan, 76
Genocide, 31
Gentiles, 48; Israeli Jewish attitudes
toward, 24–25, 58–59, 117–18;
Jewish perceptions of, 30, 35–36,
38–39, 158, 159, 169–70; attitude
toward Jews of, 40–44; American
Jews' attitudes toward, 49–50,
54–57, 94–95; perceived inferiority
of, 50–54; Zionist views of, 59–62;
Israeli insensitivity to, 167–70. *See
also* Anti-Semitism
Gerber, Jane, 36

German Jews, 160–61
German Reform Judaism, 160
God, 4–5, 6
Golus, 134
Government buildings, in Israel, 78
Goyim, 4, 35. *See also* Gentiles
Greenblum, Joseph, 51, 52, 97
Group interests of Jews, 97, 109,
112, 133
Guilt, 17
Gush Emunim, 73–74

Halakha (Jewish law), 23, 146, 148,
160; American Jews' observance of,
123–28, 180–81*n*1; Israeli
observance of, 139–42
Halpern, Ben, 36, 39, 88–89
Hammond, Phillip E., 87–88
Hanukah, 4, 15–16, 123, 139
Har-Even, Shulamit, 180
Haredim, 25, 143, 144, 155; defined,
182*n*9. *See also* Orthodox Jews
Harmony and disharmony of cosmos,
35, 36
Hasidism, 145
Haskala writers, 69
Havdalah service, 126–27
Head covering, 130
Hebrew language, 2, 69, 87
Heilman, Samuel C., 137, 138
Hellenization. *See* Assimilation
Herman, Simon, 49, 50, 61, 62
Herzog, Elizabeth, 38, 39, 51
Hevreh, 76
Hillel, 28
Hiloni. *See* Reform Judaism;
Secularism
Hispanics, 48
Historiography, 11
History, 69, 97; Jewish conceptions of,
13, 14–17; impact of, 109–10
History of Eretz Yisrael, The, 69–70
Holocaust, 4, 31, 45, 61; as symbol,
32–33, 43, 169, 170

Homosexuality, 105, 115–16, 121, 138,
181*n*3
Humanitarianism, 26, 97, 101, 118

Identity, 2, 10, 29, 166; in Israel,
86–88, 117–18. *See also* Anti-
Semitism
Ideology, 29, 154
Illegalism, 75–76
Immigrants in America, 41
Individualism, 76–77, 115, 116,
119, 133
Intellectuals, 41
Intermarriage, 10, 13, 23, 56, 166,
178*n*6; anti-Semitism and, 45–46;
attitude toward Gentiles in, 47;
changes in Jewish attitudes, 53–54
Intifada, 1, 24, 170
Isaac, 60
Islam, 4, 36, 146, 174
Israel, 4, 42, 67; as redeemer, 62–66;
American Jews' attitudes toward,
83–88. *See also* Eretz Yisrael; State
of Israel
Israel Defense Force (IDF), 81
Israeli Jews, 1, 97; spirituality of,
9–11; attitudes toward American
Jewish practices, 132–33. *See also*
Anti-Semitism; Judaism; Halakha;
and other individual concepts

Jackson, Jesse, 104
Jerusalem Post, 155
Jewish National Fund, 32
Jews without Mercy (Shorris), 111
Joint Program Plan of *1987–88,*
106–07
Joseph, Rabbi Ovadia, 25
Journalists, 41
Judaism, 1, 137, 156; as religious
culture, 5–6
—Israel and America compared, 8,
157–58; differences between, 1–3;
commitment to tradition, 159–61;

population characteristics, 161–65;
structure and environment, 165–
71; common bases, 172–75;
universalism vs. particularism,
27–28; recent interpretations of,
142–47. *See also* Conservative
Judaism; Liberalism; Orthodox
Judaism; Reform Judaism;
Religiosity; Secular nationalism

Kahane, Meir, 119, 148, 154
Kalischer, Rabbi Zvi Hirsch, 37
Katz, Jacob, 38
Katz, Shaul, 69
Katznelson, Berl, 58
Kibbutz, 71, 183*n*15
Kimmerling, Baruch, 75
Kinship, 17–18, 28–29. *See also*
Familism
Knesset, 148, 149
Knesset building, 78
Kohn, Hans, 68
Kook, Rabbi Abraham Isaac
HaCohen, 72–73
Kook, Zvi Yehudah, 73, 82
Kosher laws, 124
Kovner, Abba, 151
Kristol, Irving, 108–09

Labour party, 71, 120, 154, 167
Land of Israel. *See* Eretz Yisrael
Language, 2, 14. *See also* Hebrew
language
Law. *See* Halakha; Illegalism
Lebanon, 170
Left-wing politics, 48, 120–21, 135,
136, 153–54
Legitimization, 160–61. *See also*
Secular nationalism
Liberalism, 26, 57, 94, 95, 96–98
—of American Jews, 99–103;
dimensions of, 104–09; reasons for,
109–14; of Israelis, 114–17; relation
to Judaism, 117–22

—education and, 179*n*1
Likud party, 70, 154
Luz, Ehud, 68

Ma'ariv (newspaper), 24, 76
Majority, Israeli Jews as, 3, 168
Mamlakhtuit. *See* State of Israel
Mann, Ted, 111
Mapam party, 119, 120
Market Facts (survey research
    company), 11, 12
Masorati'im, 120, 139, 140. *See also*
    Conservative Judaism
Masoret (tradition), 5
Meaning of Galut, The (Shnitzer),
    89–90
Meimad party, 148, 149
Meir, Golda, 70
Memory, 13, 31; collective, of Jews,
    43, 47–50
Midstream, 93
Mikvah (lustral bath), 130
Militarism, 121
Military, 81–82, 101, 108, 142
Minority group, 16, 101; Jews as, 3, 62,
    113–14, 168; Jewish support for,
    102–03
Mitzvot (commandments), 125, 128
Moderation, religious, 147–49
Modernization, 3, 161; impact on
    Judaism, 5–7
Mondale, Walter, 100
Moral Majority, 43, 107–08
Moral privilege, 44
Moralism, 122, 127, 133–38, 146–
    47, 150
Mortality rate, of Arab infants, 115
Myths, 15–17

NAACP, 104–05
National Organization for Women,
    103–04
National Religious party, 74, 143
Nationalism, 148

Natural history, 69
Navon, Yitzhak, 76, 77
Nazis, 33, 42, 169
Neemanei Torah V'Avodah, 148
Nekudah, 145
Neriyah, Rabbi Moshe Zvi, 59
Newfield, Jack, 103
Non-Jews. *See* Arabs; Gentiles
N'turei Karta, 24

Obedience, 128
Obligation, 18, 19, 20, 158
Oil crisis, 7
Ordeal of Civility, The (Cuddihy), 20
Orderly society, 49
Orthodox Judaism, 8, 26, 97, 137, 138;
    attitudes toward Gentiles, 56–57;
    ritual among, 126–27; personalism
    among, 130–31; divisions in Israel,
    144–45; influence of, 162–65
Overcrowdedness, 115
Oz, Amos, 90, 142
Oz V'Shalom-Netivot Shalom, 148

Palestine, 1
Palestine Liberation Organization,
    77, 169
Particularism, 150, 165, 168; of
    American Jews, 26, 27–30;
    universalism and, 133, 134–35, 141;
    moralism and, 146–47
Passover, 32, 123, 134
Peoplehood, 29, 30–31, 74, 172, 173,
    177*n*7
Percy, Charles, 42
Peres, Shimon, 83–84
Personalism, 127, 128–32, 137, 181*n*2;
    familistic, 20–21; among Israelis,
    145–46
Petachim (periodical), 148
Pharaoh, in Jewish myth, 32, 33
Pogroms, 49
Polish Jews, 37
Politicization of Judaism, 9–10

Politics, 96; role of American Jews in, 41–42; influence of religious voters, 143–46. *See also* Liberalism; Left-wing politics; Right-wing politics; Secularism; *and individual political parties*

Politika, 119

Pollard, Jonathan, 7

Population characteristics, 161–65

Pornography, 116, 121, 144

"Portrait of the Mythical Gentile" (Clark), 50–51

Poverty, 100, 102, 115

Prager, Dennis, 44

Prayer, 128–29

Prayer in schools, 106–07

Present Tense (magazine), 7

Prisoner exchange, 77–78

Private schools, 107

Privatization of Judaism, 153, 156

Prophets, 160

Protestants, 48

Public and private Judaism, 86–87

Public opinion surveys, 11–12, 24

Purim, 32, 137–38

Purpose, sense of, 17, 18, 28

Ra'anan, Zvi, 180*n*11

Rabin, Yitzhak, 29

Racism, 61, 154

Raising Your Jewish Christian Child: Wise Choices for Interfaith Parents, 132

Rash, Yehoshua, 151, 180*n*11

Ratz movement, 119, 120

Reagan, Ronald, 100

Redemption, 35–36, 37; exile and, 57, 58, 88–89

Reform Judaism, 26, 97, 110–11; 148; ceremony in, 126–28

Religiosity, 2–3, 79, 116

—of Israeli Jews, 9–11, 30, 158–59; reasons for, 139–42; moderate camp, 147–49

—Eretz Yisrael and, 71–74

—effects of, 116, 118–19, 160–61, 162–65, 171

—party affiliation and, 120–21

—of American Jews, 123–28; personalism and voluntarism in, 128–32; religious triumphalism, 142–47, 153

Republican party, 100

Resettlement, 85, 92

Responsibility, sense of, 17, 18

Right-wing politics, 48, 70–71, 149–50

Ritual, 124–26, 128, 130, 133, 137, 139, 144, 159

Rivkes, Moses, 38

Roiphe, Anne, 47

Rosh Hashanah, 123

Rosman, M. J., 37

Rothschild Foundation, 78

Sabbath observances, 124, 126, 130, 139, 153, 154, 156

Sacks, Jonathan, 170

Sacred Survival (Woocher), 136

Sarvaney Geulah, 74

School prayer, 106–07

"Schvartzes," 24

Schweid, Eliezer, 68, 69, 73, 151–52

Scriptures, 69

Secular nationalism, 149–53

Secular universalism, 153–56

Secularism, 29, 30, 119–20, 141–42, 148, 183*n*15

Seder, 4, 123, 134

Sephardi Jews, 3, 17, 144; view of statism, 80, 81, 83; view of galut, 92; politics of, 149–50; attitudes of, 161, 162–63; response to modernity, 182*n*14

Shabbat b'Shabbato, 74

Shamir, Yitzhak, 150

Sharett, Moshe, 82

Sharon, Ariel, 149

Shinui party, 120
Sh'ma, 133
Shnitzer, Shmuel, 89–90
Shorris, Earl, 111–12
Shprinzak, Ehud, 75–76
Shtetl, 51
Shuchmacher, Yoselle, 25
Shulweis, Harold M., 102
Siddur Sim Shalom, 129, 133
Sidorsky, David, 99
Silberman, Charles, 41
Six Day War, 16, 33, 71
Sklare, Marshall, 51, 52, 97, 127,
    128, 133
Smith, Anthony, 13
Smooha, Sammy, 79
Snyder, Charles, 53
Social Action Commission (Vorspan),111
Social service organizations, 19–20,
    27. *See also* Humanitarianism;
    Liberalism
Social structure, 165–71
Soviet Jews, 10, 42, 63, 100, 108
State of Israel, 29, 142, 158, 165, 171,
    173; concept of, 5, 75, 77–83; anti-
    Semitism and, 64–66; devaluation
    of state, 77–78. *See also* Zionism
Statism, 81
Stereotypes, 50–54. *See also* Anti-
    Semitism; Gentiles
Sternhall, Ze'ev, 118, 119
Suffering, of Jews, 36, 44–45
Superiority, Jewish feelings of, 29–30,
    170, 171; reasons for, 36, 37–38;
    and Gentiles, 50–54
Supreme Court building (Israel), 78
Survey data, 11–12, 24
Symbols, 2, 3–4, 5, 8, 133, 157, 172;
    transvaluation of, 6, 7; meanings
    attached to, 9–11, 169–70
Synagogue attendance, 123, 124, 126

Tal, Uriel, 9
Tefutzot. *See* Diaspora Jews

Tehiya party, 70
Tel-Aviv University, 154
Telushkin, Joseph, 44
Temple, destruction of, 7, 32, 68, 134,
    177n2
Temple Beth Ami, 129–30
Terrorism, 89
Tikun Olam, 110–11
Tisha B'Av, 32, 130, 134
Tobin, Gary, 178n1
Torah, 4–5, 126, 137, 138
Torah V'Avodah, 115
Tradition, 3–5, 74, 140–42;
    conditions affecting, 6–7; liberalism
    and, 97, 98; reconstruction of,
    127–28
Traditionalization, 22
Triumphalism, religious, 2–3, 79, 116

Ultranationalists, 70, 73, 74, 82, 148,
    150
Ultrapietism, 25
Unger, Rhoda Kesler, 116
Union for Traditional Conservative
    Judaism, 129
Uniqueness of Jews, 29–30, 31
United Jewish Appeal, 1, 19, 45
Universalism, 94, 118, 122, 127,
    133–38; among American Jews,
    27–30, 109, 112–13; in Zionist
    ideology, 58–59, 62; among Israelis,
    146; effects of, 170. *See also* Secular
    universalism
Urban League, 104–05

Victimization of Jews, 31–34
Vietnam War, 108, 109
Voluntarism, 127, 128–32, 181n2;
    among Israeli Jews, 146; among
    American Jews, 168–69
Vorspan, Albert, 111

Walzer, Michael, 110, 112–13
Washing, 125

Waskow, Arthur, 135, 136
Welfare state, 101, 103, 113, 115
West Bank settlement, 16, 71, 73
Wiesel, Elie, 151
Willis, Ellen, 46–47, 103
Women's rights, 102–03, 104, 105, 115–16, 146
Woocher, Jonathan, 18, 27, 45, 136

Yehoshua, A. B., 152–53
Yeridah, 92
Yerushalmi, Yosef, 14
Yeshiva University, 60
Yishuv, 16, 17, 177*n*2
Yisrael saba, 180*n*10

Yom Kippur, 123, 139, 140
Yom Kippur war, 7, 142

Zakhor (Yerushalmi), 14
Zborowski, Mark, 38, 39, 51
Zemach, Mina, 11, 77
Zionism, 39; defined, 2, 4; secular, 29, 35–36, 141–42; ideology of, 58–59, 60–62; view of galut, 60, 90–91; in Israel, 64–66, 72–74; attitude toward state, 82–83; in America, 85; view of diaspora, 94; collectivism in, 115; new tendencies in, 147–48; Zionist socialist period, 150–51